THE MOVING FINGER

Writers On Writing

THE MOVING FINGER

Writers On Writing

Edited By
**HILDA DAVID &
FRANCIS JARMAN**

Om Books International

First published in 2024 by

Om Books International

Corporate & Editorial Office
A-12, Sector 64, Noida 201 301
Uttar Pradesh, India
Phone: +91 120 477 4100
Email: editorial@ombooks.com
Website: www.ombooksinternational.com

Sales Office
107, Ansari Road, Darya Ganj,
New Delhi 110 002, India
Phone: +91 11 4000 9000
Email: sales@ombooks.com
Website: www.ombooks.com

Copyright for the individual pieces rests with the authors
Preface © Hilda David 2024
Anthology © Om Books International

ALL RIGHTS RESERVED. The views and opinions expressed in this book are those of the authors, and have been verified to the extent possible, and the publishers are in no way liable for the same. No part of this book may be reproduced or transmitted in any form by any means, electronic or mechanical, including photocopying and recording, or by any information storage and retrieval system, except as may be expressly permitted in writing by the publisher.

ISBN: 978-93-5376-979-6

Printed in India

10 9 8 7 6 5 4 3 2 1

The Moving Finger writes; and, having writ,
Moves on: nor all thy Piety nor Wit
Shall lure it back to cancel half a Line,
Nor all thy Tears wash out a Word of it

—Edward Fitzgerald's
Rubáiyát of Omar Khayyám, LI

Contents

Preface: *Hilda David*	1
About Writing: *Shashi Deshpande*	7
Can You Write about Love?: *Simran Paul*	19
Writing about Sex: *T.W. Geraghty*	23
Writing about Yourself: *Peer Khan*	35
Writing about Psychopaths: *Heena Rathore-Pardeshi*	37
How to Write Funny: *Krishna Shastri Devulapalli*	48
Memory Plays Truant—Remembering and Forgetting in the Writing of Fiction: *Gita Viswanath*	55
Feeling Noir in India: *Zac O'Yeah*	63
Clues, Craft, and Characters—The Journey into Mystery Fiction: *Manjiri Prabhu*	82
Fantasy Fiction: *Francis Jarman*	94
Writing Mythology: *Suhail Mathur*	121
Writing Historical Fiction—What It Might Be Worthwhile to Keep in Mind before Embarking on This Adventure: *Christoph Werner*	133
Writing for Children: *Paro Anand*	153

Losing Higher Ground—The Short Story Today:
Anjum Hasan — 161

On Your Fingertips—Writing for Television:
Gajra Kottary — 180

Writing for the Stage: *Francis Jarman* — 187

Follow Your Nose (Why Playwrights Write):
Ramu Ramanathan — 211

Many Ways to Make a Play: *Shanta Gokhale* — 227

Poems Matter Because They Have Holes—
Making Peace with Language and Myself:
Arundhathi Subramaniam — 239

Waking Dream—Reflections on Poetry:
Randhir Khare — 261

Why Poetry Needs to Mess with Your Head:
Francis Jarman — 272

Writing Scrumptious—Using the Bengali Meal Plan
as a Guide: *Ramona Sen* — 283

On Translation: *Jerry Pinto* — 291

A Basic Recipe for Translating: *Bruce W. Irwin* — 310

One Small Step in Pursuit of Words: *Premila Paul* — 338

A Writing Life: *Anil Menon* — 355

Copyright / Acknowledgements — 363

Preface

Hilda David

So you want to be a writer? Then who better to turn to for help than successful writers—to those who once had similar dreams and ambitions, and who have fulfilled them?

Where do you start? Does one adhere to a common template to describe aesthetic considerations? Accommodating, for example, both Bhalchandra Nemade's *deshiwad* (nativism) and S.L. Bhyrappa's religious exploration? Both are recipients of many prestigious literary awards. And both prevent readers from reducing writing to easy binaries of this versus that. Can English do that in New India? Create a vocabulary which responds to the new reality? Attempt to mirror the multiple themes of day-to-day life? Bhakti philosophy, historical renditions, urban angst, rural life?

This is one for writers to look at, rather than critics, although some critics are creative writers, and some writers have written literary criticism and incisive non-fiction (a case in point is Amitav Ghosh). The time for detailed critical analysis will also come, but what you need first is insights into that peculiar activity called writing, from writers themselves.

No magicians are prepared to reveal all the secrets behind their illusions. Nevertheless, in the following pages you will find Indian and international writers, including distinguished authors, hardworking and successful practitioners, and some promising and enthusiastic newcomers sharing their thoughts on writing. What they have in common is a love of writing, and a willingness to be frank about their own work. (Let us not forget that not all writers are happy explaining what they do, in case it jinxes their creativity and causes writer's block.) It requires honesty, and a high degree of self-knowledge.

Why, in an Indian publication, have we included non-Indian writers? We probably wouldn't have done so in a work aimed at aspiring authors writing in Hindi, say, or Tamil. But your decision to write in English has certain consequences.

Our aim is to focus on divergent concepts that emanate from literary works. I was in Karnataka recently and talking to a Kannadiga scholar. He shared that the English-speaking Kannada scholars speak of Gil Ben-Herut, Phillip B. Wagoner, or Richard Eaton; while other Kannada academics speak of Shamba Joshi, Kirtinath Kurtakoti, or M.M. Kalburgi. That's when you realise that the two worlds (and their words) don't meet. In a nutshell: we need to break free from our existing compartments and silos.

Partly as a consequence of the lingua franca role of English in India, your work will be available to a very wide audience. Forget all that stuff about the colonial burden, about English being the language of an oppressor—it hasn't stopped other former British colonies from developing a rich, vibrant and home-grown literature in English. That goes not only for cultures, like the United States or Australia, for instance, where a majority of people have English as their first language, but also for West Africa, where they generally don't. This is not to say that your relationship with English will always be an easy one. See the fascinating discussion in the essay in this volume by the poet Arundhathi Subramaniam, for whom "English has meant resource and refuge, scalpel, scimitar and sanctuary over the years…"

Your choice of English not only pushes a huge door open in India; it also makes your work accessible to readers across much of the rest of the world. In that respect, you are joining a club, and your international readers will expect you to keep (broadly) to the widely accepted rules of the English language. Yet it won't be a problem if the English that you write has a distinctly Indian colouring. Quite the opposite, it will add character and authenticity. You can draw upon the tricks and tropes of what has now become arguably the world's greatest literary tradition, which is not a bad club to belong to! That we have contributions from British, Irish, North American and European writers is a reminder of the international nature of that tradition. Be aware, of course, that not everything will work with equal effectiveness in every country where English is understood.

Famously, Shakespeare's "Shall I compare thee to a summer's day?" may not always be recognised as complimentary in some of the hotter parts of the world. By the same measure, allusions that every Indian would grasp at once will be lost on non-Indian readers unless the context makes them clear, or you provide a glossary.

We have included a wide range of types of writing. In addition to the major triad of literature—drama, poetry, and their very much younger sibling, prose fiction—we have screenwriting, food journalism, and translation, both literary and technical. (Technical translation, incidentally, is a massive field of opportunity for young Indians with an interest in science and technology and a gift for language, and it pays better than poems, plays or novels do.) There are a few gaps, such as journalism, or advertising copywriting (which was Salman Rushdie's job before he became a full-time writer. Memo to the Publisher: Perhaps we could add these in the second edition?).

But apart from a traditional coverage of genres, we are also hoping to achieve something of what one might call "the Kosambi effect".

The remarkable polymath D.D. Kosambi (1907–66) enlightened Indians on a wide range of subjects, and his books *An Introduction to the Study of Indian History* (1956), *Myth and Reality* (1962), and *The Culture and Civilisation of India in Historical Outline* (1965) are eye-openers. Originally a mathematician, he also created a new approach to Indian history, scientific methodology, and modern techniques of interpretation, selection, and analysis of social problems, his ideas being vigorously expressed in his writing.

After schooling in Pune, Kosambi moved to America with his father and studied at the Cambridge Latin School till 1925. He graduated from Harvard. While at Harvard, he became interested in mathematics, history, and languages. It was here that he became proficient in Greek, Latin, German, and French, and came in contact with the mathematicians George Berkoff and Norbert Wiener. When he returned to India in 1929, he joined the Banaras Hindu University as a professor of mathematics. For two years, he taught and researched at Aligarh Muslim University. In 1932, he joined Fergusson College in Pune. Kosambi taught Pali language for fourteen years. There were further academic stays and appointments (Mumbai, London, Chicago, Princeton), trips to many parts of the world, and a wealth of publications. Kosambi's writing was a break from traditional historiography, and from the orthodoxy prevalent among middle-class intellectuals. He added a new dimension to Indian historiography, which is why we still discuss his work so many years after his death.

On a more modest scale, we too will introduce you to viewpoints which are often at dissonance with the same-old, same-old. This book is therefore not a ground-level coaching guide, or a banal "Tips and Tricks" manual ("Don't use too many adjectives", etc.), but you will find exciting ideas and serious reflection on types and genres of writing, the delights, the dangers, and the problems, from writers who know them well.

Our sincere thanks go to our contributors (often very busy people), to Suhail Mathur at our literary agents The Book Bakers, and to Shantanu Ray Chaudhuri, our editor at Om Books International.

The individual contributions represent the views of their authors, of course, which are not necessarily shared by the editors, the other contributors, or the publishers.

About Writing

Shashi Deshpande

Shashi Deshpande is one of India's most distinguished writers. Born in Dharwad, Karnataka, the daughter of the Kannada writer and scholar Adya Rangacharya ("Sriranga"), she has degrees in economics, law, and English literature. Her works include ten novels, a crime novel, two crime novellas, collections of short stories and critical essays, and children's literature. Her books have been translated into many languages, and she received the Sahitya Akademi Award for *That Long Silence* (Penguin, 1989). Among her other novels (also published by Penguin) are *The Dark Holds No Terrors* (1980), *A Matter of Time* (1996), and *Small Remedies* (2000).

~

It is a strange thought that for something so closely associated with words, created out of words, in fact, it is hard to find the words to describe the process itself. There is a huge curiosity about writing, and I am often asked questions like: Where does your writing come from? Where do your characters come from? Writers are at a loss to find an answer even for the seemingly simple question: Why do you write? The British writer Martin Amis speaks of the "deeply mysterious process of a novel arriving".[1] And Anita Desai says that to talk of writing is "to externalise a totally internal process. By doing so, I find I have quite lost the quality of secretiveness which is essential to the process."[2] As a short story writer and a novelist I have learnt this too, that there is no "one way" of writing; each writer has her or his own way. Writing is both individualistic and idiosyncratic. Young writers will find no path prepared for them by older writers. They will have to find their own path, fight against obstacles, struggle through brambles and bushes—all this without knowing whether they are on the right path or not.

If this is how it is, how can writing be taught? What about creative-writing classes, which are mushrooming everywhere? Young and not-so-young hopefuls flock to these classes expecting, perhaps, that they will learn how to write the novel they have always wanted to write. Personally, I don't believe classes can fashion writers out of just any raw material. There are, of course, students who have emerged out of these classes as writers. But I would imagine that these are people who have talent, a control over language, and have something they want to say. Such a person would become a writer anyway. The class, perhaps, taught them a few tricks of the trade and, what matters more, made them write, which, left on their own, they might not have done.

However, if writing cannot be taught in classes, there are two schools which can help a person who wants to write. One is the school of life itself. A writer writes to give expression to some thoughts, ideas, emotions—all these put into a story of people and their interactions, their relationships with one another, with their

---

1 See "Martin Amis." In: John Haffenden. *Novelists in Interview*. Methuen, 1985, 18.
2 Anita Desai. "*Feng Sui*, or Spirit of Place." In: *A Sense of Place: Essays in Post-Colonial Literatures*. Ed. By Britta Olinder. Gothenburg University Press, 1984, 105.

own selves. To write about this one needs to know and understand the emotions of love and hate, of friendship and enmity, of joy and sorrow. To know about life, about struggle, failure and success, about fears and hopes. I once heard Pandit Birju Maharaj, a famous dancer, say that the techniques of dance can be taught, but the bhavas, or the emotions, have to come from within the dancer. Which can only come through living life.

The other school where writing can be learnt is the school of reading. Reading and writing are so intertwined it is hard to separate them. Eudora Welty, the American author, said, "I don't know whether I could do either one, reading or writing, without the other."[3] I can relate to this. Long before I became a writer I was a reader. A passionate reader. From the early age of seven or eight, I read voraciously. Nobody told me to read or what to read. Nobody told me what not to read, either. But I was told not to read fiction at all, because my schoolwork seemed to be suffering from the amount of time I spent reading novels. I was forbidden to use the school library. Nobody realised then, not my teachers, not my father, himself a writer, not even I, that with this reading I was preparing myself for becoming a writer.

I have since then read books like *Emma* and *Pride and Prejudice* (Jane Austen), *Wuthering Heights* (Emily Brontë), *North and South* (Elizabeth Gaskell), *David Copperfield*, *Our Mutual Friend* and *Bleak House* (Charles Dickens), *Howards End* (E.M. Forster), *War and Peace* (Leo Tolstoy), *Crime and Punishment* (Fyodor Dostoyevsky), *The Bridge of San Luis Rey* (Thornton Wilder). I could go on and on. I did not read with the idea of becoming a writer; reading was an end in itself. What I learnt from these books was the invaluable lesson of what good writing is, of what great writing is. I learnt to love language, which is an essential part of being a writer. I found it, still find it, a marvellous and wondrous thing. But I wrote nothing

---

[3] Eudora Welty. "The Making of a Writer: Listening in the Dark." In: *The New York Times*, 9 October 1983.

in my early years. Oh yes, I had a diary and wrote in it all the rages and passions of an adolescent. But apart from this I wrote nothing but what I had to do as part of my work in school.

One of the problems of my extensive reading, as I realised when I began to write, was imitativeness. The very first story I wrote was pure Somerset Maugham (anyone recognise the name? I doubt it. So fickle is fame), a story with a proper beginning, a middle, and an end with a punch. Another story I wrote a little later was a Daphne du Maurier clone. Actually, I don't think it is a bad thing for a writer to imitate other writers. Babies imitate older children and adults, young boys and girls imitate older boys and girls—it's natural. In time they learn to be themselves. So too in writing. And, fortunately, I soon realised there was some problem with my writing, with my stories. I was dissatisfied with them even though I was getting acceptance from magazines and my stories were getting published. Nothing I could pinpoint, only a vague sense of dissatisfaction. I now realise that I felt that my writing was shallow, skimming over the surface, not going into the depths. But the dissatisfaction marked something that is important: it was the self-critic in me making an appearance.

Writing is not a self-indulgent activity; it requires you to be hard on yourself. The self-critic is a very essential part of a writer. It makes sure you are not in love with your own words, your own writing. To think that you are writing wonderfully well is to condemn yourself to never improving, never trying for excellence. The real artist is never satisfied, never complacent. Each time I have completed a novel I have had the feeling—I could have done better. Fortunately, there is also an optimist inside the writer who says, next time, perhaps. And so you go on trying endlessly for that perfect novel. Jane Austen's *Emma* is considered her "most perfect book" by her biographer Claire Tomalin.[4] But she herself thought otherwise:

---

4   Claire Tomalin. *Jane Austen: A Life* (1997). Penguin, 2000, 252.

> I am very strongly haunted by the idea that to those Readers who have preferred P&P. [*Pride and Prejudice*] it [*Emma*] will appear inferior in Wit, & to those who have preferred MP. [*Mansfield Park*] very inferior in good Sense.⁵

But the world thought, even today thinks, otherwise. And writers keep going because there is the carrot of great writing just ahead of you.

Anyway, at some time I realised that what my writing lacked was my own voice, my real voice. It is the most important step in writing for a writer to find her own voice. Writers put up certain barriers, afraid to reveal their own selves in their writing. At least I did. I remember that writing always brought up for me a picture of the curtain going up and I standing alone under the spotlight with an audience in front of me. A nightmare for one whose goal was not to attract any attention. But if you want to write, if you are a real writer, the real self has to emerge, the real voice has to be heard. No posturing, just saying what you want to say. Not aware of an audience, not being careful or restraining yourself. No worrying that you may hurt someone, harm your family, your relationships. There are ways of taking care of this, but the way is certainly not to gag yourself.

It is important not only to find your own voice, but to get the right tone, the pitch in which you will tell the story. I always think of a singer and her accompanist tuning the tanpura, both of them anxiously bent over the instrument, listening, ears cocked to the sound. Finally getting the right sound and looking at each other with a smile which says, that's it. So does the writer work towards getting the right tone. Martin Amis speaks of going on until the tuning fork is still.

---

5   From a letter to John Murray, 11 December 1815, http://jasna.org/austen/works/emma/

If anyone were to ask me what the most difficult thing about writing is, I would say the beginning. It seems wonderful to start. For quite some time, the characters have been moving in my mind, I can hear their conversation, I have the words with which to begin. I start, but what had seemed so wonderful when floating in my mind comes out stilted and banal on paper. This is terrible. A look at the pile of papers waiting to be filled up fills me with apprehension. How am I going to do it? I think of authors who have done it and wonderfully well too. "*Emma* opens with a paragraph which sends shivers of pleasure down my spine; it glitters with sheer competence."[6] Jane Austen always took a straight dive into her novels, got to the heart of it in her first few sentences. Looks easy, but it is not. I remember trying innumerable beginnings for a novel that would later become *That Long Silence* (1989). None were satisfactory. I left it alone and moved on. When I had come almost two thirds of the way, I suddenly got it.

> To achieve anything, to become anything, you've got to be hard and ruthless. Yes, even if you want to be a saint, if you want to love the whole world, you've got to stop loving individual human beings first.[7]

This was the right beginning. I was writing of Jaya, a seemingly ordinary woman, a wife and mother like many others. But this first sentence cuts away the ordinariness from her. The reader gets an idea of her real self through her idea of achievement: "You've got to be hard and ruthless."

The problem of the beginning is not confined to the first novel. You may have written a dozen novels, about fifty short stories; but each time you begin writing anything new, you are a novice. The

---

6   Fay Weldon. *Letters to Alice: On First Reading Jane Austen* (1984). Hodder & Stoughton, 2011, 96.

7   Shashi Deshpande. *That Long Silence*. Virago, 1988, 1.

first words, the first sentence, the first paragraph—all these come after a struggle. It never becomes easier. At the same time, the fact that you have overcome this problem earlier reassures you that you will be able to do so again.

None of what I learnt came from any book or teacher. I stumbled upon these things as I wrote. Which told me the most important truth about writing: that you learn about writing by writing. It's a hands-on learning. You make mistakes, you learn from them, you falter and get to know why. What can, perhaps, be taught is the craft of writing. Yet even here there is a snag. Each novel demands its own technique; there never can be a general rule. I have a penchant for the first-person narrative; it lets me go deep into a person, lets me immerse myself in the character, get the intensity I need. There was a time when, tired of the "I" narration, I tried to write in the third person. I thought it would be less narrow, give a more complete rounded picture. But it would not come. I then tried from the point of view of two people, alternating the narration. That too was no good. Finally, I realised that the story was Jaya's story, she had to tell it herself. It worked. But I must have written over a hundred pages before I got to what was really right for this novel. I have never written a novel with a linear narrative, because lives are not lived like that. Memories are constantly churning inside us, stopping us in our tracks sometimes, driving us to truths we don't want to face. Memories bring in the past, dreams and desires bring in the future. Time is not neatly carved into past, present and future.

What do you do when you have completed your novel? You do need another opinion. You have been so immersed in it, you can't see it objectively. I trust my editor; editors see flaws you don't. One editor to whom I'd sent a novel wrote to say that I had introduced thirteen characters in the first few pages and how did I think the reader would cope with that? Well, since I hadn't thought of a reader, I hadn't thought of this problem. But I recognised the truth of what the editor was saying. I hate explanations, I assume that my reader is smart. So with minimal words, I put each character into the context.

But what about when you don't have an editor? Whom do you give it to? It is necessary to give the manuscript to someone to read in order to have a feedback, to know whether it has any literary value at all. It has to be a person you trust and whose opinion you will accept. I know that some writers, specially beginners, give their work to many people. I think it is dreadfully dangerous. Each person could say a different thing and what will you do then? It is also better not to let anyone read it if you are very sensitive. Criticism can kill creativity for some people, while it puts others on their mettle.

The most important thing in writing is language. Language is needed by everyone. But for writers it matters immensely; it is the writer's tool, the medium through which the writer communicates with the world. Writers are specially sensitive to language. How you use it is one of the important factors of good writing. Poor language means that the communication is faulty. Also, fiction makes demands on a writer which other writing does not. There are so many different parts in a novel. There's straight narration, there's description, there is the authorial voice, there's conversation. Conversation is between people of all kinds, from the most illiterate to the most intelligent. Different language is needed for different characters. Women's language is different from men's language, children's language from that of adults. A writer has to use language suited to the character. Besides there is humorous talk, mundane conversation, professional talk. The writer has to take care of all these things.

The only rule which should be observed, according to me, is that the writer should not write to impress the reader. When a reader says, "I had to sit with a dictionary to read this writer," I think the writer has not done a good job. Unfortunately, many of us think that using difficult and unusual words is good writing. I believe in what Sir Ernest Gowers says in *The Complete Plain*

Words.⁸ This is one of the first books I bought after I started writing; only the dictionary came earlier. Gowers, whose books came out of the need of the government to make civil servants write better, has one basic rule: "Good English," he says, "can be defined simply as English which is readily understood by the reader. To be clear is to be efficient; to be obscure is to be inefficient." And again, "The golden rule is not a rule of grammar or syntax. It concerns less the arrangement of words than the choice of them." And therefore a large vocabulary. Which can come only through reading. I give an example of how a writer, using simple language, conveys wonderfully what is meant to be conveyed.

> From Monday morning until Saturday night, I had no advice, no counsel, no encouragement, no consolation, no assistance, no support of any kind from anyone that I can call to mind, as I hope to go to heaven!⁹

This is Charles Dickens's David Copperfield as a little boy, left all alone in London after the Micawbers leave him. The pathos Dickens wants to convey comes through very simple words and repetition. I had a lump in my throat when I first read these lines. Dickens could do melodrama as well as anyone, but here he is at his best in conveying the emotion by, as Gowers says, his choice of words.

There are two other examples I would like to quote, these the words not of writers, but surprisingly of politicians.

> Four score and seven years ago, our fathers brought forth upon this continent a new nation conceived in liberty and dedicated to the proposition that all men are created equal. Now we are engaged in a great civil war, testing

---

8   First published in 1954. There have since been many reprints and revised versions.
9   Charles Dickens. *David Copperfield* (1850). Penguin, 2004, 170.

whether that nation, or any nation so conceived and so dedicated, can long endure.[10]

This was Abraham Lincoln giving what is now known as the Gettysburg Address, speaking during the dedication of a Soldiers' National Cemetery in Gettysburg.

Long years ago, we made a tryst with destiny and now the time comes when we shall redeem that pledge, not wholly or in full measure, but substantially. At the stroke of the midnight hour, when the world sleeps, India will awake to life and freedom.[11]

These are the words of Pandit Jawaharlal Nehru, India's first prime minister, moments before India became an independent nation. Historic moments, both of them, of which the speakers are aware and which they have taken into account. Simple words which carry the weight of the occasion. Which fitted the solemnity of the moment. These are not written statements, but speeches, made by men who were not only heads of their countries, but had a grasp, a control over the language. Who knew the power of language and how to use it. Certain expressions used, like "four score and seven years ago" or "we made a tryst with destiny", give the speeches a kind of rhythm which makes them memorable, which has made them live for so long.

The spoken word sometimes makes a greater impact. For which reason, I always read out my novel to myself (behind closed doors) after it is complete. The ear catches the flaws which the eyes may miss. It is amazing how sensitive our ears are, how quick they are to take note of anything which jars. And then begins the task of revising, of editing, of rewriting. It is essential

---

10 https://en.wikipedia.org/wiki/Gettysburg_Address
11 https://www.inc.in/en/in-focus/tryst-with-destiny-speech-made-by-pt-jawaharlal-nehru

to take another look at what you have written. Now, with the computer, it is easy to change, to insert, to rewrite. But there is a danger of going on with this editing endlessly. A time comes when tweaking becomes counterproductive and you have to force yourself to stop. To write The End and send your "baby" out into the world.

Lastly, I consider it my good fortune that I have been, still am, a writer. It is not a profession, not a chore. There is something joyous about creativity. All my writing life, I have woken up in the morning eager to go to my table and start working. I often remember the words of Dorothy L. Sayers, the crime writer: "What we make is more important than what we are."[12] And therefore it is the work that matters. The joy lies in the writing, not in calling yourself, or being called, "a writer" or in becoming famous. Of course there are bad days and good days, bad moments and good moments during the writing. Times when a story almost writes itself, other times when you can't write even one good sentence. The thing is to keep going.

One of the problems of writing, creative writing, that is, is that you can never be sure of earning money through it. Never be sure that you can earn enough to support yourself (and your family if you have one), enough to be independent. Writers therefore need another way of earning money. At the same time, it is very hard to combine writing with a full-time job. I remember reading in my father's diary his anguish at having to do work which he hated in order to earn money. He wrote about a time when he was aching to write something that was urgently pressing on his mind; but his job took priority. Ultimately, he asked his assistant to take over for a day and in twenty-four hours wrote the play which had been plaguing him. Charlotte Brontë, who had to take up the job of a teacher in a school, writes in her diary:

---

12 See Eve Auchincloss. "The Lady behind Lord Peter." In: *The Washington Post*, 6 September 1981.

> I felt as if I could have written gloriously—I longed to write. [...] If I had had time to indulge it, I felt that the vague sensations of that moment would have settled down into some narrative better at least than any thing I ever produced before. But just then a dolt came up with a lesson. I thought I should have vomited.

I myself had household chores, and my children's needs, all of which had to take priority over my writing. My writing brought in very little money; it did not justify the amount of time I spent on it. And yet I was constantly pursued by the need to find time to write, I was constantly grabbing at time, I stuck to my working hours with great tenacity, I gave up everything but my household duties and my writing.

I often have people telling me that they want to give up their jobs and devote themselves to writing. I think it is a very risky thing to do. Writing cannot bear the burden of supporting an individual, let alone a family. Not everyone earns large sums, many never do. In India specially, it is impossible to earn an income through writing. Yet, one has to live. It is a hard choice, a hard decision, something which every person has to take herself. And yet, for me, the moments when I am sitting at my table, words flowing out of me, my pen gliding effortlessly across the paper, these moments make up for all the frustrations and the struggle. Not that this happens very often, but when it does, it is like tasting a slice of Heaven.

Can You Write about Love?

Simran Paul

Simran Paul is the author of *Eleven Ways of Looking at Love* (Red River, 2019), a collection of poems in which she "attempts to understand the myriad emotions of love through 11 words handpicked from world languages—*Koi no yokan*; *Ala rasi*; *Xinteng*; *Yuanfen*; *Forelsket*; *Tuqburni*; *Saudade*; *Onsra*; *Toska*; *Litost*; and *Desenrascanço*. Paul explains that these words cannot be directly translated into any other languages, but all of them have something to do with love" (*Sakal Times*).

~

How does anyone write about love?

Especially when you have never truly experienced it, given the innumerous and intricate exhibit on social and media outlets. I wonder if there is any source that particularly validates our emotion of "love", apart from we ourselves.

I can't write about love. The fact that I wrote an entire book about it surprises me to this day.

If I had to describe the emotion in one word I'd say, "controversial".

Yes, love is controversial.

The ideals around it have changed, but that doesn't mean whatever one feels can be disregarded, whatever timeline they are a part of.

The discourse around "love" is so vast that we tend to forget that it's not something you intellectually or perhaps magically find an answer to. It never was a question in the first place. And yet, the confusion it creates for almost everyone who is in love speaks otherwise. I mean, does anyone really ask for it?

Eleven Ways of Looking at Love began as a confession. Something that I would never have said out loud to the people I wrote it for. Along with being a confession, it was also an apology, *because* I never said it out loud to those I wrote it for.

The fact that I not only got to confess but had everyone read it and take away a part of the feeling, somehow made me feel accomplished. It was, however, just one part of the story, one that I got to mould into my narrative.

I remember the first time realisation struck me. I felt sick, because it was nothing like what I had read about. There were no butterflies in my stomach or a static sensation. I remember it clearly because it felt more like walking in cold spots than having someone come and share warmth, there was more anguish than ecstasy.

If I knew any less, I'd have said that I've been in love just once. But over the years, I've come to realise that's untrue. We fall in love almost every day, knowingly or unknowingly we become a part of it somehow. It doesn't have to be the exact composition of the hormones serotonin, dopamine and oxytocin in a specific order. But we feel it all, maybe one less than the other.

Unlike other aspects of life, love doesn't always make sense. It does tend to get complicated, but that's only because we, as humans, tend to infuse it with morals. In earlier generations, a lot of people had this clear notion about a soulmate. You meet a person whom you fall in love with, you commit to that person for life, and then you work like hell to save said commitment. And if you strayed from your partner, well, you were just a trash human. I wouldn't say that I'm speaking on behalf of cheating partners. But I'm also questioning the ideals that have been portrayed decade after decade with respect to commitment and relationships as a whole. Just as we have always accepted the fact that humans can fall *in* love, why haven't we ever conceded that it is just as possible for them to fall *out* of love? We read about Paris and Helen, Romeo and Juliet, even Bonnie and Clyde, but it shouldn't really set a bar for our emotions or our relationships.

Looking back on all the people I've come across till date, I realise that I haven't looked at the emotion like humans usually do. There has always been an association of fear and loss of self. If I had to explain this, I would say that I agree with what Nietzsche said, that love is the most "ingenious expression of egoism", and that his proposition that love is close to greed or the lust for possession holds true at some point.[1] My barely present optimistic side, however, refuses to let me completely agree with this. Why else would people willingly fight to the death for love?

If the person becomes special enough, you will voluntarily lose yourself to them. You would start losing at games if it meant they would win, you would start cancelling on your friends if they asked you to spend more time with them. You would even readily give up on previously important days and people if it meant you could satisfy the one you were sincerely infatuated with. I think this is what Nietzsche meant when he said there was a lust for possession. What happens when you don't do any of the things mentioned above? You either end it with the person because there hasn't been enough attention given or you end up in a toxic-free relationship with a sound person who shows Nietzsche's words to be lies.

Religion preaches about specific types of love, but I think that's of little use. If love could be schooled into categories,

---

1 See Friedrich Nietzsche. *The Gay Science* (1882), Book One, Section 14.

Shakespeare wouldn't have been so famous. Love has never had any boundaries; we created them. And we ourselves then protested against disrespecting them. Like I said earlier, love is controversial.

No matter who you love, be it a girl, a boy, a dog, a book, an idol, even a wall—all love is valid. If you feel your heart is going to burst into a puddle of heart-shaped confetti, yes, it is valid. If you feel you're about to melt into a puddle of tears, yes, it's valid. There is a lot that I need to discover about love, but if there is one thing I am absolutely sure about it is that you can't be in love without a certain degree of passion. You either feel it with everything you have, or you don't feel it at all.

There is no agreed definition of love. Some feel it in ways completely unknown to the ways you are acquainted with. But that doesn't mean it's not deep or any less meaningful. It gives them the same sense of support and belongingness that it gives you, maybe even more so.

Even if I became familiar with this emotion in a much more negative way than I would have liked, I don't regret one bit of it. There was the perseverance of falling in love, and there was strength in letting go of it. Loneliness and lies make for a good poet; past lovers make for better poetry.

Writing about Sex

T.W. Geraghty

T.W. Geraghty is a veteran Irish writer, journalist, and intercultural commentator.

~

It's simple—just don't. The trouble is that sometimes you can't avoid it, and for two good reasons.

The first is that, whether we like it or not, sex is a vital part of our lives. No one writing about human beings can ever completely overlook sex. As the Roman playwright whom we now call Terence (Publius Terentius Afer) wrote, more than two millennia ago, in *The Self-Tormentor*: "I'm human, so any human interest *is* my concern."[1]

The second reason is that for most people sex is quite a big turn-on—and that goes for both readers and writers. Not that you should become obsessional about it, because then you will no longer be writing about the human condition and suchlike

---

1 *Homo sum: humani nihil a me alienum puto.* In: Terence. *The Comedies.* Transl. Betty Radice. Penguin, 1976, 104.

serious matters; you will be writing about your own hang-ups, and possibly creating *pornography*. The etymology of that comparatively modern word is revealing: it derives from the Ancient Greek words for "harlot" and "writing", and means roughly "writing about whores", i.e., producing writings that are intended to inflame lust. Your creations may achieve that, but I am hoping that that wasn't their main purpose.

Sex is not love. In fiction of earlier days and even, until quite recently, in films, sex was supposed to take place only in marriage (and marriage isn't love, either). When, more adventurously, it *didn't*, it was because true love had just blossomed, and so marriage couldn't be far away. (There is a historical–institutional parallel to this, in that some cultures used to allow young people to start sleeping together once they were betrothed, that is, once they were "promised to each other".)

Alternatively, it was because those in the books or films who were making the beast with two backs were low-class riffraff, evil rapists, degenerates, dodgy foreigners, or "loose women", for none of whom a happy ending was needed.

In films the blossoming of love might be signalled by a passionate kiss, in soft-focus, accompanied by powerful, swelling music. Wow, they are going for it! There would then be a cut from pre-coital "Before" to post-coital "After": a scene showing the couple in relaxed, intimate mode. If the film was French or German, the couple might now also use the familiar form of the Second Person, *tu* or *du*, instead of the formal *vous* or *Sie*, to address each other, indicating a major change in their relationship.

There would be no sign of disappointment, or (from the perspective of the male participant) of that notorious condition that "after coitus every animal is sad, except for the cockerel and the human female".[2] Regarding this common if less than optimal

---

2   *Post coitum omne animale triste est sive gallus et mulier* (or similar), usually attributed to the second-century physician Galen of Pergamon.

outcome of sexual intercourse: not many writers have dared to go there. After all, who wants to read about the plunge into gloom and disillusionment that so often follows the excitement and challenge of seduction? The "After" that is more like a crashing hangover than a romantic afterglow?

A notable exception is Dan Jacobson's sardonic retelling, in *The Rape of Tamar*, of a piquant Old Testament story. After the eponymous event, Amnon rages at his victim, his half-sister Tamar:

> In other words, when all was done, it was "just another fuck".
> The words, I hasten to add, are Amnon's, not mine. They were said to his sister when he drove her out of his house the next morning. He uttered them in an absolute paroxysm of moral outrage, as if *he* was the one who had been assaulted and betrayed.
> "If you knew what I've been through!" he screamed at her; at least, it sounded like a scream, though his voice never rose above a whisper. "If you knew what I've suffered! For what?"
> [...]
> Just another fuck! Eloquent phrase! Say what you like, Amnon deserves to be called a man of the highest and most inflexible principle. It wasn't any common guilt or remorse made him turn on Tamar; but disappointment. Definitely, disappointment.[3]

He calls her a whore, a slut, a bitch, and even worse things, and hurls her clothes at her.

> "And I thought ... How could I have imagined? ... Another world! And nothing there! You go to the end

---

3   Dan Jacobson. *The Rape of Tamar* (1970). House of Stratus, 2015, 75.

of everything, you risk everything ... Just another fuck! Look at it, look at it lying there!"⁴

While Amnon is not a Nice Person, even by the low standards of Old Testament princes, and his treatment of Tamar is shameful, not only during the rape of course but afterwards too—as she herself tells him, "What you are doing now, Amnon, is even worse than what you did to me last night"⁵—he would not have been the first man (and certainly not the last) to be overwhelmed by the disappointment that immediately followed the gratification of his passion.

In everyday life, sex may take place without love playing much of a role (more often than not, a cynic might add). This is the way human beings behave, and have always behaved, however much the moralists, romantics, spoilsports, prudes, and religious authorities might wish it to be otherwise.

Sex tends to involve the interlocking of two bodies, with only a small number of options for physical connection available. On the other hand, the number of "positions" that can be adopted in the course of making those connections is far greater, albeit that most of the positions—regarded as too strenuous or uncomfortable, or viewed as ridiculous—will be unknown to many couples. The curious reader is referred to such well-known sex manuals as the *Kamasutra* of Vatsyayana or *The Perfumed Garden* of Sheikh Nefzawi, as well as to more recent works with titles like *The Joy of Sex*.

But sex is far more complex and difficult than that. There is a mental dimension to it too, of "sex in the head", involving fantasies and projections, obsessions, morbidities, and perversions. Every

---

4   Dan Jacobson. *The Rape of Tamar*, 76. In the Biblical account, we learn that after the rape "Amnon hated [Tamar] exceedingly; so that the hatred wherewith he hated her was greater than the love wherewith he had loved her. And Amnon said unto her, Arise, be gone" (2 *Samuel* 13:15).
5   Dan Jacobson. *The Rape of Tamar*, 77. Which is very like what Tamar says to Amnon in the Biblical version (2 *Samuel* 13:16).

person who engages in sex has a different set of needs and desires; to paraphrase the famous opening of Tolstoy's *Anna Karenina*: "All experiences of love are similar; every person experiences sex in their own way."[6] It would be a fool's game to offer models for "how to do it" from the works of established writers (as opposed to examples of "how *not* to do it", for which see further below).

When you write about sex, you write from your own experience; from what others have told you (and were they being honest?); from what you have read (the same applies); or from your imagination (a most dangerous source). The more you go into detail, the more likely your reader will find your description unconvincing, peculiar, uninteresting, or even repellant. And do you want people speculating that your account is a direct description of your own sexual behaviour, and as a consequence perhaps despise, laugh at, or even pity you?

In writing about sex, it is better to keep it simple, or even skip it altogether, and in earlier times that was easy to do. But writers today don't really have the convenient option, available to writers of the past, of drawing a discreet veil over the nitty-gritty of what went on between the sheets. If you do that, however, or play safe by sticking to standard generic descriptions, many of your readers are sure to complain that your work is unadventurous and dull.

You can take refuge, for your descriptions of the rumpy-pumpy, in metaphor, but it is difficult to come up with effective and original ones. Many fine metaphors for orgasm, for example, have already been taken, whether it is the exploding fireworks in James Joyce's *Ulysses*[7] or the earth moving in Ernest Hemingway's *For Whom the Bell Tolls*.[8] Use any of those and you will be scorned as derivative.

---

6 "All happy families are alike; each unhappy family is unhappy in its own way." Leo Tolstoy. *Anna Karenina* (1873–77). Transl. Richard Pevear and Larissa Volokhonsky. Penguin, 2006, 1.
7 James Joyce. *Ulysses* (1922). The Bodley Head, 1960, 477.
8 Ernest Hemingway. *For Whom the Bell Tolls* (1940). Arrow, 2004, 166–67.

On the other hand, if you try too hard to be original you run the risk of making a fool of yourself. This is well-documented in the history of the Bad Sex in Fiction Award, presented by the magazine *Literary Review*.

> Since 1993, the Bad Sex in Fiction Award has honoured the year's most outstandingly awful scene of sexual description in an otherwise good novel. Drawing attention to the poorly written, redundant, or downright cringeworthy passages of sexual description in modern fiction, the prize is not intended to cover pornographic or expressly erotic literature. The Award was established by Rhoda Koenig, a literary critic, and Auberon Waugh, at that time editor of *Literary Review*.[9]

Among the recipients of the prize ("winner" seems inappropriate here), the runners-up, and the "honourable mentions", there have been many of the outstanding names in modern English writing. Because the novels have generally been "otherwise good" (it is one of the rules of the award that they should be), we should take pains to spare their authors' blushes—the excerpts that follow have thus (contrary to good scholarly practice) been left anonymous.[10]

Yet where to begin? Perhaps with an unconventional take on sex?

> Katsuro moaned as a bulge formed beneath the material of his kimono, a bulge that Miyuki seized, kneaded, massaged, squashed and crushed. With the fondling, Katsuro's penis and testicles became one single mound that rolled around beneath the grip of her hand. Miyuki

---

9   https://literaryreview.co.uk/bad-sex-in-fiction-award
10 Though if you are feeling malicious you can find them online without much effort.

felt as though she was manipulating a small monkey that was curling up its paws.

A small monkey curling up its paws? A cardinal rule when writing descriptions of sex is to avoid the ridiculous (unless you are writing comedy, that is), because it will distract your reader's attention from the main action and rob the scene of its erotic tension. Laughter—like thinking of yesterday's rice-pudding or your grandmother—is a most powerful anaphrodisiac.

You should certainly try your hardest to keep control of the language, rather than letting it flop about all over the place, as it does here:

> Eliza and Ezra rolled together into the one giggling snowball of full-figured copulation, screaming and shouting as they playfully bit and pulled at each other in a dangerous and clamorous rollercoaster coil of sexually violent rotation with Eliza's breasts barrel-rolled across Ezra's howling mouth and the pained frenzy of his bulbous salutation extenuating his excitement as it whacked and smacked its way into every muscle of Eliza's body except for the otherwise central zone.

A snowball that is also a rollercoaster? The "pained frenzy of his bulbous salutation"? Oh dear. And is it helpful, in a passage of frenzied action, to slip in highfalutin' words like "copulation", "salutation" and "extenuating"? No one joyously engaged in the activity being described here would likely choose such words. Note the unusual expression "central zone". Note also the long, run-on sentence without punctuation—ah, the breathless, incoherent excitement of sex!—as in the following example too:

> …oh the sheer ecstasy of lips and tongues on genitals, either simultaneously or in alternation, never will I tire of that silvery fluidity, my sex swimming in joy like a fish in water, my self freed of both self and other, the quivering sensation, the carnal pink palpitation that detaches you from all colour and all flesh, making you see only stars, constellations, milky ways, propelling you bodiless and soulless into undulating space where the undulating skies make your non-body undulate.

There is enough undulating going on here to make you feel seasick. But it is surely only good old sex that the author is describing? And not some epochal astronomical event? Yet cosmic comparisons are only too common in bad descriptions of sex, as are elaborations on the "earth moved" narrative (Hemingway has much to answer for).

> Brida surrendered herself entirely. The forces of the world were penetrating her five senses and these were becoming transformed into an overwhelming energy. They lay down on the ground between the rock, the precipice and the sea, between the life of the seagulls flying up above and the death of the stones beneath. And they began, fearlessly, to make love, because God protects the innocent.

Yes, sex is a big and exciting event, we know that, but it's not as though it's never happened before in human history. If you make the description *too* portentous (and thereby pretentious), you will come across not as a gifted prose-poet but as a silly, immature person.

Occasionally an author will seem to be becoming excited not so much by the sex itself as by the metaphors used to describe it—as in the following example, food:

> She smells of almonds, like a plump Bakewell pudding; and he is the spoon, the whipped cream, the helpless dollop of warm custard. She steams. He applauds, his tongue hanging out (like a bloodhound espying a raw chop in a cartoon).
> She is topped with melted apricot jam. It makes her shine. Beneath that: the spongy gold, the give, the softness. Then still further down, the firmer butteriness of a thin-baked layer of crumbling shortcrust.

It is so easy, isn't it, to find yourself sidetracked by food! But it is not very flattering for the lady object of the gentleman's passion.

> I kissed the soft bristles in the hollow of her armpit, then I kissed the smaller hollow of her clavicle. I moved up to her mouth, which smelled of ripe melon. Not the wound-red Tuscan watermelon, but the pale-green variety I had bought in Naples once, and which had grown, so I was told, on the wild coast of Barbaria.

Get a grip, young man (you want to shout), and stop rambling. If you want to give us a guide to the fruit and vegetables of Italy, go ahead; otherwise, please concentrate on what you are doing!
Some writers find it hard to resist motoring imagery.

> She picks up a Bugatti's momentum. You want her more at a Volkswagen's steady trot. Squeeze the maximum mileage out of your gallon of gas. But she's eating up the

road with all cylinders blazing. You lift her out. You want to try different kinds of fusion.[11]

Others prefer equestrian metaphors: "Now his big generative jockey was inside her pelvic saddle, riding, riding, riding [...]."

Or they may go for even stranger images, as when the sexual act is compared to "a lepidopterist mounting a tough-skinned insect with a too blunt pin".

Sometimes the writing contains details so preposterous that you wonder whether a gremlin didn't access the author's computer overnight to add them surreptitiously to the text.[12]

> She unbuttoned her shirt. They stood there. Skin to skin. Her brownness against his blackness. Her softness against his hardness. Her nut-brown breasts (that wouldn't support a toothbrush) against his smooth ebony chest. [...] She could feel herself through him. Her skin. The way her body existed only where he touched her. The rest of her was smoke. She felt him shudder against her. His hands were on her haunches (that could support a whole array of toothbrushes), pulling her hips against his, to let her know how much he wanted her.

I shall never see that everyday object, the toothbrush, in quite the same light again.

---

11 This kind of obsession may be commoner than we realise. On a trip to Japan, I was once stuck for a whole day in my hotel room because of the torrential rain outside. Out of boredom I zapped through the TV channels and discovered a pornographic film that showed a man having sex with his car. I watched the whole ninety-minute film, in open-mouthed astonishment. We live in a world of wonders.

12 Or as we used to slip the word "cabbages" at random intervals into our homework assignments, to check whether our teachers were actually reading them?

Men and women experience sex differently, therefore it would be surprising if they didn't *write* about it differently. Male descriptions tend to stress the dynamic nature of intercourse, with verbs of action and images of force, domination, and conquest. Female descriptions are often focused on states and feelings, and more likely to use images of inclusion, enfolding, and belonging. Whenever men try to write about sex from a feminine perspective or women from a masculine one they are both treading on very thin ice.

That goes not just for beginners, but also for the so-called "great writers". One of the most admired American novelists of the twentieth century (again, no names!) makes one of his female characters comment that a certain man has "the longest prick in Christendom". Well, we men have all heard by now that women can also "talk dirty", but like *this*? Somehow, I think not.

Up to a point it can be done, though, without the thin ice giving way. William Maltese is a prolific and successful American writer of pornography. He has written, using several pen-names, for different kinds of reader: erotica for straight men, gay pornography, and erotic novels for female consumers of "Romance" fiction.[13] Nonetheless, I would suggest that those of us who are less talented than William are better advised to stick with what we know.

There is much to be said in favour of discreet accounts of sex.[14] This is not just a question of taste or style. There is a deeper reason. In almost every other kind of writing, narrative precision and descriptive detail are to be lauded, but not necessarily when it comes to sex. No detailed account will ever meet the expectations of more than a handful of readers, because we are all so different (and individual) in our sexuality. Why not therefore let the reader's

---

13 He can be found at www.williammaltese.com/bio/.
14 Or, as the comedian Robert Webb puts it, in his autobiography, and noting that he couldn't track down the quotation "but maybe you know it": "Sex is vital to the novel. Fucking is not" (*How Not to Be a Boy*. Canongate, 2017, 174).

imagination take over, filling in, in his or her mind's eye, the lesser details in whatever manner is individually satisfying?

A good erotic novel or short story will, over time, be found more rewarding than a pornographic video. As is also the case with horror writing—where the horror has more impact when you allow your imagination to fill in the gaps, tapping into your own darkest personal fears and nightmares—so erotic writing, too, is more effective when it leaves space for the reader's imagination to paint in what they privately, and most intimately, find sexy.

Writing about Yourself[1]

Peer Khan

———⋅⟫⟪⋅———

Peer Khan is a discreet pen-name, used by this writer only for poetry. He is composing a series of sonnets on aspects of India, questions of moral responsibility, and the nature of creativity.

~

Writing about yourself, the hardest task
Is how to frame the questions: how to know
Which ones to leave unsaid, which ones to ask
(Though where hurt beckons, that is where you'll go).
You'll fall into the deepest, filthiest part
Of what you were, a horror without name.
Below the rag-and-bone shop of the heart[2]

---

1 The writer warns how poets must, while aiming to achieve transcendence, first dig into their past and relentlessly confront what they find there. However, drawing on such personal material in their work may (if they have been honest) make them deeply vulnerable.

2 The "rag-and-bone shop of the heart" and "those ladders" are references to W.B Yeats's famous autobiographical poem "The Circus Animals' Desertion" (see, too, the essay by Randhir Khare, "Waking Dream:

Lurk, deeper still, long memories of shame.
Your work (those ladders) will then be your course,
A path to lead you slowly to the light,
But should your finer spirit's wingèd horse
Suddenly lift you to the steepest height,
The unforgiving spotlight of disgrace
May catch you yet, naked, in that high place.

Reflections on Poetry", in this volume).

Writing about Psychopaths[1]

Heena Rathore-Pardeshi

Heena Rathore-Pardeshi is an award-winning author, developmental editor and scriptwriter. With over nine years of experience in creative writing (fiction and creative non-fiction), the craft of storytelling, English, French and Greek literature, and backed by courses from prestigious universities like Harvard and Yale, Heena works as a freelance editor and scriptwriter and analyst (for adaptations). She lives in Pune with her ten rescue cats in a house full of books.

~

Writing anything is hard because it doesn't only take a good eye and a good hand in the art itself, but also involves deep exploration of the self, taking in both the good things and things that might not be pleasant at all.

---

1 The terms "psychopath" and "sociopath" are often used interchangeably but are entirely different. Many of their traits may be similar, but the distinctive ones are not applicable to both in the same way.

The activity of writing can sometimes feel overwhelming if done constantly over time, because a writer, at least one who practises their craft faithfully, will eventually stumble upon things about themselves and about who they are that they might not like. These things can include powerful emotions, feelings, and desires.

Emotions and feelings have a great deal of influence on one's writing. There is a famous saying in the writing community: *No tears for the writer, no tears for the reader.* And I believe firmly that if a writer is not emotionally involved in their writing, they can hardly expect their readers to be swept away by it.

My writing is heavily emotional, and it is not only because I am an emotional and intuitive person, but also because I have suffered from dysthymia (a form of chronic depression) and complex post-traumatic stress disorder since a young age. As a result, I have developed the compulsive tendency to dissect my emotions, and writing helps me not only to dissect but to process these emotions on a micro-level. It does get obsessive for me most of the time, as the need to write is very strong whenever I go through an emotional turmoil, but in the end it is what gives me peace.

So, to put the bare and ugly truth before you, writing is neither as easy as people think it is, nor as simple as they think it ought to be. What I am talking about here is writing in general, but if I am to pick out a specific theme, it gets even tougher. When it comes to writing about darker themes and emotions, it gets particularly tricky. It would be no exaggeration to say that writing to scare the readers and creating negative characters is akin to living a nightmare over and over again. I adhere to the same principle of "tears" in writing for dark themes and emotions too: *No scare for the writer, no scare for the reader.* It's as simple as that.

This means that writing about dark themes, and especially about dark characters, is a huge task. Unfortunately, it is an area of expertise for me because I have been writing about dark characters for the last seven years. For instance, my book *Deceived* (Citrus, 2019) explores dark psychological aspects of all its characters, going into the depths of the psyche of three in particular—two of whom are sociopaths, and the third a psychopath. The psychopath is the antagonist of my story.

Characterisation

Characters are not just *written*—they are created from scratch, and thoroughly developed to display realistic traits like those of real people. It is like planting a tree—you need to first sow the seed, water it, give it ample sunlight, protect it from rain, add necessary fertilisers, care for it, and nurture it, after which it will slowly grow, giving you the desired fruit or, in the case of writing, the desired effect. Personally speaking, for me characters are as important as the story itself, because the story is always about characters; hence, a writer cannot afford to have a weak character, no matter what genre they choose to write in or what story they end up telling.

Now, when we talk about writing about psychopaths it further ups the ante, as it is dangerously close to the edge of darkness that we all try to stay away from as writers. Writing about them not only requires a substantial amount of research but also entails discovering their motivations, the way they think, the way they function, and the way they may react to a stimulus. To create a character who is a psychopath, the writer will have to explore the uncharted dark territories of their mind, emotions, and motivations, which for me is the scariest part of working on such characters. Yet while the entire world knows how evil psychopaths can be, we as writers must let go of such prejudices or opinions and open ourselves to experiencing and understanding their drive, their trauma, and the problems they may face because of their distinctive mental disorder.

Let us take as an example the most famous of all fictional psychopaths: Norman Bates (in Alfred Hitchcock's film *Psycho*, 1960). Norman is *a certain way*, but he is that certain way *because* of something, and that something is what we, as writers, need to explore. If you would like to dig deep and try to understand at least one of the possibilities of this character's development, I would recommend the TV series *Bates Motel*, which in five seasons (2013–17) explores Norman's past from a unique perspective. It is, of course, *one* of the possibilities. But that, in fiction, is how things work.

We need to stroll through the uncharted territory of a psychopath's psyche in order to create a fictional psychopath, which makes it necessary to understand their childhood. It is childhood that lays the foundation for how a person turns out when they have grown up. While working on any character, especially the flawed ones, what is of utmost importance is to explore their childhood carefully and craft it according to how their motivations are developed, and all this must be done in accordance with the stake, the involvement, that they have in the main story.

Another thing to keep in mind is mannerisms and body language. People with severe mental illnesses suffer from comorbid conditions like obsessive-compulsive disorders, depression, anxiety, aggression, impulsivity, substance-use disorder, etc., and all these conditions combined will have a very distinct effect on the way they behave and react. Their body language will be heavily influenced, as will their way of speaking and their overall temperament. For example, the antagonist in *Deceived* is an obsessively organised person. He simply cannot tolerate seeing things out of order or messy, gets agitated easily, and will often react violently. This element was so important in the book that I had to constantly keep his traits at the back of my mind because they needed to reflect in everything he did—the way he lived his day-to-day life, his profession, and his habits and behaviour, especially around others.

Is the character exhibiting psychopathic tendencies the main character, one of the secondary characters, the antagonist, or just a foil character?[2] Establishing their role in the book will determine the extent of the characterisation needed, i.e., the amount of detailing you will need. For example, if your psychopath is simply a foil character, you won't need too much and can simply work out a basic profile for them. On the other hand, if the psychopath is your main character, you will have to build them up from scratch.

The reason for sweating over characterisation is that characters drive the story forward and make it come alive. If you go wrong in characterisation, the chances are that your story will fall flat on its face.

If you have a psychopath as your protagonist, or as a secondary figure with a substantial role in the story, you'll have to work on the following aspects of their character:

- Appearance
- Attitude
- Body language
- Childhood
- Habits
- Manners
- Medical history
- Motivations
- Nature
- Personality
- Significant past incidents in their life
- Thoughts

---

2 Foil characters are used as a foil to highlight qualities of the main characters. They are generally polar opposites of the main characters. Authors use them to bring out the qualities of their main characters indirectly. For example, Draco Malfoy is a foil to Harry Potter's character in J.K. Rowling's *Harry Potter* series, and Sansa Stark is a foil to Arya Stark's character in George R.R. Martin's *A Song of Ice and Fire* series.

Character Arcs

Character arcs are an essential tool when it comes to creating realistic characters. Working on the character of a psychopath, we usually defy the norms and follow one of what are probably the two least popular character arcs in writing.

Flat Arc: This is when the character does not go through any kind of emotional or personal growth or decline—they end just as they started. This usually happens when you have a character who is either genetically a psychopath or is shown as one right from the start of a story.

Negative Arc: Here, the decline or emotional downfall of the character is shown. Thus, the arc would be a downward curve on the graph. Let's have a look at these in more detail.

In the flat character arc, as far as emotional or overall personal growth and transformation are concerned, none can be seen. But it should be noted that, while there is no growth, there is no significant decline either. This usually happens when the character knows about their *inner truth* and embraces it without any remorse. As most of the deviance in the arc is based on false belief relating to inner truth, you can see why this character arc is called a flat arc. There is nothing that the characters need to learn about themselves or find out about their life or anything important related to it. They either already know it, or it is never revealed to them, thereby extinguishing the scope for growth or decline.

When we begin our story, we generally either show a person who is already deranged and psychopathic, or we use their traits to aid us in the plot. Unless we are going into depth about how they became the way they are, and we are using their character as a psychopath right from the start, a flat arc is appropriate. For example, Norman Bates is a psychopath from the start in *Psycho* (by Robert Bloch) and that is how he is in the end too, so no major transformation happens, except for the occasional fluctuations in his tendencies in some instances. This is a flat arc. On the other hand, in the series *Bates Motel* (developed by Carlton Cuse, Kerry Ehrin and Anthony Cipriano), the character of Norman is completely taken apart and dissected throughout the series. In it, Norman Bates metamorphoses into a psychopath. The creators dwell on the question of *how Norman became the way he did*, exploring the negative character arc.

In a negative character arc, the character ends up in a *worse state* than at the start of the story. This is usually done by showing the mental decline of a character or their loss (of a possession, a person, or something of great importance to them). In a negative arc, the emotional downfall of a character is shown in detail and the story is scripted accordingly. This arc is therefore mostly used when you want to explore the *how* and the *why* of your character's state. If you have a psychopath as your main character and you go into their backstory in detail, revolving your story around how they became a psychopath (if, in fact, that is the case) it would be a negative arc, a downward curve on the graph. For example, Norman Bates in *Bates Motel*. Other examples that could illustrate negative arcs are most of the characters of George R.R. Martin's *A Song of Ice and Fire* series; the two that immediately pop up in the mind are Eddard "Ned" Stark, who dies because of his loyalty to the dead king and dearest friend, alone and knowing that his entire family would be targeted by Cersei next, and Robb Stark who starts off as the son of the newly made king's hand and then, after a series of elaborate events, dies brutally in the Red Wedding.

The flat and the negative arc are not popular amongst writers of fiction because using them requires a certain degree of expertise. They are also dangerous to work with because, should you fail to pull them off in the way you intended, the chances of disappointing the reader are great indeed. That is why, in most cases, writers of fiction prefer other types of character arc that focus primarily on the growth and transformation of their main characters.

Research

Working on a character with any kind of physical or mental illness, it is essential that the writer does a fair amount of research, so as not to put out inaccurate or misleading information regarding the illness they are portraying. Most novice writers think that research has no place in fiction, but that is wrong. Your fiction must be grounded in reality, to make the foundation of your work and the core ideas stronger. Also, it will serve you well to remember that whatever you are writing about may be read by a person going through that very same illness, so falsifying facts is not acceptable. I am not referring to dramatic exaggeration. Dramatic exaggeration of facts is okay; falsifying them is not. Make it a rule, and you will be able to write about tricky or important topics in a better way.

You won't use all your research in the story. No. Your research is important for you, as a writer, to be able to grasp the full extent of what you are working with, for you to be able to understand your character inside out, to be able to visualise them and create them in the right way. To be able to find an appropriate tone and voice for the narration as well as in dialogues. In short, to be able to put yourself in their shoes and be able to feel and think like them.

Writing about a psychopath is also hard because we not only have to create their character realistically, we also need to understand them—whether as writer or as reader—on an emotional plane. So, while working with such a character you must be sure not only about their motivation and their stake in the story but also about their backstory, personal history, genetics, and family background. As these characters fall into the category of emotionally traumatised individuals, you need to do the right amount of research to be able to understand their thinking and be able to strike a good balance.

Just as all writers have different ways of writing, they also have different ways of researching. But some things are rudimentary, and here is a list of steps that I think are necessary while you are doing the research work for a diabolical character such as a psychopath:

- Start with basic internet research.
- Interview people behind the websites and blogs that you find the most useful.
- Interview doctors and therapists who deal with mental illnesses or any other illness you are going to be using in your work.
- Study past cases by digging them out of your local or online library archives.
- Watch as many true crime documentaries as you can on personalities similar to your fictional character in order to understand how they behave and to learn their mannerisms and body language. Pay close attention to how they react, respond, and talk.
- Talk to people who might have closely encountered or interacted with people exhibiting traits like those of your main character.
- Read non-fiction accounts in books and articles on this subject and study the characterisation of such people that you find there.

After doing your research, use everything you have learned to build your character and to set the tone of the narrative. I normally go for epistolary chapters in the form of letters or diary entries, as they offer a deeper and more intimate perspective. But I am only able to do so after I have spent at least four to six months researching and learning about my characters.

Once you have mastered the research and the characterisation, you can easily create your own unique, morally deviant, and emotionally distant psychopath, who will stay with your readers, revisiting them when they least expect it, long after they have turned the last page of your book. I receive messages and emails telling me how some of my readers are still haunted by my characters and their doings, and although on the one hand I feel bad for them, on the other I rejoice, as a writer, because it is then that I know that I have done my job successfully.

It is important to keep reminding yourself to take breaks while researching and working on dark themes and characters, because if you are a writer worth your salt you will have to "get into the head" of your character. This comes with its own set of problems—it unsettles you in a psychological way that is very hard to avoid. Working on the development of characters who were mentally deranged, I suffered horrible dreams that left me feeling restless throughout the day. The research proved especially difficult, as I had to sit through long videos or read lengthy texts about the traumas of these men and women and do so attentively enough to be able to take notes so as to understand how they think. That took a toll on me and my mental health. I do strongly suggest not pushing yourself too hard during the research phase, and that you take breaks in between to reset your mind.

Promises and Payoffs

Promises and payoffs are a subject not much touched upon in most books on writing. It wouldn't be wrong to say that most new writers don't even know what they mean.

Promises are the expectations that a writer sets up for their readers at the beginning of a story; payoff is simply the meeting of those expectations or promises. Most writers make a lot of promises and raise their reader's expectations by creating a great hook for their story, through a truly interesting, entertaining, and involving inciting incident.[3] Yet as soon as the middle section of a

---

3   Inciting incident: An event that draws the reader into the story and sets everything else that happens in motion.

novel is reached (in a novel with a traditional three-act structure), most of those promises will start to fall apart and, more often than not, by the end of the middle and the beginning of the final part even the writer may have forgotten them! Then readers will feel dissatisfied or disappointed, claiming that the book started well but later failed to live up to their expectations.

The main reason why this happens is that writers often pour hour after hour of hard work into the opening part of their book, but rarely plan the ending. And so if a writer has worked first on the beginning and only much later scripted the ending of their novel, those promises will likely be forgotten. The best way to not let this happen is to work on the beginning and the ending of your novel together. For example, if you're using the basic three-act structure, work on the opening (act 1) and final part (act 3) first. The middle section (act 2) can always be dealt with after you've figured out how your story will begin and how it will end.

As writers, we owe it to our readers not to disappoint them, and I truly believe that once a writer has mastered promises and payoffs that is unlikely to happen.

How To Write Funny

Krishna Shastri Devulapalli

Krishna Shastri Devulapalli is a humour writer, columnist, screenwriter, novelist, playwright and illustrator/cartoonist. His novels include *Ice Boys in Bell-bottoms*, a 1970s bildungsroman, *Jump Cut*, a seriocomic thriller set in the Tamil film industry, and the comic *The Sentimental Spy: The Family Bond*. His other works include a humorous epistolary play, *Dear Omana: Notes on How to Be a Literary Sensation*, with the backdrop of the Indian publishing industry, and a book of non-fiction, *How to Be a Literary Sensation*. He has co-edited *Madras on My Mind: A City in Stories*, and writes regularly for *The Hindu*, *Deccan Chronicle* and *Scroll*, among other journals. He is currently at work on a detective series for the web, and a feature film. His forthcoming books include *The Artful Dodger: How I Side-stepped Life with Movies, Books and Music* and a sequel to his first novel titled *Rally Days and Disco Nights*.

~

One way of doing it, I guess, would be by holding your pen between your big toe and long toe. But jokes aside (a promise from a humour writer you should never take at face value), at the risk of incurring the wrath of the other contributors (which, as a writer of humour, is one of my primary goals), let me tell you unequivocally that, in this anthology, my piece was the most difficult one to write. And that includes the essay on writing erotica. In fact, I asked the editor if I could do that piece instead. (But—with neither nudge nor wink—he said that that opening had already been filled by someone more qualified.) Because I thought I had a better chance of doing a how-to piece on humour taking a route spattered with humours (that's a synonym for body fluids) than one in which I had to list out the whys and hows of writing comedy.

The point I'm trying to make is that a writer of erotica has a better chance of making a how-to piece sexy (or funny, most certainly) than a writer of humour has of making a similar piece funny, let alone sexy. And that is precisely the crux of humour writing. For a bona fide humour writer, being funny at all times is not just critical but non-negotiable. Being mildly funny or occasionally funny is as shameful to a practitioner of humour as not writing about loss and redemption is to a writer of literary fiction. So pathological is this unhealthy need to be wildly funny at all times that the writer of comedy would feel done out if he couldn't slip a gag into his mercy petition.

So we come to Rule Number Two. (Where's Rule Number One, you ask? Well, Paragraph One of this piece contains Rule Number One: To be a humour writer, you have to be an inveterate displeaser.) Unless being funny has been a biological requirement from your infancy, a predilection which has got your face into intimate encounters with open palms and blunt instruments and which hasn't taught you a thing except seeing the world around you, including the funeral of a close relative, especially the funeral of a close relative, as a set-up for a cartoon, limerick, story, essay, novel or script, do not attempt humour.

Which brings us to Rule Number Three: do not attempt humour. You can attempt the CA entrance exam, doing the plank, or understanding Sadhguru. And possibly succeed, after having failed a few times. Comedy, on the other hand, is brutally unforgiving. You cannot *attempt* it. Like you can't attempt poetry. Or defusing an IED. Because the results can be catastrophic for innocent bystanders. Unfunny comedy is worse than unintentional comedy. So if you *must* attempt humour, do it privately. Very privately. On the other hand, attempt bomb-dismantling at a poetry session or attempt performance poetry while a bomb is being defused, and you could succeed at humour.

Other rules: if you think P.G. Wodehouse is funny, don't write humour. If you think words like "waddle", "dodder", "harrumph", "blather", "croak", etc., are funny, desist from writing humour. If you like to forward jokes, give humour writing a miss. If your family thinks you are hilarious, most likely you are not. Also, if you're a bigot, sexist, misogynist or moneylender, humour may not be your thing.

With the hows out of the way, this essay would be incomplete if we didn't address the why. Because the why, in a way, is the how. And to get to the why, we need to start with the when. (Swami Nithyananda, please note.)[1]

I think I began valuing being funny above all else while quite young. The obvious reason would have to be Father. He was a professional illustrator and writer of comics before there was such a profession in India. (Today, when we speak of comics, we mean Marvel and DC's superheroes, blood-curdling Japanese manga and their many demented by-blows. I don't know how anyone can miss the irony that there is not a *thing* comic about any of the books which come under the genre called comics today.) Not that Father did humour exclusively. Along with his popular comic

---

[1] Swami Nithyananda (born Arunachalam Rajasekaran) is an Indian godman, who is known among his followers as Nithyananda Paramashivam or Paramahamsa Nithyananda. Following the charges of rape and abduction filed in Indian courts, he fled India and has remained in hiding since 2019. In 2020, he announced the founding of his own self-proclaimed island nation, Kailaasa.

creations, Dumbu (a kind of Telugu Dennis the Menace), and an anthropomorphic dog with a mind of its own called Bhairav, he did picture stories belonging to the historical, folklore and crime genres, too. But the funny stuff was what got me.

And for a serious-looking guy who seemed to intimidate house guests without even trying, Father was funny in real life, too, when he chose to be. As was his father, my grandfather, a guy known pre-eminently for being a romantic poet. Mother was funny but in a totally different way. While Dad and Granddad specialised in deflationary humour, Mother played elaborate pranks, utterly oblivious to their consequences, and said completely inappropriate things that women of her time didn't say in public. Whether she was clueless or having everyone on, it's hard to say.

But it wasn't as if anyone at home told me, "Naanna, when you grow up, it's important you be funny, okay? That's how you conquer the world." My folks were many things, not all good, other than funny, both intentionally and unintentionally. But of all the qualities on offer, I picked funny. If I was a Korean child (I have been "accused" of looking like a mix of several kinds of "Far Eastern" but that's another story), going through the traditional fortune-telling custom of *doljabi* on his first birthday, among the calligraphy pen, the book, money and the other items before me, I would have picked up the whoopee cushion.

Now that I have somehow managed—obliquely though, I must admit—to talk about the hows and whens of humour, let's talk about the whats. There are two principal ingredients to comedy, which are as indispensable to gin and tonic as gin and tonic: truth and the Establishment.

Is your joke based on truth? Because, if it isn't, it could never be funny. A caricature would be a good example to illustrate the importance of truth in comedy. Would a caricature work if it didn't, first and foremost, provide a proper likeness of the subject? The base of all caricatures is the person herself. And a clever, not to mention cruel, manipulation of the feature(s) most suited for exaggeration. If one were to do a caricature of Stan Laurel or Aamir Khan, it would be near-impossible not to make the ears extra-large. Likewise, caricatures of Angelina Jolie, KCR[2] and Jennifer Lopez would be hard to do if they didn't amplify the mouth, nose and posterior respectively.

Coming to Ingredient Two: the Establishment. For a satirist, the target is *always* the Establishment. The satirist's raison d'être *is* fighting the Establishment. Let's take a leaf out of our glorious past—real or otherwise—that infallible ready reckoner for everything today. Can you imagine our homegrown satirists Tenali Rama, Birbal or Gopal Bhand[3] siding with the king? These characters existed for the sole purpose of making the megalomaniacal king see the error of his ways.

How terribly unfunny our folklore would be if our jesters mocked the peasant and propped up the king.

In other words, the underdog is the comedian's principal ally and weapon.

What happens to a humour writer when he hears a joke? Does a joke become to him what blood becomes to a surgeon or sex to an adult entertainer: business as usual?

For one thing, I can tell you, my reaction isn't normal. When I hear a funny line in a movie or show, I don't laugh. Or giggle or titter or guffaw. I find myself letting out a piercing "ha", clapping loudly and hitting pause. This is as much to savour the line or gag as to tell my poor wife—immediately—*all* the reasons why it's funny, what it reminds me of, who the writer's influences

---

2 Kalvakuntla Chandrashekar Rao, the first chief minister of the state of Telangana. Refer to his photographs to get an idea of how his nose is tailor-made for a caricature.
3 Tenali Rama, poet, scholar, thinker and a special advisor in the court of the Vijayanagara king, Krishnadevaraya. Birbal, one of the nine jewels in the court of the Mughal king Akbar, known for his wit. Gopal Bhand, court jester in medieval Bengal, in the court of Raja Krishnachandra (1710–83), the king of Nadia.

could be, how I would have taken the gag further by going in this direction or that, and, above all, why I'm so cool. (I permit myself this eccentricity exclusively in my own home, I add. And my wife has been patient with my genuinely disturbing behaviour. This and the rest. For over a quarter of a century.)

While watching *The Chair* on Netflix the other day, I found myself doing my annoying yelp–applaud–pause routine. It was a scene in which two senior professors (and these are seriously senior), who might be facing termination of their employment, are talking of the injustice of it.

"They can't do this to us, you know," says the younger of the two. "Considering we are in the prime of our lives."

The older prof's response is a whiny, extended fart. While I pretty much keeled over at the sheer brilliance of that gag/non-line employed to illustrate the stark contrast between what is being said and what is, what got me was the line that followed.

The windy professor conversationally asks: "Was that you or me?"

This is pure comedy genius. Just the juxtaposition of those three "lines", the economy of it all. And like all great comedy, the undeniable tragedy encompassed within.

I thought it was a terrific reworking, most likely unintentional, of one of my all-time favourite comedy lines, which is ironically from a silent movie: *City Lights*.

After an all-night binge, Chaplin and his drunk millionaire buddy are so out of it that their car has gone off the road and is hurtling like a misguided missile down the sidewalk. As pedestrians leap out of the renegade vehicle's path, passenger Chaplin says something to the drunk driver. We can't hear what he's saying, obviously.

The dialogue card comes on a second later: *Don't you think you're driving too fast?*

The driver responds to his companion. The dialogue card: *Oh, am I driving?*

Which in turn reminded me of an old cartoon in *Punch*. Two bleary-eyed winos are sitting side by side on a park bench. It is night. There's a cartoonist's crescent moon above the city skyline. One of the fellows has his arms outstretched and his hands clenched like he's holding something. The caption: *I'm tired. Why don't you drive for a bit?*

I could go on. Playing a kind of reverse *antakshari*[4] of jokes, gags and punchlines—from books, movies, shows and personal experience—each beginning where the previous one left off, going all the way back to when I was in the womb listening like a modern-day Abhimanyu[5] to my dad's stories.

In essence, why and how do you write humour? You do it because you can't help it.

---

4   A spoken parlour game played in India. Each contestant sings the first verse of a song that begins with the consonant of the Hindi alphabet at which the previous contestant's song ended. The word is derived from two Sanskrit words: *antya*, meaning end, and *akshara*, meaning letter of the alphabet. When these words are combined and an "i" suffixed, the term means "the game of the ending letter".

5   Warrior from the ancient epic, the Mahabharata. Son of the Pandava king Arjuna, he is celebrated for his strategy of breaking through the *chakravyuha*, a formidable and labyrinthine military formation. A folktale separate from the epic claims that Abhimanyu learned this from Arjuna while still inside his mother's womb. However, he was unable to hear the bit about how to exit the chakravyuha, and this incomplete knowledge contributed to his demise.

Memory Plays Truant

Remembering and Forgetting in the Writing of Fiction[1]

Gita Viswanath

Gita Viswanath is a Vadodara-based writer. She has taught English literature at school, college, and university levels, and is currently Academic Fellow, Forum on Contemporary Theory, Baroda. Dr Viswanath is the author of *The "Nation" in War: A Study of Military Literature and Hindi War Cinema* (Cambridge Scholars, 2014) and the novels *Twice It Happened* (Vishwakarma, 2019) and *A Journey Gone Wrong* (Vishwakarma, 2022), as well as academic papers in the field of film studies and literature. She has also published short stories and poetry in journals and made a number of short films.

~

---

1 I am deeply indebted to Sumana Roy, Tanushree Podder and Priya Sarukkai Chabria for their inputs, and equally grateful to Dr Aarati Mujumdar of the Modern College of Business and Science, Muscat, Oman, where parts of this essay were delivered in September 2018 in a lecture on the creative process.

> What you end up remembering isn't always the same as what you witnessed ... so I need to return briefly to a few incidents that have grown into anecdotes, to some approximate memories which time has deformed into certainty. I can't be sure of the actual events anymore; I can at least be true to the impressions those facts left. That's the best I can manage.
> —Julian Barnes, *The Sense of an Ending (2011)*

Fiction connotes a narrative coming from one's imagination—unreal, untrue. Experience on the other hand is real, true, something we go through rather than imagine. But the twain shall meet, as we will see! How does this happen? What does the process of mining one's memory to write fiction, clearly a creative progression, involve? In this essay, I would like to examine the role of memory in the writing of fiction. The relationship between memory, experience and imagination has been at the centre of debates over the writing of fiction for a while now.[2] As illustration, I would use instances from my own novel, *Twice It Happened*. I would also share some views of other novelists whom I interviewed for the purpose of this article.

According to Robert J. Sternberg, we use memory as a vehicle to restore information from experience.[3] Memory and its various forms are central to the processes involved in the preservation and recovery of information that we gather through our senses from the world around us. We also derive our individual identities and forge relationships through our memories of ourselves and others.

In order to understand the role of memory in the writing of fiction, we need to examine the creative process of writers and surely there are as many processes as there are writers. Let me deploy the metaphor of cooking to explain the creative process. The first

---

2   See, for example, *New Directions in the Philosophy of Memory*. Ed. Kourken Michaelian, Dorothea Debus & Denis Perrin. Routledge, 2018.
3   *The Nature of Cognition*. Ed. Robert J. Sternberg. The MIT Press, 1998.

stage, and this is a purely subjective point of view, is the gathering of ingredients. The ingredients, in the case of writing, would primarily be ideas of all kinds. What do I write about? The answer to this question comes from inspiration from various sources. The books I read, the people I meet, the places I experience—all of these are recorded in memory to be retrieved for future use. At this point, we are merely gathering ingredients; we may proceed with cooking immediately or, most likely, we may not. There is an element of randomness in this process. We are not even collecting ingredients to suit one particular recipe; we could just be picking different ones in arbitrary, unconscious ways.

We then progress to the next stage of cooking: marinating the meat or vegetables. It is an indisputable fact that marinated meat (or veggies) tastes better, as it has absorbed the flavours and tastes of the different herbs and spices. When ideas seep into our consciousness, some remain and some vanish. The ones that remain are worth writing about. Now that I have marinated the meat (or veggies), we come to the most important stage in the process: cooking it; in the case of writing, we now have to cook up our story. It is at this point that I stir the plot gently if I am cooking a psychological drama or briskly if I am cooking a murder mystery. I work self-consciously on the conflict-action-resolution arc that is integral to any form of writing. I choose my narrative form, my temporal and spatial settings and of course flesh out my characters as they move about acting their roles in my plot. I also garnish my work with a flourish of similes, metaphors, and other literary devices. Broadly, this is how a creative product comes into being.

However, the moot point here is, how do we rely on our memory in the various stages of cooking our story as outlined above? Memory plays truant, as a character in my novel has said. Highly selective, memory can be distorted, also determined by whom we are disclosing our memories to. Clarity therefore is alien to the faculty of memory. Events get twisted out of shape in the process of recall and may barely resemble our experience or even our early memory of it. The temporal dislocation between the time of events, the time of recall, which can be multiple times, and the time of writing dismantles the notion of memory as reliable. Does that mean we abandon our task of writing? Certainly not! This is when we bring in the faculty of imagination that transcends our sensory perceptions. The greatest works of art or even scientific discoveries and inventions could never have been produced without the power of the imagination. Through a combination of memory and imagination, we move on to cook up our story.

The use of memory would lead us to the next tricky question, of whether fiction is in fact autobiographical. After all, there is no such thing as pure fiction, there never can be. As Berntsen and Rubin have noted, autobiographical memory refers to one's knowledge not only of specific past episodes but also of whole life periods, as well as the overall course of one's life.[4] How then does this memory seep into one's writing? Deep-seated regrets, childhood trauma, unarticulated pain, anger at certain institutionalised forms of oppression and so on do find a way into one's writing. While it is cathartic for the writer, it is by no means entirely a window into the writer's own life. Also, for me personally, authenticity is a cherished value. I would find it extremely difficult to make my character a nuclear scientist, for instance. I know nothing of their innermost anxieties, insecurities, and ambitions. Since I have no experience here, even if I tried to write based on conversations with nuclear scientists. I would still feel inadequate to represent their lives in my writing.

Sumana Roy, the author of *Missing: A Novel* (2018), concurs:

> Memory and imagination are related to each other in a way that we do not always acknowledge. They often

---

4 See *Understanding Autobiographical Memory: Theories and approaches*. Ed. D. Berntsen and D.C. Rubin. Cambridge University Press, 2012.

blur—what we imagine about people becomes part of our memory. Memory is my reservoir—even a memory of things imagined. The characters I have so far created in my fiction have mostly been based on people I have known, and therefore my memory of them.[5]

Dylan Trigg has argued[6] that the memory of places we experience is fundamental to a sense of self. Thus, the selection of locales one is familiar with and can portray with warmth and affection is a crucial stage in the creative process. *Episodic memories* (remembrance of personal experiences that took place at a particular place and time) are intertwined into the creative process.

Tanushree Podder, author of nine works of fiction, says:

> Much of my writing is inspired by the culture and customs of places I visit. For instance, the location of my detective series is based on a small town located at the foothills of the Himalayas. While scouting for an appropriate location, I recollected the nuances and fine points of the place where I spent two years. Similarly, notes on the Mughal architecture made during my visit to the structures came in handy while writing the two books set in the Mughal era.[7]

In my own case, the village of Gajulupur in which a large part of the narrative unfolds is based on Gownipalli, a village in Karnataka, which is the ancestral home of my father. The action that takes place here and, descriptions of life in the village evolve

---

5   From an interview with the author. Sumana Roy's *Missing* is published by Aleph.
6   Dylan Trigg. *The Memory of Place: A Phenomenology of the Uncanny*. Ohio University Press, 2013.
7   From an interview with the author.

through the memories of the writer and the characters, Nagamma and Chitra. Thus, there are three levels of consciousness. First, my own memory of the village and, secondly, the memory I bestow to Nagamma and Chitra who are a generation apart. The first-person narratives in a way become an extension of the authorial voice without the characters becoming entirely *raisonneurs*, embodiments of my viewpoint.

There are varieties in memory such as long-term, short-term, declarative, episodic, and so on. Without going into unnecessary detail, it will suffice to say that this remarkable capacity of the human brain to remember and forget can be creatively utilised in writing. To go back to the characters in my novel, memories manifest themselves in different ways, depending on the character's temperament, circumstances, and psychological profile.

Sridhar's memory is raw despite all the years. His resentment towards his family remains unhindered by the march of time.

Aditya, on the other hand, develops an indifference towards his family over time. His memory is processed in such a way that the bitterness of the past is not allowed to taint the present.

Nagamma's memory is the kind that lingers, simmering in her consciousness under a façade of resignation. Her memory of a long-held secret is kept on the backburner throughout her life, occasionally forcing itself to the forefront. Her hardnosed pragmatism lets her live out her daily life in relative peace.

Chitra's is an eidetic memory that can recall even the minutest detail of life in a cantonment as well as emotions experienced at different points in time.

Nagamma's stories to the children in the large extended family are evidence of the play of memory and imagination in the process of spinning a yarn. As she herself admits, "So, what if I'm telling you a real-life story; I still have to imagine some parts. Or else would you be interested in listening to me?" (95). Into our memories, we add dollops of imagination in order to tell a tale.

However, there is really no absolute and reliable way in which the human brain can recall the past.

This brings us to the notion of the unreliable narrator in fiction, to borrow a term from Wayne Booth.[8] Unreliable narrators are embodiments of the unreliability of human memory. In my own novel, there are three first-person narratives and each narrator may qualify as an unreliable narrator.

The first, Jyothi, is the recipient of extra-terrestrial messages from her aunt Nagamma. Unable to cope, she ends up with a nervous breakdown.

The second, Nagamma, herself, narrates her story after her death. Her voice is the disembodied voice of a woman on her way to the other world.

The third, Chitra, tells her story through emails several years after her event-time, during which she experienced deeply complex relationships.

In all these narrations, the wide gap between event-time and narration-time results in dependence on memory, which as we have shown is highly inconsistent. Does this mean there is no value to these narratives? Where then does Truth, if there is an absolute Truth, come into play? Ultimately, does it matter to the writer or the reader if there is memory in imagination, imagination in memory, fiction in memory or memory in fiction?

Pune-based poet and novelist Priya Sarukkai Chabria goes beyond memory as mere individual memories of a given person. She understands memory in a Jungian manner as the repository of the recollections of a civilisation.

> Memory is the nebulous changeling we carry which shapes us; it is a site of grief and gladness. In my speculative fiction *Clone*,[9] I focus on the historical import of memory

---

8 See Wayne C. Booth. *The Rhetoric of Fiction*. University of Chicago Press, 1961.
9 Zubaan, 2018.

and the sense of responsibility this carries in the face of fake and spurious history-making. I "use" the mined memory of characters down centuries to suggest our plural histories. For memory is linked to ethics, morality, minorities, artificial monoculturalism. In literature, we use our imagination to return to truths; therefore, we need to base our writing on facts, not fiction. Literature's power is to probe what makes us human.[10]

Thus, truth, even if relative, cannot be sabotaged, as this leads us to the question of historical memory, which may have disastrous consequences for societies, civilisations even. Events that occurred at a particular point in time are documented and memorialised through various means, such as academic works, fiction, cinema, visual art and so on. Memories are mined by people in power in accordance with their ideologies, to create narratives that could have unsavoury results for certain sections of society. These issues are indeed fraught, making the domain of memory and its use in fiction highly contestable.

---

10 From an interview with the author.

Feeling Noir in India
Zac O'Yeah

Zac O'Yeah grew up in Sweden where he worked in the music business before retiring early, at twenty-five, and coming to India. After a successful book debut in 1995, his authorial career has included travelogues, cult detective novels (two of which are currently being adapted into cinema), children's literature, and the acclaimed Gandhi biography *Mahatma!* which was ranked as the best Swedish non-fiction book of 2008, and his writings have been translated into more than twenty languages in Europe, India, China, Russia, and elsewhere. Zac O'Yeah has written for over ninety-nine different publications in Europe, India, China, Russia, and elsewhere. He has had a long involvement with theatre, as a playwright, designer, producer, and occasional performer, and he currently writes songs and directs videos for a disco punk band known as The Ändå. Previous jobs worth mentioning include being International Secretary of the Swedish Writers' Union, a bodyguard, and a dishwasher in a pizzeria. He is married to the author Anjum Hasan and his most recent book is the critically acclaimed foodie travelogue *Digesting India* (2023).

~

The Globalisation of the Crime Scene

The classic detective character, be it the scholarly Sherlock Holmes in the late nineteenth century, the hardboiled Philip Marlowe in the early twentieth, or the feminist Lisbeth Salander now in the twenty-first, has always been an urban explorer and a bit of a misfit; obsessive and neurotic, constantly probing what goes on in our cities after dark, the stuff that most of us remain blissfully clueless about—whether made up or real, fiction or fact, who can tell? Does it matter?

No and *yes*. I go to New York and buy an Ed McBain paperback or Paul Auster's *The New York Trilogy* (1985–86) to feel I'm in town; in Stockholm I pick up a Sjöwall-Wahlöö pulp novel or another instalment of the *Millennium* trilogy for local colour. Before visiting Mumbai, *Sacred Games* (2006) by Vikram Chandra does the needful. Not the web-TV series, I'm talking about the book. Books do things to the imagination and it doesn't matter much that McBain fictionalised the Big Apple as Isola, or that much of Chandra's city can't actually be found on maps. It is atmosphere we readers are after.

I've always felt that every self-respecting metropolis ought to have its own detective novel series. In my native Sweden, there are villages like Fjällbacka, with a population of less than one thousand in real life but nevertheless the setting for multiple serial-killer hunts in book after book. Realistic? How many semi-professional serial-killers would it take to decimate a thousand peasants? It defies logic, but you read the books because Fjällbacka is depicted as quaint and yet appears to have a dark side. That, in a nutshell, is the success story of the detective novel and why it is a global sales phenomenon, keeping publishing houses alive and kicking.

Location matters. The popularity of "crime fiction guided walks" grows around the world in the footsteps of the booming thriller industry—whether it be classic Sherlock Holmes tours in London (which include a visit to the mock-up of Sherlock's apartment at 221B Baker Street, "the world's most famous address") or Philip Marlowe bus rides in Los Angeles. (The late Raymond Chandler, incidentally, loved showing visitors the settings for his plots.) When I recently bought a ticket for the guided "Millennium Walk" to see locations from Stieg Larsson's trilogy in Stockholm, there were tourists from Europe, Asia, and America in the group. Even the tiny Swedish village of Fjällbacka arranges for visitors to have a peek at the fictional murder sites as featured in Camilla Läckberg's bestselling crime novels. In Mumbai you can go on guided visits to the places mentioned in Gregory David Roberts's *Shantaram* (2003) or Suketu Mehta's *Maximum City* (2004). Trailing fictional heroes and villains is a global pastime.

So it follows that place, milieu, atmosphere are oh-so-important for a fictional sleuth. In the case of my own creation, the semi-heroic wannabe hero Hari Majestic, the hallowed ground is the mean streets of Bengaluru's (formerly Bangalore) bustling Majestic area. I chose to set my "Majestic Trilogy"—comprising the novels *Mr Majestic* (2012), *Hari, a Hero for Hire* (2015), and *Tropical Detective* (2018)—there for several good reasons. Until fairly recently, crime fiction used to be dominated by Anglo-American locations and concerns, but nowadays you have global bestsellers set in places like Botswana (admittedly written by a Scot) or Japan (often but not always written by the Japanese). So why not Bengaluru?

A pioneering crime writer when it comes to using Indian locations, H.R.F. Keating became slightly notorious for having written much of his "Inspector Ghote" mystery series without having been to India. He apparently picked Bombay by flipping randomly through an atlas. He did visit the city much later, once the series was a hit. In the 1980s, Ismail Merchant was filming *The Perfect Murder*, which is why Keating found himself in India—for a cameo in it. In his how-to manual titled *Writing Crime Fiction* (1986), Keating states that all the world's exotic locations are there to be used by an author and "it is not altogether necessary, if your mind is constructed that way, actually to visit your chosen locale". I beg to differ.

Beantown Thrills

The protagonist of my novels, Hari Majestic, was a week-old orphan when found under a seat in the third row at Majestic Talkies. That's how he got his surname. Now demolished, the popular cinema also lent its name to the whole area (which is shown as Gandhinagar on the map) where Hari has his haunts. In his twenties in the first book, he is a reformed tout who has turned into something of an unofficial trouble-shooter, a Mr Fix-it. People come to him with their problems—missing siblings, cheating spouses, suspected scams—and since he knows Bengaluru like his own nostrils, he is the perfect private investigator. It is through his eyes that we observe the changes in the city, the gradual gentrification of the Majestic area where bazaars give way to shopping malls and pawnbrokers to ATMs. So, for example, in the third novel, when he is in his thirties, Hari finds himself guarding an ATM, a symbol of the increasingly digital world that has encroached on a traditional bazaar area.

I doubt I could have imagined such a character without having spent decades in Majestic or, indeed, Bengaluru. For the record, Majestic is a somewhat seedy urban district sprawled out like a tattered red carpet in front of the railway and bus stations, its streets crammed with Art Deco cinema halls (once, it had the largest number of theatres per square kilometre anywhere), semi-shady bars, and the rock-bottom hotels of backpackerland.

I first set foot in Majestic long before I thought it might be a good idea to write detective novels; in those days I was merely a traveller trying to figure out how to survive on less than a shoestring. In Majestic, back in the early 1990s, it was possible to get a room for under 90 rupees a night, which suited my budget. If I stuck to simple vegetarian fare like idlis, vadas and dosas, I could hang out for a month on practically nothing. Coincidentally, many years later, reading the gangster memoir *My Days in the Underworld: Rise of the Bangalore Mafia* (2013) by newspaper proprietor and social activist Agni Sreedhar, I discovered that gangsters frequented the very same vegetarian eateries in Majestic in those days, hatching gang-war plans over plates of vada-sambar and tumblers of filter coffee.

I still recall, in vivid Technicolor and wide-angle panoramic memories, the morning when I first got off the train, and filled my lungs with the nippy but slightly greyish Deccan air. I'd been travelling for some time through the harsher north of India—and I'd had my encounters with touts in the usual tourist traps of Delhi, Varanasi, Agra, Rajasthan—but the sudden, unexpected homely vibe that is provided by easy-on-the-pocket food, affordable accommodation, jolly people and an abundance of cheap beer came as a pleasant surprise. There were no special tourist attractions in Bengaluru, so therefore no need to carry out any sightseeing agendas. I spent my days in bookshops around Mahatma Gandhi Road and at those nameless second-hand bookstalls that used to proliferate due south of Kempegowda Circle. Luckily, the distance between these intellectual havens and the nearest pub was rarely more than fifty steps, so as day turned into night my brain would be further stimulated by chilled UB lager.

Later I realised I also liked it because Majestic is cosmopolitan enough to accommodate pretty much everybody. As if to prove it, I discovered a thriving migrant food culture—humble eateries serving the best Kerala-style biryanis in town or Bengali canteens with authentic mustard fish. In the same streets, temples stood next to cinemas with their larger-than-life cut-outs of cine gods, separate mythological universes, cheek by jowl.

Once I'd spent enough time walking about, the street grid, curiously, reminded me of my old hometown some 8,000 kilometres away—the port city of Gothenburg—the main exception being there's no harbour here. But the way the streets were laid out gave me unsettling flashbacks, and the fact that there was always a bar around the next corner, made me feel that I was walking on very special ground. My type of ground.

The fecundity of Majestic was beckoning me, it seemed, waiting for me to do something literary with it.

The Seedy Germs

Like no other place I had known, the city appeared to have a will of its own, growing uncontrollably like a frontier town in the Wild West. In a street corner where I one day discovered a stylish colonial-era bar, there'd be a glass-and-steel shopping mall with a top-floor food court coming up before I had time to drink up my beer. The kaleidoscopic nature of it intrigued me: just when I thought that I knew my whereabouts, I took a second glance and the kaleidoscope shifted and everything changed.

The eternal construction sites, the suburbs at the city's edges pushing its limits another kilometre out with every passing year, nay day, might occasionally make one feel melancholic, an emotion well worth tapping into for a writer. But art produced in a city like this could also, I thought, defy ordinary imagination, the way that Bengaluru itself does, seeming to expand fast enough to swallow the entire world.

But after a good decade of living here, I still hadn't seen a local detective novel in the bookshops. My favourites, Premier Bookshop run by Mr Shanbhag, Bookworm owned by Mr Krishna, and of course Blossoms Book House started by Mr Mayi, all of them in the Cantonment area's Church Street, did stock Asian crime stuff—Japanese thrillers by Keigo Higashino, *Bangkok 8* (2003) by John Burdett, a few translated Bengali detective story collections, *The Blaft Anthology of Tamil Pulp Fiction* (2008), and second-hand copies of out-of-print 1970s pulp classics such as the

Jaz Zadu series about a north Indian IMFL-guzzling James Bond-like character who "attracts beauties and bullets with equal ease".

In that first decade of the 2000s, some truly heavy crime novels were written about the "maximum city" of Mumbai: the aforementioned Vikram Chandra's *Sacred Games* clocked in at 900 pages and Gregory David Roberts's *Shantaram* was a little heavier at 936 pages. In their hardcover editions, both could be used as murder weapons. Slimmer and really hardboiled, and with distinct early-1990s Mumbai settings, were three striking novels written by Ashok Banker. I still remember reading *The Iron Bra* (1993), a gory story of a female investigator, Sheila Ray, whose finger rests lightly on the trigger as she defends her family's reputation and takes on gangsters in an unforgettable shootout. The overcrowded city's construction sites were a crucial component in the tight plot. Tragically, my own copy, which was bought in Patna, is long lost and second-hand copies cost $129 from an online bookshop. So Mumbai has had its share of writers who painted the city as black as noir gets, but the rest of the country had been left out. In those days, the genre was still a rather new phenomenon in India—though more recently a bunch of outstanding writers have penned great pulp. To name a few notable titles: Eshwar Sundaresan's hate-crime novel *Behind the Silicon Mask* (2013), largely set in the US, Somnath Batabyal's unscrupulous rookie journo on the Delhi crime beat in *The Price You Pay* (2013), and Ankush Saikia's series of extraordinary thrillers set in India's northeast.

But still, there hadn't been much written on Bengaluru at that time, despite the fact that it is one of the world's fastest expanding cities. So that was why I decided to pen my own *Mr Majestic*. One thing led to another, one idea spawned the next, and soon the matrix of the first novel began to unfold. I wanted to avoid creating a stereotypical literary detective—the overweight, middle-aged, cynical, divorced cop (if male) or the curious spinster aunty (if female), or any of the other varieties of "classic" investigator characters.

I'd seen plenty of Kannada action movies and become a fan of the wacky ones by Real Star Upendra, the king of cool and one-liners. I wondered what a literary equivalent of such films might read like. After all, Indian cinema follows a different logic from Western, so shouldn't that colour the literary plot and its protagonists as well?

As far as I understood, a typical Indian film contains, within itself, the elements of every cinematic genre: a romantic movie will also have a villain who plots nefarious mischief as well as a clown who makes us laugh until we cry. A comedy is likely to have heroics of the nail-biting kind as well as romantic entanglements which will bring tears to our eyes again. An action film, too, will have serious comical aspects in it, the latter seeming to enhance the thrills rather than defusing them—as we cinemagoers of India very well know. If a Western film attempts the same, critics and audiences are likely to judge it as being all over the place; it is simply impossible to imagine Sylvester Stallone singing, dancing and horsing around on a mountain slope, and then going on a shooting spree. At the most he can wisecrack once. Or twice. But this same impossibility is not only possible in India, it's an integral element of every really big blockbuster. This has obvious roots in that ancient Indian theory of dance, theatre and music, the *Natya Shastra*, which teaches us that any artistic work must have a dominant mood, rasa, with supplementary elements added on from the eight possible emotions or bhavas, such as comedy (hasya), terror (bhayanaka), heroism (vira) and, naturally, also love (rati).

By contrast, Hollywood cinema (and Western storytelling by and large) seems to operate according to the classic strictures of "the dramatic unities"—as propounded from Aristotle onwards and refined in the era of French Classicism—according to which credibility in theatre is created by avoiding mixed registers and hybrid art forms such as, for example, tragicomic romances. This tendency remains very much alive in the West.

But I set out to write a romantic tragicomic thriller in Bengaluru—which was to become the first book in the "Majestic Trilogy", the eponymous *Mr Majestic*.

The Reality Check

I prepared myself well. Having read enough translated Bengali detective fiction featuring the brainy sleuths Byomkesh Bakshi (created by Saradindu Bandyopadhyay) and Feluda (by Satyajit Ray), who seemed to be far too derivative of the Sherlock Holmes persona for my taste, I decided that a reality check was required. So spotting a sign for a detective agency one day, I dropped in. Already on the staircase I got the feeling that I wasn't going to find either deerstalker topis or chain-smoking private eyes with bourbon in their hipflasks. There was a notice saying that job applicants must be well-groomed, freshly shaved and have a proper haircut. I touched my own chin and realised that I should have visited a barber first.

It turned out that an Indian detective bureau is like any open-plan office; this could be, say, an accountant's chambers or even a low-end call centre, if it weren't for all the staff looking so ex-army. They also didn't care much for PR, I found, when I asked for a public relations person: the receptionist simply told me I couldn't expect to get any information. After too many questions that were left unanswered, I was eventually ushered into the glass cubicle where the head of the bureau sat behind a desk covered in promotion materials for his spiritual guru.

Brimming with excitement, I asked my first question: *What do real detectives work with?* The boss replied, "That I can't tell you, because it is secret."

I tried again: *If I wanted to hire you, what could you do for me?* He stared out through the window and those all-detecting eyes lost themselves in the distance. "Supposing you wanted to buy that house over there and needed to know who owns it, we could find that out."

I looked at the house, but, no, there were no suspicious criminals lurking on its roof terrace. Besides, if I wanted a house, I might go to a real estate agent rather than a secret agent, but I found it wiser to say: *So, is that what detectives do for a living?* He shook his head vigorously. "Not at all; I just said that supposing you wanted to know."

And how much would it cost me to hire you to do that? He looked at me doubtfully and said, "That I can't say, it's secret."

So instead I turned to Google and found out everything I needed to know. During this lengthy research process, another Swedish writer—Kjell Eriksson, whose books have been shortlisted for the Best Swedish Crime Novel Award so many times that I've lost count—popped into Bengaluru, also planning to write a thriller set here. Being generous by nature, I took him around Majestic to show him what a perfect location I had scouted. But he didn't find it exotic enough. As we sat in a dingy bar, Status—off Kalidasa Road, which seemed like an auspicious address—the veteran writer gulped down some Knockout Super-Strong, leaned forward over the stained tablecloth, and told me: "I want to discover something that genuinely speaks to me: it is psychologically important even though the reader may not notice much of the behind-the-scenes work."

After another sip, he continued, "Much of what I put in my books has a symbolic value to me. Now you shouldn't think that I'm being pretentious, but I mean that things acquire a meaning to me when I write them down: a small detail can be of utmost importance."

Such as a squirrel he saw jumping off the ledge of his hotel window, which he described to me vividly and which went on to get a bit part in the novel. As did my good self, I discovered later, after his thriller had been published as *The Hand That Trembles* (2011): I found myself featured as a nameless, pushy-pesky foreigner at an expat dinner party. But cosmopolitan Majestic didn't make the grade for the master writer. Being an ex-gardener (before he became a full-time novelist), Eriksson decided he'd much rather set his plot in the flowery environs of the city's Lal Bagh botanical gardens, where a foreigner is found labouring without a work permit, a man who turns out to be a long-time missing, presumed dead, Swedish politician on the run.

Eriksson is one of those writers who don't plan a lot; he told me that he never wrote a synopsis, but would let the story develop, along with its own twists and turns, as he keyed it into his laptop. Walking around in Bengaluru, for example, helped him imagine what kind of life the politician had led here during his sixteen years as a missing person.

So, is it the writer who finds his setting or is it the setting that finds a suitable writer? It certainly began to look more and more like it may have been Majestic that picked me, just as Lal Bagh appealed to Eriksson, rather than the other way around. It's a two-way communication between place and story.

It does happen that I'm asked by readers how I dare to write so audaciously about, or manage to credibly capture, a place which I obviously don't belong to. But sometimes the most evocative descriptions of milieus are written by those who have had limited access to them—writers such as Martin Cruz Smith, who in the pre-internet days depicted life behind the Iron Curtain with seeming accuracy after only having spent a few days there. "Seeming" is perhaps the key word here. A crime novel is, like any novel, a contract between a writer and a reader. The readers will feel obliged to read only so far as they feel persuaded by what they are reading. By these criteria, Smith's "Arkady Renko" books rank high—they are extremely vivid stories of a Moscow-based investigator against whom life is always conspiring.

Each book in the series is a gripping story of Renko's battle against impossible odds (he's usually as good as dead by the last page), but taken together the novels also form a historical narrative spanning the final stages of the crumbling Soviet Union and the years of Glasnost and Perestroika, mirroring the upheavals and brutal capitalism of the noughties that were to follow, with mafias, oligarchs, remnants of withering communism, and bleak Vodkaholism.

Smith has obviously read up on his subject, yet that alone can't account for the effectiveness of the local colour, which seems completely convincing to me. (I grant, though, that I've altogether only spent twenty-four hours in Moscow.) Indeed, Smith has received a lot of praise. *The Guardian* wrote that "when Smith is at his best, it is impossible to tell how much is research and how much imagination", and Bengaluruan literary columnist Pradeep Sebastian noted that Smith "is not merely America's greatest thriller writer, he's one of their best writers, period". Today, the first novel in the series, *Gorky Park* (1981), is, paradoxically, one of the major reasons for tourists to visit the self-same amusement park—though in those days it was so difficult to go to Moscow that the movie version, starring William Hurt and Lee Marvin, had to be shot in Finland instead.

As it turns out, prior to writing *Gorky Park*, Smith managed to make a quick visit with a tour group in 1973. Of the two weeks in Russia, he spent six days in Moscow, ditching the group as often as possible to take long walks and collect details. Not speaking a word of Russian, and without a camera (a camera-toting foreigner might have caught the attention of the KGB), he used sketchbooks to document people and places. *Gorky Park*—despite its non-American hero—became an instant surprise bestseller, catapulting the hitherto obscure pulp writer (who had penned Nick Carters for a living) to global fame. The book was, naturally, banned in Russia, where Smith was put on the KGB's list of dangerous agent provocateurs, making the novel something of a cult read for Muscovites (if they could lay their hands on a copy).

Smith's success must be largely attributed to how tirelessly he ferrets out the mundane details of daily life with which he adorns his plots. Each book usually takes him three to four years to research and write. He once said to an interviewer:

> I only write about what I am curious about. That means I know nothing about it at all, and have to find out. And that always takes a while to get together, and then even longer to figure out how to make fiction from it. Then you only ever use the smallest amount of what you have learned.

Although *Gorky Park* was planned as a one-off thing, investigator Arkady Renko has continued his detective work through multiple sequels and was well into his fifties in the latest book I read about him, and as stubbornly alive as in the first book. And, some years ago, Smith himself was spotted doing more research in Moscow—where he has been taken off the "enemy of the state" list.

Me and My Workmates

The other night, Patrick Bryson and I sat in a bathtub filled with beer—at least, that's the kind of luxury we dreamt we were going to earn by our penmanship. We were actually in a bar in Connaught Place in his adopted hometown, New Delhi, and we utilised the happy hours until well beyond the restaurant's closing time by pre-ordering enough KF Strong to cover every inch of the table. What luxury. Indeed, Bryson wouldn't have to pay till much later that night, when he went home to a seriously annoyed wife who found him rolled up into a ball outside the apartment door. (This is also known as the football position, because by adopting it modern husbands are well prepared to get kicked by their better halves who are unlikely to hit any vital organs.)

Bryson had an interesting day job as a consular fraud investigator and his debut novel, *The Sad Demise of Manpreet Singh* (2014), is set in that world—his protagonist, Dominic "Biscuit" McLeod, scrutinises spurious visa agents and is led by a trail of dead applicants to uncover high-level corruption. As a writer, Bryson considers himself a Delhi local, just the way that I'm a Bengaluru local. It feels good to have colleagues with a similar mindset and to know that I'm not the only "firang" detective novelist around. Regarding this thing about being a "local", Bryson went on to explain: "That's very important for writing a crime novel, as you have to deal with a lot of inside information—the stuff about a city and a population that isn't really publicised elsewhere, and it's hard to make it up unless you have witnessed it first-hand. Coming from outside allowed me to write it truthfully without being embarrassed, and it gave a certain sense of perspective."

[Burp] *So that'sch your modusch operandi?*

Bryson rinsed his tonsils with beverage and then pointed out, "What happens is that you end up having two cultures, without belonging to either. This is a great process for the protagonist in a crime novel—like my hero, Biscuit McLeod—because the investigator is the person who has to be in that world of crime, without being a criminal. There is that line from Chandler: 'Down these mean streets a man must go who is not himself mean, who is neither tarnished nor afraid.'"

The lights at United Coffee House kept growing dimmer or maybe it was just me getting drunker. *Oh yeah, I've heard that one. Scho what about it?*

"To paraphrase that, Biscuit—and this is something I share with him—had to walk down the mean streets of Delhi and Punjab without being from either place."

Ex-cowboy and ex-war correspondent Tarquin Hall is another colleague, like Bryson married to an Indian lady, and also resident in Delhi. His Vish Puri, Most Private Investigator series was compared to Alexander McCall Smith's *The No. 1 Ladies' Detective Agency* set in Botswana. However, the evening that I met him in a rundown Delhi bar in Def Col market, he had spent the day hanging out with illegal bookmakers for a story. Somebody had threatened to beat him up, so he too needed a beer badly.

I obliged and ordered a couple of pitchers. Hall told me how he began his literary career by writing non-fiction books (such as the brilliant autobiography *Salaam Brick Lane*, about a crazy year in his own life) but switched over to pulp at a point when non-fiction was paid ridiculously low rates in the West. The advance for a travelogue barely covered his expenses. At around the same time, he did a story for UK newspaper *The Sunday Times*, about Indian private detectives, and he found their cases fascinating from a social point of view.

My memory of our conversation is hazy, but I recall him remarking that his detective series was really a personal chance to further explore India. What is typically Indian is, for instance, the importance of the family. Mind you, despite meeting me in a seedy bar, Hall is himself a dutiful Punjabi son-in-law, while Puri's mummyji is almost a co-detective in the crime plots. For those who haven't read a Vish Puri mystery yet, suffice it to say that the protagonist is not another hardboiled detective, but rather something of a jolly social explorer, frequently handling cases that are family-related—such as prenuptial check-ups and absconding maids, often to comical effect. And whereas Sherlock Holmes infamously smoked opium in his notorious pipe, Puri is addicted to greasy pakoras.

But unlike Arthur Conan Doyle, who got trapped into writing more Sherlock Holmes stories by fans who wouldn't let him kill off the detective, Hall is certain that he will write no more than twelve Puri novels in all. Then it will be time for something else.

However, what struck me as significant about this new generation of writers was that their vision of India is much more nuanced and far better informed than that of earlier Western writers. Take *The Moonstone* (1868) by Wilkie Collins, which was a pioneering crime bestseller, and subsequently hailed as one of the greatest detective stories of all time by the likes of T.S. Eliot, G.K. Chesterton and Dorothy Sayers. Although essentially now unfashionable, it was advanced for its day and age. It featured red herrings and thefts committed under trance, it introduced a professional detective from Scotland Yard (other early mystery stories published during the nineteenth century tended to favour brainy amateurs), and it threw in a locked-room murder to boot.

The eponymous Moonstone, belonging to an idol and stolen by a corrupt British soldier in the aftermath of the battle of Srirangapatnam (not far from Bengaluru), gives three Brahmins reason to travel all the way to inauspiciously foggy and spooky Yorkshire, masquerading as a band of juggling gypsy fakirs. The mysterious priests are, in a way, the real heroes and they eventually retrieve the sacred jewel and take it back to its home.

Collins never visited India, but he started a fashion in popular pulp: the sacred but cursed jewel, as well as the secret Oriental society, would both feature in innumerable thrillers. It is probably no coincidence that such exotic ingredients were used to spice up mysteries when the British Empire was at its mightiest.

Consider "The Adventure of the Speckled Band" (1892)—Doyle's own favourite Sherlock Holmes story. It has suspicious gypsies and weird wildlife (a cheetah and a baboon) frolicking outside a British mansion. The murder weapon is an extremely deadly Bengali swamp adder, trained to kill. Although quite unscientific (Bengal never exported swamp adders to be used by Western murderers simply because there are no swamp adders anywhere in India), the corrupting influences of colonialism loom large and the culprit, if you recall, turns out to be a Calcutta-returned, brutish, British, self-taught snake-charmer.

Indian exotica also featured in "The Crooked Man" in which the Mutiny plays a pivotal role—the suspect is a British soldier captured by rebels and kept as a slave in Darjeeling, who after escaping from their clutches learns conjuring tricks from Punjabis before returning to Britain as a queer sideshow attraction. There's also a doped mutton curry in "The Silver Blaze", while in "The Adventure of the Three Students" one suspect is "a quiet, inscrutable fellow; as most of those Indians are". Not to mention the fact that his sidekick, Dr Watson, had served in colonial India—unlike Doyle himself.

Carrying on this pulp fiction tradition of stereotyping, G.K. Chesterton wrote several detective stories in which a Catholic priest battles the superstitions of the Orient. In "The Salad of Colonel Cray"—a short story in the collection *The Wisdom of Father Brown* (1914)—a British officer appears to have been cursed by monkey-worshippers while looking for strong Trichinopoly cigars in south India; other stories feature an enigmatic Indian conjuror ("The Wrong Shape"), a perhaps cursed sacred ruby ("The Red Moon of Meru"), and so on.

Later in the twentieth century, tropes such as the motif of purloined Indian jewels were recycled in two Agatha Christie plots (*The Secret of Chimneys*, a novel from 1925, and the short story "The Rajah's Emerald"). Furthermore, she tried out a piquant murder weapon in *The Big Four* (1927): a toxic chicken curry, presumably effective because the spiciness hid the taste of poison. (Poisoning was incidentally Christie's preferred murder method.)

Simultaneously, an avalanche of "thugs" and other colourful sects lavished their thuggery on numerous superficial flicks. A sampling: *Gunga Din* (1939), starring Cary Grant; *Sabaka, the Hindu* (1953), starring Boris Karloff (better known for his portrayal of Frankenstein's monster); *The Black Devils of Kali* (1955), starring Lex Barker (who also played Tarzan in five jungle flicks); *Zarak* (1957), starring Anita Ekberg; *The Mystery of Thug Island* (1964), starring nobody you'd ever heard of; *Help!* (1965), starring The Beatles; the James Bond movie *Octopussy* (1983), starring Roger Moore; *Indiana Jones and the Temple of Doom* (1984), starring Harrison Ford; and *The Deceivers* (1988), starring Pierce Brosnan.

Entertainment epics that sustain popular prejudice are as endless as they are mindless and this "eastern influence" wasn't limited to India. There was, for example, Fu Manchu waging his own version of jihad against the West with ray guns and poisoned prostitutes. Nastier and far more long-lived than any other megalomaniac, Fu Manchu debuted in a story by Sax Rohmer in 1913 and survived the author's death in 1959 by becoming the inspiration for several 1960s cult movies starring Christopher Lee. Lee is best known for playing Dracula in B-film shockers produced by the ultra-low-budget Hammer Studios, whose success formula can be summarised as the two Bs: Boobies and Blood.

Gradually, with the Western pulp writer maturing intellectually, the idea of evil Orientals fell out of fashion. Recent Hollywood attempts to produce Fu Manchu sequels have failed because of the character's political incorrectness—after all, such films might harm the already precarious US trade with China. I can't for the life of me recollect any major motion picture or crime novel with Kali-worshipping thugs over the last three decades with the growth—coincidentally?—of post-liberalisation India as an export market for the West.

How Fiction Works or Doesn't

How is it that when you start reading a story, focussing your eyes on those tiny black squiggles of ink on a page in a book, you leave your location—a dentist's waiting room, an airport lounge, your bedroom—and enter another space, imagined by a novelist, maybe years ago, maybe far away in another country? You're in Delhi or Stockholm or London, and then you read a story set in Bengaluru—and zoom, you *are* in Bengaluru.

It's magical. There's no widescreen, no projector, none of those 5.1 sound systems—and still you see the place, hear its noises, and smell its air in the pages of a good book. To me, that's the greatest miracle that storytelling can offer us.

To perform this magic as a novelist is an intuitive and tricky process. You hope for the worst for your characters (that is, as much high-voltage drama in their lives as possible) and pray that you'll get away with what outrageous adventures you've dreamed up. Yet the end product must be perfectly logical, as readers want to believe that what is obviously made up is, indeed, true.

Writing books is, essentially, a bit like trying to stay alive in Bengaluru: it's a chaotic activity; you must kill your darlings, tear into pieces what you've previously written, and rewrite upon the ruins of your earlier ideas; and you need to stretch your limits, conquer new ground, and attempt the impossible—just like Bengaluru itself does each day. When I observe Bengaluru or stroll in it, I feel I'm walking through a manuscript forever in progress, a poem that will never be completed but always remain in flux.

Clues, Craft, and Characters

The Journey into Mystery Fiction

Manjiri Prabhu

Manjiri Prabhu is an award-winning international author, a short-film-maker, and the founder/ director of two successful festivals: PILF (Literature) and IFSI (Spiritual). She has directed over 200 children's TV programmes, more than fifty short fiction and travel films and has authored twenty books. Dr Prabhu has been acknowledged as a pioneer in India among women writers of mystery fiction, and she has a diverse global fan following. She is the first female mystery author to be published outside India and has been labelled as the "Indian Agatha Christie".

~

[…] in one moment, every drop of blood in my body was brought to a stop by the touch of a hand laid lightly and suddenly on my shoulder from behind me.

I turned on the instant, with my fingers tightening round the handle of my stick.

> There, in the middle of the broad bright high-road—
> there, as if it had that moment sprung out of the earth or
> dropped from the heaven—stood the figure of a solitary
> Woman, dressed from head to foot in white garments [...][1]

The first legendary meeting of Walter Hartright with Anne Catherick in *The Woman in White* sets the indisputable tone for a perfect mystery novel. It dives deep into the mysterious atmosphere, brings forth the unexpectedness of the incident, describes the setting, and introduces two striking, unique characters all in one go, thus allowing us, the readers, to imagine what lies ahead in the novel.

Edgar Allan Poe wrote the first short story with a detective as a central character titled "The Murder in the Rue Morgue" (1841), thus inventing the mystery genre. But it was eighteen years later, in 1859, that Wilkie Collins published *The Woman in White*, which has been hailed as the first mystery novel. It was followed by *The Moonstone* in 1868, considered to be the first detective novel.

Wilkie Collins set a high standard for other writers to follow, as he laid the foundation for mystery and detective fiction. A master of the genre, his exceptional plots and characters are still looked upon as unparalleled classics.

But first things first.

Imagine a cauldron of boiling curry; red, glossy, and mouth-watering with the choicest of spicy ingredients with outworldly aromas, garnished with a contrasting dash of green coriander and kept steaming hot on a continuous flame. That for me signifies a mystery novel. A cauldron of curry that stimulates your sense organs, the spice that tickles your brain, and the continuous hot flame of surprise that holds your attention at boiling point.

Simply put, a mystery novel is a gripping story that will keep you hooked, curiosity pushing you to turn the pages, the

---

1 Wilkie Collins. *The Woman in White* (1859). Wordsworth, 1993, 16.

characters drawing you into their stories and engaging you in a game of guessing till the final shocking revelation—the grand truth that will leave you reeling.

In one sentence: there is a main protagonist, a crime that takes place, suspects, the process of solving the crime, and, finally, the truth.

Or to give it a formal definition: a novel which uses intrigue (secret scheming), craft (skill in planning, making, or executing) and craftiness (the use of subtlety and cunning) to play games with the mind of the reader is mystery fiction.

I have written mystery novels since I was a kid and I consider writing mystery fiction a unique skill. It is a complete art form which touches almost all emotions, stages and elements of life and encompasses other genres within itself. It can comment on socio-political issues and offer deep insights into the human psyche—all under the guise of an entertaining mystery story. As such, I feel it is the definition of a complete novel.

Any well-written novel relies on its five important pillars: Plot, Characters, Narrative (the structure of the novel), Research, and Backdrop/Setting/Ambiance

The plot is of course the heart of the novel. The grand idea that makes you put pen to paper and weave a world of mystery through its different stages. It is a combination of P for Planning and Pacing, L for Logic, O for Originality, and T for Technique. An important reminder, tag, post-it—call it whatever you wish—there is no option to being original. I cannot emphasise this enough. An original plot is something that you can claim for eternity. The rest is all inspired or borrowed.

In a nutshell, a Plot becomes memorable when you Plan and Pace your story in a Logical and Original manner, using different narrative Techniques in writing. With these guideposts, a story can move from any location to anywhere else, and swing from one emotion to another, using credible characters.

Sometimes in mystery fiction the main character is forced into such a situation that he must take on the role of a detective. Then he sets out to untie puzzling knots that have entangled his life. Often the main character himself or herself is a professional detective charged with the task of solving a complicated case. In either situation, what is important is the systematic unearthing of clues, a motive for the crime that rings plausible, the gradual unravelling of the story like the unfurling of a rolled carpet, and the final grabbing of the main culprit or criminal—all in one clean sweep.

The moment you utter the word detective, the image of Sherlock Holmes comes to mind. And especially Sherlock with a magnifying glass in hand. Or Hercule Poirot with his twirled moustache and egg-shaped head. Or, more on our home TV ground, Karamchand with a carrot in his hand. The impressions are so firmly imbedded in our heads that it takes time and effort to replace them with something more contemporary. And even original.

When I create characters or detectives, I consider the play of different dimensions and levels of mind. To put it simply:

The way you communicate with the outside world, with your physical looks and appearance, is the first dimension. It is your first impression.

The way you *look at yourself*, in your mind's eye, with an honest opinion of yourself based on critical appreciation, is the second dimension.

The way you *think* on the inside, in the privacy of your inner world—your thoughts, analysis, fantasies, emotions which you would rather not share with anyone—is quite another dimension.

And your subconscious mind, the one that *even you* need to be aware of and fathom, which often appears in your dreams or guides you like an inner voice, is the fourth dimension.

A good character and especially a good detective ought to have a layered combination of all four dimensions, such as makes detective fiction unputdownable.

The biggest feat of writing detective fiction is of course creating original sleuths. Sleuths who have not been created before. Who have a modus operandi uniquely different from those of their predecessors. Someone who can snatch your attention from the first page, sweep you into their world and keep you interested till they finish solving their case. Someone who (not only through the plot) also gets you as a reader totally curious and addicted to them as a person, to their issues and to their personal story. A four-dimensional detective is not just interesting but intriguing. Human. Grey (that is, not black or white). Someone to love or hate. To follow or unfollow. A reminder of what life can offer or not. Often wise, sometimes blundering, messing up relationships and committing mistakes. But always emerging triumphant and victorious, because that is what distinguishes a detective from other characters. The assurance of success. The assurance that all their efforts, analysis, mistakes, actions will lead to one thing and one thing only: justice. Which justifies the creation of this unusual novel-form in which, ironically, the reader's satisfaction is determined by how artfully the reader is deceived!

And that's what I have tried to do with my characters. I work with imagination, not realism. I wouldn't want readers simply to relate to the characters, I would want them to admire them, to aspire to be them. I would like emotions to be the point of connection, not actions. In a way, I would like readers to be in awe of my detectives. They are special, uncommon. With a kind of uniqueness, although not unrealistic. Definitely not superheroes, but displaying the superior qualities of a fine, distinctive, analytical mind.

When I wrote my Stellar Investigations Series, I wanted to create a character who was modern, willing to experiment with the new, but with her roots firmly grounded in a traditional upbringing.

Sonia Samarth is in her twenties, with the laudable goal of wanting to change the world, with modern views, yet grounded in Indian culture, sensitive and emotional to a fault and so balanced in her idea of justice that sometimes she sympathises with the criminal. But what really sets her apart is the way she solves crimes—she uses Vedic horoscopes to solve the cases. Sonia also loves to dance to ear-splitting music, which gets her deductive juices flowing and helps her to interpret situations from a fresh angle, just the way I envisioned her in my dream!

My relationship with my detectives is very special. I see them in my dreams or they appear like a flash before I write about them. They create themselves. I saw the vision of a young girl, dancing with wild abandon to loud music, before Sonia Samarth made an appearance in *The Cosmic Clues*.

Another character, Re (pronounced as ray) Parkar, appeared like a brooding, intense man standing on the edge of a lake, his back turned and his ponytailed head gleaming in the sun. Re Parkar is an investigative journalist with a psychic bent. He gets visions of a place he has previously visited and knows that something terrible is going to transpire there. Insightful. Sensitive. Dignified and yet possessing a wry sense of humour and wit, Re is different. He is enigmatic. Even a bit unfathomable. Yet with his heart in the right place. Sometimes confusing the readers as to his intentions. Sometimes endearing. A complex, multilayered character whom I loved creating. Sporting a ponytail and silver-rimmed glasses, carrying his cameras and playing a flute. He also possesses a heightened sense of smell and imagination and he is, for me, satisfactorily different.

These characters share an "inside" bond and know the complexities of the story very well. Together, these detectives and I need to discover the truth of the plot, and the detective helps me as an author to deceive the reader, enabling me to keep alive the element of surprise so essential to a mystery novel. We are co-conspirators and voyagers on the same journey. Sometimes we grow together. Like I did with Sonia Samarth. Her journey was mine, her process of self-discovery was mine, and so was her growth as a detective and a person. She wasn't me but she grew into me.

I can safely say that my characters have arisen out of some part of my soul and are actually my soulmates. For example, Magdalena Lindberg from *Voice of the Runes*. In fact, I am in awe of her. Magdalena (or Maddy) is a woman you cannot take lightly. You either love her or you hate her. You certainly cannot ignore her. The range and intensity of the emotions she portrays in the novel, her determination to succeed and the wild abandon with which she loves Re left me breathless. I admire her tremendously and often wonder from which part of me she was born—from my brain, or my heart.

The narrative of a mystery or a suspense novel or a thriller usually follows a set pattern. Cosy mysteries work around limited backdrops—a house, a town, a family, a community or a group—and walk at a steady pace. Thrillers are faster paced, and can zip across the world as the story unfolds through multiple viewpoints. Suspense novels can widen their scope and fall within the realm of cosy mysteries, and can be psychological noirs as well as dark, electrifying thrillers.

I have always experimented with narratives and structures within the framework of a mystery or suspense novel, even a thriller. There is a certain charm in breaking rules, placing yourself in seemingly impossible plots and trying to bind them in reason and logic, creating bridges between history and the contemporary, travelling across the world for intrigue, noir, and mystery.

For example, *The Cosmic Clues* (2004) and *Stellar Signs* (originally *The Astral Alibi*, 2006) are collections of crime cases or short stories within a novel. This is a unique format which I call a "serialised novel". Multiple complex cases are solved throughout the novel and characters can come and go. But what binds the stories together are a base plot and certain key characters, the most important being Sonia Samarth, the world's first Astro-Detective. Her modus operandi, Indian Vedic astrology, is used not like a magic wand but as a scientific tool of exploration. When Sonia reaches a dead-end in her deductions she uses horoscopes, as a map to point her in the right direction and like an X-ray to probe into the minds of the criminals. And that is what made these cosy mysteries difficult to write—not only finding plausible plots that would allow the use of horoscopes, but the sheer variety that would break the monotony of the plots. My mother, Shobha, who is a renowned astrologer, played a huge role in the scheming of the stories.

Another challenge I took up was to write thrillers that unfold in less than forty-eight hours across global locations. It began with *The Cavansite Conspiracy* (2011), a standalone romantic thriller in which the protagonist Koyal Karnik is accused of stealing a rare Cavansite[2] as well as killing her best friend. What ensues is a chase sequence which moves from Pune to Hamburg to the island of Sylt to end in a thrilling finale in London, all in forty-eight hours. The challenge was managing the time difference and the flights within the stipulated time. To complicate matters, I gave the novel a countdown, timewise, and each chapter begins with the time of the day, almost as if the novel were unfolding in "real time". Imagine then, what a task it was for me to stick to reality and juggle between the flight timings and flight durations, including the time it takes to travel to the airport and the time differences between two countries, amidst all the action of the plot. I literally sat with a flight schedule, planning a minute-by-minute itinerary, and laid out a map with minute detailing as Koyal managed to dodge the police as well as other criminals. It was mind-boggling but oh, so satisfying!

However, I actually began writing destination mysteries and thrillers with *The Gypsies at Noelle's Retreat* (2013), which features India's first teen detective Riva Parkar, a member of an all-girl rock

---

2 A much sought-after collector's mineral most frequently found in the Pune area.

band, "The Gypsies". Riva and her band are invited to perform at a Writers' Retreat in France. The mystery unfolds through thrilling clues that take Riva and her friends all over Paris and to nearby Giverny, landscapes which provide a charming European backdrop to the story.

It was around the same time that I finally decided to put into motion my long-term dream of basing a thriller in Salzburg, at the Schloss Leopoldskron where the film *The Sound of Music* was shot. A delightful city and a palace steeped in history form the backdrop to a contemporary mystery plot. And that is when Re Parkar made an appearance in my life. *The Trail of Four* (2017) is a mystery thriller that takes place in forty-eight hours, leading Re, the investigative journalist, on a strange trail set seventy-five years ago by the Jewish-American director Max Reinhardt. In the process, not only does he retrieve the stolen, 300-year-old heart of an archbishop, he also saves the city of Salzburg from destruction.

This was, I believe, my most ambitious novel up to that point, not only because it was set entirely in a European city, which would act like a character, but also because of the scope and grandeur of the plot. The three most important elements of the novel were the massive research that had to be undertaken; extracting a thread out of the popular history of the palace and of Salzburg, and intertwining it with a rational, contemporary plot; and, finally, laying the trail. Of the three, laying the trail was the most difficult. I must have walked through the Schloss at least fifty times, figuring out clues and identifying ancient frescoes and engravings, as well as trudging the old streets of the city laying clues and finalising the pillars of Salzburg that had to be fictionally destroyed! It wasn't easy, I admit, but the sheer madness of that journey and then the rapturous delight of completion were incomparable. The whole experience took mystery and thriller writing to a different level for me.

In the sequel to this destination thriller, Re moves from Salzburg to the 350-year-old Lund University in Sweden. *Voice of the Runes*, a thriller about soul connections, was a learning curve for me. When Professor Heinz of the Runology Department drops dead in the middle of his annual lecture, everyone is shocked. With clues written in runic letters, Maddy (Magdalena Lindberg), the professor's assistant, who also practises runic divination, offers to help Re as he steps into a maze of intricate Nordic signs and symbols on a hunt for the truth. Terrifying incidents follow with escalating speed, plunging the university into the depths of fear as Re unearths a startling truth.

There were two main elements in the writing of this novel. The first one was the amount of research needed, which was overwhelming because the foundation of the plot lay deeply embedded in an ancient Germanic language of symbols called runes. Runes or rune stones are an inherent part of Scandinavian culture. I had to study and understand the rune signs and symbols and their connection to Norse mythology. The process also involved driving for miles and walking long hours down Swedish country lanes to actually find the rune stones strewn all over the region. We discovered rune stones in cathedrals, by the lake side, and some even beside the road. What I am trying to say is that research can sometimes give you the thrills, and chills, and make you sweat! But if you love what you are writing, everything is worth the while. With Re by my side (in my imagination of course), I too learned about the mystical nature of the runes and rune stones and revelled in the process.

The second element was the narrative. Usually, a thriller employs multiple viewpoints to cover greater ground and lead the reader on a fast-paced chase across the landscape of the book. I knew that I wanted to do it differently. I decided that I wanted Maddy to narrate the story, for it was after all her love story. Writing a destination thriller from a single point of view, which was not that of the detective, and with the story unfolding in thirty-six hours, in nail-biting romantic suspense, was indeed a challenge. I trust I passed the test that I set myself. The novel, to my mind, is a narrative success and, believe me, Re helped me on that intriguing journey.

Every writer strives to put his or her best into their work. Good research, planning and implementation, undergoing an exhaustive journey of creation. But there is also a secret ingredient, one that sets a good novel apart from a mediocre one.

Let me give you an example. *The Trail of Four* takes place in a palace in Salzburg, so the locale is fascinating. Detective Re is fascinating. There is an exciting, fast-moving plot that unfolds in forty-eight hours. Taken together, that should be a deadly mix, right? But it's not enough. A good detective novel works with emotions, with people who need to rise above their problems and resolve seemingly impossible situations. And herein lies the human element. That emotional touch which makes a novel unforgettable—even a "commercial" detective novel.

Another aspect that is crucial to my mystery novels is the creation of mood. I heavily (and happily) depend on nature for atmosphere creation in the novel. Rain and mist feature prominently in almost all my novels. Somehow, I connect to these natural phenomena, and I think that they bring out the flavour of the mystery. They are perfect metaphors for expressing suspense, mystery, nostalgia, revenge, repentance, lust and romance. I am so loyal to the rain and mist that I even titled one of my novels *Silver in the Mist*.

And, of course, the big question remains: how to keep the reader guessing? What will make him say "Aha!"? An element of surprise, of course! One of the highlights of a successful mystery novel is keeping the surprise element intact and running throughout the novel like a flowing river, until the climax plunges from the top of the hill like a fully-fledged waterfall and drenches you in surprise. Literally!

I believe that we often write what is deep within us, in our fourth dimension, unknowingly creating characters that reflect our innermost thoughts, a complex, sometimes turbulent world, although it may not be obvious. The point is to be able to do justice to this inner world, consciously, with a brutal honesty and without inhibitions, so as to create an effective work of art, no matter what the genre. This process can be simple or complicated, but it has to be meaningful to you. The transition from the inner world to paper will be lengthy and lonely, but expressive and cathartic and, most importantly, representing you in its fictional form. Your characters speak your words (unless they decide to take matters into their own hands!), the plots move in the directions set by you, your emotions mark the emotional makeup of the situations—each word is your creation, springing from your inner world. Like a combined offering of the four dimensions—an intense journey. It is up to us, as authors, to ensure that it is meaningful and enjoyable for everyone.

Finally, we would do ourselves a great service to remember that writing a mystery novel is like writing an exam paper—one that you simply cannot afford to fail! Ultimately, your success as a mystery writer will lie in how well you spring over the creative fences that you set up for yourself and land on your feet, firmly, like a roaring tiger.

Fantasy Fiction

Francis Jarman

What is fantasy fiction? It draws on many different genres, such as science fiction, satire, fairytale, fable, political or religious allegory (both utopias and dystopias), children's fiction, historical fantasy, horror, travel adventure, and romance. If you tried to represent it visually, you would end up with a complex Venn-diagram of overlapping sets. Yet all examples of fantasy fiction have one thing in common: the worlds that they present are not identical with our "real" world.

People say "write about what you know"—write about things that exist, and with which you are familiar. That is not bad advice, but imaginative writers have always gone beyond that, writing from the heart, and from their dreams, and the writer of fantasy fiction describes a whole *world* that does not exist, except in his or her imagination. That is a great challenge, as well as an opportunity.

This imagined, created world is a *secondary world*. The first important text on secondary worlds was penned by J.R.R. Tolkien, though it's not *The Lord of the Rings*, but his 1947 essay "On Fairy-Stories".[1] The term was later used by W.H. Auden

---

1   J.R.R. Tolkien. "On Fairy-Stories" (1947). In: *Tolkien on Fairy-Stories*. Ed.

in a lecture, "The World of the Sagas", given at the University of Kent in 1967 and included in a volume, published a year later, entitled *Secondary Worlds*. Auden explains how secondary worlds come about at least in part because of the author's dissatisfaction with the primary world. He lists five "principal grievances" (and how secondary worlds are a response to these).

- We are born into the real world without our consent, but secondary worlds are there because we choose to make them
- We have little freedom of action, but in the secondary worlds that we make we are omnipotent
- Instead of having only limited knowledge and understanding, we are omniscient and all-understanding
- Our primary-world experiences are often profane, unimportant, or boring, but from a secondary world "we can exclude everything except what we find sacred, important, enchanting"
- Evil and suffering are an insoluble problem; because we find them so fascinating, we will not exclude them from our secondary worlds (unless we are writing "arcadian" fiction), but we will include them "in a simplified, more comprehensible form". Thus in fairytales the characters, instead of being potentially good or evil, will be either one or the other, and unmistakably recognisable by their appearance, beautiful or ugly, and, unlike in real life, "good is always ultimately victorious; the nice guys are rewarded, the bad guys punished".[2]

Yet even writers of conventional or "realistic" (i.e., non-fantasy) fiction set in the present create secondary worlds, because while the author's world may seem to be the actual world, it has

---

Verlyn Flieger and Douglas A. Anderson. HarperCollins, 2014.
2 W.H. Auden. "The World of the Sagas." In: *Secondary Worlds*. Faber, 1968, 51–52.

been refracted through his or her consciousness. The author is never absent. As the novelist Paul Bowles pointed out, "Whatever one writes is in a sense autobiographical, of course. Not factually so, but poetically so."[3] Without wanting to drift into the tricky philosophical territory of Bishop Berkeley and solipsism, let us just say that a good writer's created world will be recognisably their own, in its feeling, tone, and moral dimensions.

Graham Greene's "Greeneland"—a seedy world of suffering, everyday evil, and religious guilt—is a famous example. The term was supposedly coined by the critic Arthur Calder-Marshall, in an article that objected to Greene's "Catholic" philosophy and rejected a particular scene in his Mexican novel *The Power and the Glory* (1940) as both aesthetically and factually wrong.[4] Calder-Marshall happened to know Mexico very well. However, he was missing the point in complaining that this wasn't Mexico, because it *wasn't* Mexico—it was "Greeneland"!

What Graham Greene offers us is his very personal take on our real world. The secondary worlds that concern us here, however, and to which I shall restrict the use of the term, are those that don't even *pretend* to be ours, whether in the present or in some period of the past. They make that clear by signposting "Here be dragons!" (or something similar), there being no dragons in the real world—though more about those dragons a bit later.

It would be almost a fool's undertaking to attempt a detailed taxonomy of fantasy fiction, given the huge range of genres involved and the existence of so many mixed forms, with new genres being identified and named on a regular basis. "Gothic literature" admittedly goes back several centuries, and "fairytales" are even older. "Magical realism" has established itself firmly in mainstream modern literature and been practised by major

---

3   "Paul Bowles" (interview with David Seidner). In: *Bomb*, 4, Fall issue, 1982. At https://bombmagazine.org/articles/paul-bowles/
4   Michael Shelden. *Graham Greene: The Man Within* (1994). Minerva, 1995, 284–85.

writers like Gabriel García Márquez, Günter Grass, and Salman Rushdie. Other genre-names, like "sword and sandal", "sword and sorcery", or "gaslamp fiction", are reasonably self-explanatory. But "Grimdark"? "Steampunk"? "Splatterpunk"?

Still, as a starting point, and before discussing a few of the problems faced by those intending to write fantasy fiction, we could—instead of trying to list the myriad subgenres of fantasy—perhaps begin by considering where the secondary worlds of fantasy are *located*, with regard to the real world, because that is the first and most important choice that the fantasy writer needs to make.

1. **The secondary world is an invented country located in the real world and not wholly unlike real countries**

"Ruritanian fiction", as it is sometimes called, is named after a fantasy kingdom, located somewhere in Central Europe beyond Dresden, that was invented by Anthony Hope in *The Prisoner of Zenda* (1894) and *Rupert of Hentzau* (1898). This is a romantic world of court intrigue, swashbuckling adventure, swooning passion, scheming villains, attractive rogues, thrilling swordfights, last-minute escapes, and gorgeous uniforms. Ruritania might seem preposterous and unbelievable to us today, but it would have seemed less so to earlier generations of readers, few of whom would have been familiar with the many statelets that once dotted Central and Eastern Europe, and the Balkans.

By a freak chance, Hope's gentleman-hero Rudolf Rassendyll finds himself crowned king of Ruritania in place of his near-identical cousin, the rightful king, who has been drugged by his enemies in a dastardly plot to sabotage the coronation. When those same enemies later kidnap the drugged monarch, Rudolf is obliged to continue the pretence of being king until his cousin has been rescued, all the while beating off attempts to assassinate him.

Far-fetched, of course, but why not? Escapist adventure stories are allowed a certain latitude in this regard. Yet in what is almost a case of life imitating art, a twentieth-century Rudolf, the dashing English sportsman C.B. Fry, was reportedly offered the vacant throne of Albania. He wisely turned it down. The man who did eventually become king, Zog I (1928–39), had a short but eventful reign, surviving (it is said) more than fifty-five assassination attempts before an Italian invasion caused him to flee to Greece.

Violet Needham wrote a series of "Ruritanian" novels for children, set in three invented European countries, "the Empire", the Kingdom of Flavonia, and the Duchy of Ornawitza, at different points in their history. The real Europe barely intrudes (though in one novel, there is a visitor from England). Several of the novels are charming and atmospheric: *The Woods of Windri* (1944) effectively creates a sense of "mediaeval Europe", while *The Changeling of Monte Lucio* (1946) is set slightly later and involves elements of Italian Renaissance intrigue. Needham wrote nineteen novels altogether, including straightforward historical fiction for children. Remarkably, she didn't begin writing until late in her life and published her first book at the age of sixty-three.

2. **The secondary world is a place of exotic fantasy hidden away in a part of the real world**

There are many examples in literature of such exotic fantasy worlds (usually located on remote islands, or in mountain fastnesses). Thus, in Sir Arthur Conan Doyle's *The Lost World* (1912), intrepid British explorers discover a lost native tribe, a race of ape-men, and dangerous prehistoric creatures somewhere in the Amazon Basin.

Some of these novels are much more than escapist fantasies. The hero of Jonathan Swift's *Gulliver's Travels* (1726) visits the distant but imagined realms of Lilliput, Blefuscu, Brobdingnag, Laputa, the Land of the Houyhnhnms and Yahoos, and several others, as well as the real but, to Swift's contemporaries, almost equally exotic kingdom of Japan. But Swift's masterpiece, often encountered as a "children's book" reduced to little more than its Lilliput chapters, is actually a cutting satire on the politics, culture, and ideas of his time.

"Lilliputian" and "yahoo" have both entered the English language. So too have "utopia", from Thomas More's account (*Utopia*, 1516) of an imaginary ideal society, and "Shangri-La", the name of a fictional mountain paradise in James Hilton's *Lost Horizon* (1933), a place where everyone lives in peaceful harmony. However, in the cynical early twenty-first century, in the light of what the world has become and how difficult it would be to achieve them, fictional utopias have arguably gone out of fashion.

3. The secondary world is our own world, but shaped by a different historical development

A secondary world may be only slightly different from our own, perhaps because of the different outcome of a historical event. This is sometimes called *alternate history*. A world in which the Allies lost the Second World War, as in Philip K. Dick's *The Man in the High Castle* (1962) or Robert Harris's *Fatherland* (1992); Franklin D. Roosevelt lost the US election 1940 to the Nazi-sympathiser Charles Lindbergh (Philip Roth's *The Plot against America* (2004); or the Reformation never happened, as in Kingsley Amis's *The Alteration* (1976).

In Robert Reginald's *Nova Europa* novels, the world is different because the Roman Emperor Julian *didn't* die suddenly, under mysterious circumstances (perhaps treacherously murdered in battle by one of his own men, a Christian), before he could stem the rising tide of Christianity. Or, as the author half-explains:

> For those of you who care about such things, [this] is an alternate history set in a Europe whose geographic features are similar or even identical to our own, with the major (but not sole) divergence from our timeline having

occurred in the year 363 AD. I'm sure that all of you remember the events of that *annum* with as much clarity as I and can immediately pinpoint the fork in the road of time without any further help on my part.⁵

Many works of alternate history involve time-travellers changing history through their interventions, or guardians preventing this from happening, and these rightly belong to the broad family of science fiction.

Others have an obvious moral or political message, such as John Hersey's *White Lotus* (1965), in which China has defeated the United States and the eponymous Arizonan heroine is sold into Chinese slavery; *Noughts & Crosses* (from 2001), a series of novels for young adults by Malorie Blackman set in a world in which it was Africa that colonised Europe and not vice versa; or Margaret Atwood's *The Handmaid's Tale* (1985), a grim dystopia of patriarchal oppression of women. Much lighter than Atwood's story is the Norwegian feminist satire *Egalias døtre* (1977, translated as *The Daughters of Egalia*), by Gerd Brantenberg, in which "wim" rule over "menwim", and the teenage manwom Petronius, terrorised by gangs of aggressive girls, has to learn to wear an uncomfortable item called a peho! The most renowned modern political dystopia is George Orwell's *Nineteen Eighty-Four* (1949).

Historians have also played the "what if?" game, which they call *counterfactual* (or *virtual*) history. Unlike novelists, they are *not* expected to allow their imaginations free rein, but to keep to a stringent analysis of the likely outcome of a particular event occurring differently to the way that it did—for example, what would probably have resulted had Hitler been killed in the 1944 assassination attempt. A number of anthologies are available, including those edited by Niall Ferguson (*Virtual History:*

---

5   "Author's Note" prefacing Robert Reginald. *The Dark-Haired Man, or, The Hieromonk's Tale: A Romance of Nova Europa*. Ariadne, 2004, 6.

Alternatives and Counterfactuals, 1997) and Robert Cowley (*What If?: The World's Foremost Military Historians Imagine What Might Have Been*, 1999, and its successor volumes).

4. The secondary world is ours, but set in a prehistoric past

Robert E. Howard's stories about Conan the Barbarian (from 1932) take place in an earlier, "Hyborian", version of our world located in time between the fall of Atlantis and the rise of known ancient civilisations.

> KNOW, oh prince, that between the years when the oceans drank Atlantis and the gleaming cities, and the years of the rise of the Sons of Aryas, there was an Age undreamed of, when shining kingdoms lay spread across the world like blue mantles beneath the stars—Nemedia, Ophir, Brythunia, Hyperborea, Zamora with its dark-haired women and towers of spider-haunted mystery, Zingara with its chivalry, Koth that bordered on the pastoral lands of Shem, Stygia with its shadow-guarded tombs, Hyrkania whose riders wore steel and silk and gold. But the proudest kingdom of the world was Aquilonia, reigning supreme in the dreaming west. Hither came Conan, the Cimmerian, black-haired, sullen-eyed, sword in hand, a thief, a reaver, a slayer, with gigantic melancholies and gigantic mirth, to tread the jewelled thrones of the Earth under his sandalled feet.[6]

This is the epigraph with which the first of the classic Conan stories, "The Phoenix on the Sword", begins. Note how many of

---

6   Robert E. Howard. "The Phoenix on the Sword: A Conan Story." In: *Weird Tales*, December 1932.

the names echo "real" historical names, just as many of the themes in these tales are reminiscent of historical events and content.

"Conan" became an industry, encompassing stories and short novels by Howard and others, films, and comics, with many derivative creations set in similar imagined worlds. This is one of the commonest templates for modern writers of fantasy, though it is quite a challenge to live up to the panache of Howard's original invention.

5. The secondary world is parallel to ours, but accessible from it

A common device is to have the protagonist of the story find a secret "door" from their world into a completely different one. Let us take four famous examples, all supposedly books of "children's or young adult literature".

J.K. Rowling's *Harry Potter* series hardly needs an introduction. Parallel to the ordinary world of the "Muggles" there exists a world of wizarding, in the form of castles, streets, shops, and even railway platforms[7] (!) that are invisible to non-wizards and cannot be accessed by them.

The other three series contain more obviously serious content, or even a "moral".

The heroine of Lewis Carroll's *Alice's Adventures in Wonderland* (1865) falls down a rabbit-hole and enters the dreamworld of Wonderland; in *Through the Looking-Glass, and What Alice Found There* (1871), Alice climbs through a mirror into the fantasy world. In both books she wakes from her "dream", but both end with speculation about the nature of what has happened. Far from being simple children's stories, the *Alice* books are richly filled

---

7 Trains to the Hogwarts School of Witchcraft and Wizardry leave from "Platform 9¾" at King's Cross Station, London. This is located between the (real) platforms 9 and 10 of that terminus and can be accessed—if you are a wizard—by passing through a brick wall.

with mathematical references, philosophical conundrums, and literary parodies. (A more conventional version of the "Was it a dream?" framework for fantasy can be found in the 1939 film *The Wizard of Oz*, in which Dorothy is knocked unconscious during a tornado and finds herself in the Land of Oz, from which she later returns by waking up.)

In *The Lion, the Witch and the Wardrobe* (1950), the first novel in the seven-book series *The Chronicles of Narnia* by Tolkien's close friend and academic colleague C.S. Lewis, the Pevensie children discover in the eponymous item of furniture a "door" to the magic realm of Narnia (in the other novels there are different "doors"). The story contains a strong, sometimes cloying, Christian allegory, with the noble lion Aslan offering himself in sacrifice, being humiliated and killed, but then rising from the dead.

By the end of the cycle, the metaphysical elements and the relationship between the different worlds have become distractingly complex. This, however, is nothing compared to the rich metaphysical vision of Philip Pullman's trilogy *His Dark Materials*, in which the basic secondary world, loosely reminiscent of our own in the Edwardian Era, eventually proves to be only one of many parallel worlds in a "multiverse".

Crossing between worlds can be a dangerous undertaking. It is not always advantageous for human beings to become aware of existences that may lurk just outside their sight—such as the monstrous "Great Old Ones" in H.P. Lovecraft's horror stories of Cthulhu, for instance.

6. **The secondary world is not ours, but it resembles it in many ways and is governed by similar laws**

What if the secondary world is not obviously similar or even identical to our own, but merely comparable, like a version of our world on a planet in another galaxy? It will have the *feeling* of our world, in one of its historical periods, and yet be slightly different.

It will follow laws like the laws of the real world, so there will probably be no magic.

This was the model that I chose for my novel cycle *The Gardens of the West*.[8] The secondary world I describe is very like the late Roman Empire, shortly before its collapse in the West. The "Citizens" (i.e., Romans) have come under pressure from more vigorous "barbarian" peoples, some of whom seem capable of incorporation within the Empire (like my "Horse People", based on the Goths), while others are cruel and demonic-looking (my "Blood-Drinkers", based on the Huns). It is a time of social and cultural turmoil, as a revolutionary new religion (the "Slave cult", with many resemblances to early Christianity) supplants the traditional belief systems.

This approach has the advantage that you don't need to research everything with meticulous care, as you ought to when writing a historical novel, so that you save a lot of time and don't live in constant fear of committing some dreadful howler of an anachronism (such as having your ancient Greeks smoking tobacco, or your Crusaders eating potatoes). Nevertheless, I hope that my created world does have a convincing Late Roman feel to it. I have included authentic details of Roman life, of cooking, coinage, and cosmetics, for example, but no tobacco, potatoes, chocolate, or items made of plastic. And I have tried to give each of my focalising characters a mindset, knowledge, and expectations appropriate to their background, so that they don't come across as nothing more than modern people in fancy dress.

7. **The secondary world is not ours, but it resembles it in many ways, though it is governed by different laws**

George R.R. Martin's *A Song of Ice and Fire* novel sequence is the best-known modern exemplar of such a "half-familiar" secondary

---

8   Four volumes so far: *The Eagle's Wing*, 2015; *The Hour of the Fox*, 2018; *What the Hawk Sees*, 2021; *Waking the Beast*, 2023 (Wildside). A fifth (concluding) volume is planned.

world. Martin's invention and inventiveness have been much-admired, rightly so, and much copied. Yet creating a radically different world is hard to do without consciously or unconsciously falling back on material from actual historical epochs. To my mind, Martin over-eggs his pudding by drawing on too many different sources—the Wars of the Roses, the dazzling courts, poisoners, and banking cities of Renaissance Italy, the Vikings, mediaeval France, the Mongols—with dragons and zombies added to an already queasy mix, so that the end result is not always easy to digest.

8. The secondary world is not ours, has little resemblance to it, and is governed by different laws

J.R.R. Tolkien's Middle-earth is the most famous example of such a created secondary world, though you might argue that (far from it being totally unlike our own world) there is much about it that reflects a familiar kind of Merrie England nostalgia, with its simplified issues and jolly acceptance of the inferiority of (good) lesser beings like women and (bad) lesser beings like orcs.

Tolkien himself used to insist that Middle-earth was not an imaginary world: it was "this earth, the one in which we now live, but the historical period is imaginary",[9] in other words a phenomenon not unlike the Hyborian realm of Robert E. Howard's Conan the Barbarian; however, this is unconvincing.

Middle-earth has inspired many imitations, but also worlds created more *in reaction* to Tolkien, by writers who are not fervent admirers: for example, Melniboné in Michael Moorcock's *Elric* novels, an alternative world that is part of a multiverse. Melniboné is a strange place of sorcery, hedonism, and cruelty, with a distinctive aesthetic style; its inhabitants are humanoid rather than human.

---

9   *Letters of J.R.R. Tolkien* (1981). Ed. Humphrey Carter. HarperCollins, 2006, 239.

The world of Christopher Bunn's *Tormay Trilogy* is much closer to Tolkien than, say, to Martin or Moorcock, and magic plays an important role in this story (for older children) about a youngster who, coming from nowhere, saves the world from the evil darkness that threatens to overwhelm it.

9. The secondary world is far off in outer space, or set in the far distant future

These are classic scenarios of science fiction. The story may be set on Earth, but many centuries, or even millennia, hence; even more often, it will be in outer space, perhaps in a different galaxy. Unfortunately, not all creators of science fiction succeed in rising to the challenge of imagining the radically different, and their creations simply rehash familiar storylines, situations, quandaries, and moral debates of humankind, though in exotic garb; the television series *Star Trek* was notorious for this.

Science fiction has peopled the universe with exotic beings, races, and civilisations. In an early example, *The First Men in the Moon* (1901), H.G. Wells (sometimes described, along with Jules Verne, as "the father of science fiction") imagines an insectoid lunar race called the Selenoids.

Wells's Selenoids are far from being the first invention of this kind. In the second century AD, the satirist Lucian of Samosata described (in the ironically named *True History*) an incredible journey to the moon, and a war between the moon and the sun. Unlike most other writers of fantasy or science fiction, however, he prefaces his account with a warning to the reader. After criticising earlier writers for their "so-called histories of their travels describing all the huge monsters, and savage tribes, and extraordinary ways of life that they had come across in foreign parts", he adds:

> I shall be a more honest liar than my predecessors, for I am telling you frankly, here and now, that I have no intention

whatever of telling the truth. Let this voluntary confession forestall any future criticism: I am writing about things entirely outside my own experience or anyone else's, things that have no reality whatever and never could have. So mind you do not believe a word I say.[10]

If Lucian was an ancient satirist of fantasy, Terry Pratchett is a modern one. The world of his *Discworld* novels is a flat one resting on the backs of four elephants standing on the back of an immense turtle; there is also a (far less interesting) Roundworld that resembles our own. Although Pratchett makes fun of almost everything, and invents a great deal, the turtle-supported world is *not* actually his invention: the "Geoterrapinist Theory of the World" can be found in many cultures, including in the Hindu tradition.[11]

~

Some secondary worlds are difficult to locate. The setting of the first two novels in Mervyn Peake's *Gormenghast* sequence is a crumbling, vaguely mediaeval castle full of unusual characters. Gormenghast is cut off from and not explicitly part of our world, but neither is it a magic realm or part of a parallel universe. The "fantasy" effect is achieved not by sorcery or dragons, but by the unsettling atmosphere brilliantly created by Peake's writing. In the third novel, however, the protagonist leaves the castle and travels to a modern city of cars, factories, and helicopters.

10 "The True History". In: Lucian. *Satirical Sketches*. Transl. Paul Turner. Penguin, 1961, 249, 250.
11 For instance, in the *Siddhāntasundara* of Jñānarāja (c. 1500). The British philosopher John Locke referenced this tradition in *An Essay Concerning Human Understanding* (1689), describing an Indian "who, saying that the world was supported by a great elephant, was asked what the elephant rested on; to which his answer was—a great tortoise: but being again pressed to know what gave support to the broad-backed tortoise, replied—something, he knew not what" (II, 23, 2).

Where to locate your secondary world might be the most urgent question needing to be resolved when you embark on a fantasy novel, but there are other problems that should not be overlooked.

Dragons, Etc.

Are you going to have dragons?

As Tolkien pointed out, talking about dragons, fairies, or a "green sun"—none of which exist in our primary world—is not hard to do, but to make a secondary world "inside which the green sun will be credible" demands a higher level of skill.[12]

All novelists will have a problem in convincingly describing what they haven't themselves experienced, and that applies not only to dragons but also to phenomena that *do* exist in the real world.

For example, how many authors who include swordfights and battle scenes in their stories (and who doesn't?) have any practical knowledge of fighting with hand weapons? It isn't merely a question of mugging up on the techniques, which can be done from books. How many authors have ever faced an opponent intent on skewering them, crushing their skull, or hacking into their body with a sharp piece of metal? Fighting in the ancient world and in mediaeval times was a terrifying, gory business.

So too (though this is less well-known) was the more artistic rapier fencing that by Shakespeare's day had become established among the higher social classes, and which has become a staple of swashbuckling adventure films and stories:

> Rapier fighting in the Italian style required completely different poses and techniques to the old sword and buckler. It was all about thrusting the tip of the sword into the other person; cuts and slashes were discouraged

---

12 J.R.R. Tolkien. "On Fairy-Stories", 61.

as being dangerously slow. [...] You couldn't slice an arm off with a rapier but you could pierce your opponent's eye or stick them in the stomach, and, moreover, if you followed the fashionable technique you could do so very fast. [...] Whereas the cut and slash of buckler fighting, within the constraints of well-behaved practice, could be countered by skill, rendering the fights generally non-lethal, the thrust of a rapier and dagger fight could be the undoing of even the most able swordsman. A rank beginner could get lucky and spear his more skilled opponent almost by accident.[13]

More modern weaponry can also create problems. Plenty of people have fired a gun, whether at a fairground, while hunting, as a member of a rifle club, or during military service, but who has personally been shot and wounded (as quite often happens to heroes on the run)? I remember discussing this with a foreign student of mine, a young man who had been shot and gravely injured during a political demonstration in a country with a thuggish totalitarian government. His description of what it was like didn't match anything I'd ever read in a novel.

None of us can do without dead bodies, whether of tragically killed buddies or of clinically dispatched villains, but how many writers have seen a real corpse close-up, and not just on television newsreels? Have touched one, or had to move it?

Most of us have our protagonists galloping backwards and forwards on horseback, but have you done that yourself? I've ridden on donkeys, ponies, camels, and elephants, but never, except very gingerly, on a full-sized horse, and I almost made a catastrophic mistake in one of my novels in a riding scene. Fortunately, the mistake was spotted by someone who read my first draft, just in

---

13 Ruth Goodman. *How to Behave Badly in Renaissance Britain*. Michael O'Mara, 2018, 180-81, 184.

time for me to correct it. The same is true for fantasy situations like riding on a dragon, but here you may get away with almost anything because there is no one who, having ridden a dragon in reality, might inconveniently pop up to tell you that your description has got dragon riding seriously wrong.

There are no dragon riders, but there *are* expert swordsmen and horse riders who have the potential to cause you embarrassment. Those scenes will therefore need to be carefully researched, and imaginatively effective. The fantasy author will be faced with greater practical difficulties than novelists who write about domestic or workplace situations. A lot will depend on the writer's ability to make their more dramatic narrative convincing, and one could even argue that fantasy fiction needs to be *better* or at least *more carefully* written than conventional fiction, as it is so much easier to make a fool of yourself.

There is a trap that some fantasy authors fall into of over-relying on dragons and other exotic beasts. Your book is a novel, not a fantastic menagerie—although that has been done, too, by the way, brilliantly, by Jorge Luis Borges in *The Book of Imaginary Beings*[14]—and if it doesn't have a compelling plot and believable characters no amount of "dragon business" will save it from crashing like a lead balloon. Your dragons might fly (in your imagination), but your novel won't.

The same goes for supernatural figures such as fairies, or others with magical powers like witches and wizards, whom I have chosen not to include in my own novels. (I have included figures who are merely *believed* to have magical or supernatural powers, because such superstitious beliefs were common in the past.) A skilled writer should be able to conjure up magic out of the everyday, without the need for it to be present literally. Or as Douglas Adams puts it, "Isn't it enough to see that a garden

---

14 J.L. Borges with Margaritta Guerro. *The Book of Imaginary Beings* (1967). Revised, enlarged, and translated by Norman Thomas di Giovanni. Avon, 1969.

is beautiful without having to believe that there are fairies at the bottom of it too?"15

Characters and Types

A feature of many fantasy novels is that many of the figures are flat, two-dimensional, and unchanging, and you may even hear the advice to make your characters memorable by going for clear, archetypal figures: the spurned lover, the trickster, the superhero masquerading as a hobo (or the potboy waiting to blossom into a superhero), the cunning villain's thuggish bodyguard, the innocent youngster robbed of his inheritance, and so on. If you have different "races" in your novel, it is all too easy to make the elves elf-like (as you would imagine elves, based on the elven creations of earlier writers); the orcs, unspeakably revolting; the wizards, complex, unfathomable, and predictable only in their unpredictability; the dwarves, dour little fellows who are rather tediously obsessed with minerals.

But this is laziness. Archetypes soon become stereotypes, and why should an elf or an orc not be fully capable of experiencing a learning curve, of developing, of feeling self-doubt, of behaving "untypically"? We are no longer allowed to get away with stereotyping the French, the Germans, or the Japanese in this manner. Some of the minor characters may remain "types", in the brief time that we interact with them, just as people whom we encounter briefly in everyday life will have labels attached to them by us that they never lose, but the principal characters should be properly fleshed out, and made as interesting as you can manage. George R.R. Martin, in his preference for what he calls "gray characters" over black or white, surely gets this right:

---

15 Douglas Adams. *The Hitchhiker's Guide to the Galaxy* (1979). In: *The Ultimate Hitchhiker's Guide to the Galaxy: The Complete Trilogy in Five Parts*. Pan, 2017, 74.

I look for ways to make my characters real and to make them human, characters who have good and bad, noble and selfish, well-mixed in their natures. Yes, I do certainly want people to think about the characters, and not just react with a knee-jerk.[16]

It might be true that simplicity and two-dimensionality are what some readers of fantasy fiction prefer: another dose of the familiar, and (to coin a phrase) no distraction from the action. That is not a path that we should choose, because if you give in to the temptation to treat your characters in this way you will not be writing novels, but the fictional equivalent of a video game.

Evil, Cruelty and Violence

The problem of evil in the world that has so obsessed theologians and philosophers might not seem much of a problem when your world is one of noble, shining heroes and black-hearted, irredeemable villains—a fairytale world. But if you don't address it, your novel will be either (1) comparatively adult fiction best suited for (older) children (like *The Hobbit*) or (2) slightly childish fiction better suited for adults (like *The Lord of the Rings*); what it will *not* be is adult fiction for adults.

What happens to all those orcs and goblins in Tolkien? It seems that they are evil lesser beings who deserve no mercy. They are knocked down (and forgotten about) like the villainous opponents zonked or taken out in violent computer games. During the battle for Helm's Deep, Legolas and Gimli actually engage in a competition to see who can kill the most enemies.[17] Some

---

16 Tasha Robinson. "Interview: George R.R. Martin continues to sing a magical tale of ice and fire." In: *Science Fiction Weekly*, 6, No. 50 (190). https://web.archive.org/web/ 20020223190420/, http://www.scifi.com/sfw/issue190/interview.html
17 J.R.R. Tolkien. *The Lord of the Rings* (1954-55). Single-volume edition.

readers might be reminded of the grim "head-chopping" contests between Japanese officers at Nanking, testing their samurai swords on helpless Chinese prisoners.[18]

After each of the three great battles in *The Lord of the Rings*, the battlefield would have been littered with the dead, the dying, or the seriously injured, but as far as the enemy are concerned the author's general attitude seems to be "just get rid of them"...

The battle for Helm's Deep ends with the total extermination of the defeated, fleeing Orcs, who are conveniently hoovered up by the Ents of Fangorn.

At the battle of the Pelennor Fields, the enemy fight on until there is a blood-red sunset,

> ... and not one living foe was left within the circuit of the Rammas. All were slain save those who fled to die, or to drown in the red foam of the River. Few ever came eastward to Morgul or Mordor; and to the land of the Haradrim came only a tale from far off: a rumour of the wrath and terror of Gondor.

On the other hand, we are told that many on the side of the heroes "were hurt or maimed or dead upon the field", and respect is paid to their memory.[19]

The final battle in front of the Black Gate ends in total defeat for the forces of Sauron. His human allies, the Southrons and Easterlings, either fight to the death, or flee, or beg for mercy, but dehumanised ones like the orcs are in one sweeping rush removed from the landscape:

> The creatures of Sauron, orc or troll or beast spell-enslaved, ran hither and thither mindless: and some slew

---

Unwin, 1978, 558f.
18 See Iris Chang. *The Rape of Nanking* (1997). Penguin, 1998, 55f.
19 *The Lord of the Rings*, 882.

themselves, or cast themselves in pits, or fled wailing back to hide in holes and dark lightless places far from hope.[20]

After Aragorn's coronation, he pronounces judgements and receives ambassadors. We learn that he pardons the Easterlings, makes peace with the peoples of Harad, and frees the slaves of Mordor, giving them "all the lands about Lake Núrnen to be their own".[21] But there is no mention of the orcs, trolls, and suchlike. What place could they possibly have in Aragorn's Brave New World?

War is always cruel, and the fate of the defeated has often been harsh, but there have also been examples of compassion and magnanimity on the part of the victors that offer fantasy authors an alternative to just wiping out the verminous enemy. There is the famous image of the victorious Ashoka horrified by the death and destruction he has wrought on Kalinga, "deeply pained by the killing, dying and deportation that take place when an unconquered country is conquered".[22] Or the Duke of Wellington, who never lost a major battle but, according to his biographer, would be overcome by melancholy or even tears after his victories.[23]

There is one striking instance of generous compassion in Tolkien: a moment of pity for the loathsome Gollum. Frodo has just said that he is "as bad as an orc", and that he is an enemy, and therefore "deserves death"; but Gandalf disagrees.

> Deserves it! I daresay he does. Many that live deserve death. And some that die deserve life. Can you give it

---

20 Ibid. 985.
21 Ibid. 1005.
22 From the Thirteenth Rock Edict, quoted in Charles Allen. *Ashoka: The Search for India's Lost Emperor*. Little, Brown, 2012, 413.
23 Elizabeth Longford. *Wellington: The Years of the Sword* (1969). Panther, 1972, 131.

to them? Then do not be too eager to deal out death in judgement. For even the very wise cannot see all ends."[24]

The principal argument for not killing Gollum is that he might have a role to play in the unfolding story, so—better to wait and see, and in the meantime let the creature live. There is kindness in doing so, of course, but it is not a sophisticated moral position. We are in a shame culture here, not a guilt culture.

If that is one of the problems with violence in fantasy fiction, another is the tendency to go in for vivid descriptions of physical cruelty (what in extreme cases is known as "torture porn"). This is a recurring feature of the works of many of the more recent fantasy authors. Reacting against what was perceived as the twee mediaevalism of Tolkien's "heroic fantasy", they created "more realistic" settings that are dark and grim, fictional embodiments of Thomas Hobbes's notorious characterisation (in 1651) of man's natural state as one of "continuall feare, and danger of violent death", and of human life as "solitary, poore, nasty, brutish, and short"[25]—so much so that works of this kind have come to be known as "Grimdark fantasy".

Let us give these authors the benefit of the doubt and assume that they are *not* indulging perverse sadistic fantasies, and that the violence is *not* gratuitous, but a reflection of the brutality of the culture being shown. Even so, the cruelty will quickly become sickening, and sickening because we are not *of* that culture, but of one that is softer and kinder; alternatively, we may become hardened to the suffering, and blasé about it. Or, even worse, such accounts (who knows?) might encourage a certain kind of reader to want to copy what is being described. If you absolutely must have them, let the dosage of flayings, gougings, and mutilations be calculated very carefully.

---

24 *The Lord of the Rings*, 73.
25 Thomas Hobbes. *Leviathan* (1651). Penguin Random House, 2017, 103.

I don't accept the argument that wallowing in nastiness is excusable because "the world was like that". The European Middle Ages (and most other epochs of human history) may indeed have been grim and dark, a difficult place to survive in if you were a woman or a gentle, sensitive male, but your fictional secondary world is one that *you* have created. It is *not* the Middle Ages, and it is up to *you* what you make it. If you overindulge in sadism and thuggery, some of your readers may begin to wonder about you.

A third problem is the way that some writers use violence to add interest to the plot, whether it is by expunging a significant figure and thus "reshuffling the cards" of the story, or by "fridging",[26] i.e., killing, raping, or maiming a female character in order to awaken the (male) hero's protective feelings and stir him to take revenge. George Martin is ruthless in disposing of comparatively major characters—surely Ned and Robb Stark, Khal Drogo, and Joffrey Baratheon all exit the plot too early (and Ned Stark was even a third-person narrator a few chapters before his removal from the story)? But this is a weakness found in many writers, including even the great E.M. Forster.[27] In my own novels I have been reluctant to kill off any of the major characters, unless for a good reason derived from the plot.

Sex

Sex is another problem arising out of the black-and-white nature

---

26 The term was inspired by an episode in the *Green Lantern* comic series: the hero returns home to find that his girlfriend has been murdered and her remains left in the refrigerator.

27 The death of Lilia in *Where Angels Fear to Tread* (1905) is necessary for the plot, but the accidental death of Lilia's child less so; in *The Longest Journey* (1907), the accidental death of Gerald (killed playing football!) is abrupt, slightly ridiculous, and comes far too early; in *Howards End* (1910), the accidental death of Leonard Bast (of a heart attack, after being hit by a falling bookcase!) is similarly over-melodramatic plotting. Being a character in a Forster novel can be a dangerous business.

of fantasy fiction. If you are allowing yourself dragons and wizards, why then stick with flawed, realistic, all-too-human sex? Many fantasy stories are peopled by hulking, lantern-jawed jocks and stupendously endowed sex goddesses, superhuman creatures who shake the earth when they couple. There is a place for them: in comics. Nothing against comics, but your work is intended to be a novel, surely, and so you will probably want your readers to empathise with your characters rather than just admiring their superhero qualities. Not that you should overdo the realism, and have your male protagonist battling with erectile dysfunction, or your heroine laid low with an embarrassing STD, merely to make them more believable.

You might feel uneasy about the crude, male-chauvinistic nature of the sex content of many popular works. Even major fantasy authors have come in for criticism. John Norman's *Gor* novels have attracted the ire of feminists for their Nietzschean themes of bondage and submission. Here are the opening lines of one of the novels:

I am Zia.
There is a light metal collar on my neck.
It encircles my neck closely.
It is locked there.
I cannot remove it.
Masters will have it so.
Too, my thigh is marked with the cursive *kef*.
Masters will have it so.
I am a slave girl, one of many, on the planet Gor.
We are not important. We are commodities, goods, properties. We are owned.[28]

---

28 John Norman. *Quarry of Gor* (Gorean Saga; 35). 2019, from the Kindle edition.

But do resist the temptation to go in the other direction—of prim political correctness. You are writing fantasy, and fantasy must appeal to deep layers of your (and your reader's) emotions.

That said, there is a certain market for a kind of fantasy literature in which tough sisters hang out together and kick a lot of male butt, and every male character is wimpier or nastier than the last, but it's only a niche market.

The Economy, Stupid[29]

Too often the realms in fantasy novels contain major cities whose existence is hard to explain. What do the inhabitants live on? Where do their food and drinking water come from? If your city is deep inland, or stuck in the middle of a desert, or perched on a mountaintop, where is the road, river, or canal system to carry the necessary supplies? How does the city pay for these products? Do the inhabitants manufacture something that can be exported and, if so, where do they derive the raw materials from?

There will often be a noble elite of warriors, but, apart from their fighting skills, what underpins their wealth and privilege from day to day? There might be some sort of hierarchical feudal system in place, based on holding land from your liege lord and owing him services, but that alone would not explain the more luxurious lifestyle of the masters and their families. Do their tenants pay in kind, or perhaps pass on a tithe from the modest profits that they make from the land, after they have sold the results of their harvesting, shearing, and slaughtering?

If the latter, are the payments made in coin? And if so, what denominations are there? Very few real historical cultures have been able to sustain a trimetallic denomination set of gold, silver, and base metal coins for long, even when they had access to

---

29 A phrase popularised during Bill Clinton's successful 1992 American presidential election campaign.

sources of precious metals, but the characters in your story will need gold to pay ransoms or tribute, silver for wages and trade, and copper coins for everyday purchases. Many historical cultures suffered from a shortage of coin, with mediaeval silver pennies, for example, being split into halves and quarters to make up for the lack of small change; and the precious metal coinages were often reduced or debased until the whole economy began to totter.

Few fantasy authors have concerned themselves with such banalities. In Tolkien, we learn the source of the wealth of the dwarves, and that the might of Sauron and Saruman is powered by underground workshops manned by slaves, but how much are we told about the economy of the great city of Minas Tirith, other than that there are roads nearby, and "quays and landings"?[30] If you want your secondary world to be convincing it needs to have the "feel" of a functioning system. That does not mean that you must invent an enormous number of minute details of everyday life—just enough for the reader to be able to accept your world as plausible.

~

One final point: You no doubt hope that your writing will be noticed among the vast number of fantasy novels and stories now easily available, as conventional publications but also online and through self-publishing. Why should it be noticed, though? It may help if you can come up with some element that makes *your* story unique and memorable—a standout feature.

That is not an invitation to silliness. Don't try to out-Pullman Pullman, with "mega-multiverses"; or outdo Tolkien and Martin, with immense battles involving millions of warriors mounted on mythical beasts. Don't give your hero (or heroine) ridiculous and unbelievable superpowers. Don't populate your world with whimsical, cuddly creatures. I'm thinking more of distinctive

---

30 The Lord of the Rings, 780.

creative details.

Philip Pullman has the brilliant invention of the dæmon, the inner self of a person manifested in the shape of an animal companion.

George R.R. Martin has (no, not the dragons) the Wall, guarded by the Night's Watch.

In Tolkien it is the One Ring; the Harry Potter books have quidditch; my own novels, blood magic.

Frank Herbert's *Dune* has melange ("spice"), to mention just one example from science fiction (the great SF writers are clever at this sort of invention).

But whatever you do, write as well as you can, don't insult the intelligence of your readers, and believe in the world you create.

Writing Mythology
Suhail Mathur

―――⋅❧⋅―――

Suhail Mathur is not only a successful literary agent (The Book Bakers), who has guided more than a thousand authors to publication, he is also an award-winning novelist. He has also been a former cricket commentator and a senior creative professional at one of India's biggest television networks.

~

When I was approached for a contribution to this book—and on mythology—I joked to myself that I had possibly been given the most difficult topic to write on. Difficult not because there is a lack of subjects to address, but difficult purely because of how sensitive our religions—and thereby the stories associated with them—have become in the last few years.

Difficult? Or even impossible? In fact, is "mythology" even the right word? At one end of the Indian spectrum you will find sophisticated, secular readers for whom these tales are charming, exotic fantasy, like stories of the Greek or Norse gods. At the other end you will find people for whom Krishna or Rama are deeply and meaningfully woven into the daily fabric of their lives, and are not flippant entertainment figures. And, since this is a spectrum, in-between you will find many complex positions involving belief, tradition, respect, affection, commitment, ritual—and politics. Express your thoughts about how to write Indian mythology, and you are stepping on thin ice.

My very first encounter with the world of mythology via the written medium was when I was less than four years old. I remember my parents taking me to a cosy little gift shop at night and asking me to choose between a red-coloured toy of a man with a parachute or an Amar Chitra Katha mythological comic book on Lord Ganesh!

Much like any child, getting both would've been the best. But therein lay an important lesson for me. And I vividly remember how my mind worked at that instant, even though this happened around thirty years ago. I knew my parents were asking me to choose not because they couldn't buy me both the items but because they wanted me to learn the art of prioritising. Now that I knew I had to pick one, I thought on my feet and came to the conclusion that the toy, however good, would last me a few months or a couple of years at best. But the book ... the book could possibly last me a lifetime. Yes, this is precisely how I thought even as a four-year-old. I made my decision and it changed my life.

I was introduced to an enchanting world of gods, demons, fantastical elements, curses, boons and morals—the rich tapestry that Hindu mythology provides. Even as I work on this essay, that Amar Chitra Katha, the very same one on Lord Ganesh, still adorns my library! And I didn't have to wait too long to cross to the other side, from consumer to creator, and begin to earn, courtesy our mythology.

It was 1996, and Amar Chitra Katha had put up a "match the following" contest in one of their issues. As luck would have it, after being blissfully sucked into the vortex of reading these spectacular stories, I knew every single answer. I requested my parents to send in my entry, and a few days later I received an envelope from the ACK team saying that I had won the contest and with it the princely sum of ten rupees! It would take me many years to realise that the contest I had read about in 1996 had a closing date for entries in 1984, two years before my parents even met. And the gift, much like all of Santa's gifts, was from my mom and dad. But, yes, these were my first earnings through mythology.

It seems only fair that many years down the line I brainstormed with an author, Rajesh M. Iyer, who had spent several years at Amar Chitra Katha in a senior role, to write the biography of the man who made our childhood so special: Anant Pai or, as he was lovingly called, Uncle Pai, which was incidentally also the title of the book, which became a huge success and was acquired by a leading production house for a visual adaptation.

While we were generously and suitably remunerated for it, I couldn't help but think that these earnings derived ultimately from that mythological book I had been given all those years ago. And the amount this time was considerably more than what I had previously received!

Writing books in India is not a highly lucrative activity and almost all authors carry on in their regular jobs while they write. This is irrespective of the genre, be it mythology or something else. With more and more publishers entering the field and thereby even more authors, the numbers that make a bestseller have constantly gone down, which may not necessarily be a bad thing if you want to tom-tom about it, but economically the numbers simply do not add up if you wish to become a full-time author. The emphasis here is on the word "author", not "writer", as it is much easier to be a writer and sustain yourself. Articles, columns, screenplays and dialogues are all examples of writing and can be highly paid assignments, but they cannot be equated with authoring a book.

There was a time when a book used to be called a bestseller if it sold 10,000 copies or more. With time, the numbers kept dropping, to 5,000 and then to 3,000 and 2,000. Since Covid, publishers have reduced print runs in general and so these days if someone manages to sell a thousand copies the book will be considered to have done well, since it would have finished or would be close to finishing its first print run. It would have made its way to several online bestselling charts and would be a fairly talked about book. So far so good. But now let's get down to the numbers.

Average royalties on paperbacks vary from 7 to 10 per cent on MRP (maximum retail price). For our example, we will take the best case scenario of 10 per cent. Let us say that the book is priced at Rs 350. A book selling a thousand copies would be celebrated in the post-Covid era, but, still, let's triple the number. Suppose an author sold not a thousand but 3,000 copies of his book and received a 10 per cent royalty on the MRP of Rs 350. It would mean that the author is getting Rs 35 on the sale of each book. Now multiply these thirty-five rupees with the 3,000 copies and the amount you get is Rs 105,000.

At first sight, the sum of Rs 105,000 looks rather good. But consider the timeframe involved. It would have taken the author perhaps a year to write a well-researched mythological fiction or fantasy. And then it would have taken another year for the sales figures to come in. Which effectively means that in two years the total amount you would have made after writing a highly successful book would be Rs 105,000, i.e., Rs 52,500 per year, or less than Rs. 5,000 per month. And remember we are taking the best-case scenario and negating the time a publisher would take to publish the book, which could be another year.

The question that arises is: why write if even the better numbers are so dismal? The answer that I always give is simple. You write for the love of literature. You write because you enjoy it. You write for appreciation and acknowledgment. But writing a book alone won't solve your financial problems. So keep that job running, but find time to pursue your passion until the moment comes when you achieve the runaway success that will enable you to turn it wholly and solely into your profession. Ideal advice? Maybe not. But prudent and practical advice? One hundred per cent!

When I wrote my first book, *The Bhairav Putras*, I wanted to write a predominantly historical revolutionary thriller with dollops of mythology. I wanted to tell the story of a Dark God, and Lord Bhairav was the perfect choice. Not only is it interesting to write about a lesser-known god because it gives you that much more material to play around with and create a stronger narrative; I also chose him to be the titular character because I worship his child form, Batuk Bhairav.

The book did extremely well, and as a result I was invited to several literary festivals. I remember that there was a barrage of mythology themed books coming onto the market around that time, and some might feel that I had just jumped onto a successful bandwagon, but the truth is that when I started writing *The Bhairav Putras* none of these successful mythological books had yet been released. Also, it was a genre I felt comfortable with. At any other time, and irrespective of how mythological books were faring, this would have been the book I first came out with.

India's history and mythology have always fascinated me. But simply zeroing on the genre is not enough. It is necessary that you treat it with respect. So when I wrote *The Bhairav Putras*, whose story traverses the time period from 1936 to 1942, I ensured that the events of the book fitted the timeline of actual historical events seamlessly.

My second book, *The Hunt for Rama's Bow: Adventure One of the Vishnu Chronicles*, which came out a little more than two-and-a-half years after my first one, was complete even before I had published *The Bhairav Putras*. The wait was deliberate. I was aware that I had written a strong first book. But I was also aware that if I submitted my second book *after* the first had become a hit and garnered appreciation, the chances of its success would increase hugely. And that is precisely what happened. I was particularly keen that Om Books International should publish the book, given their fine track record in the genre, and as luck would have it my script was accepted within a day of submission.

Write what comes naturally to you. But don't forget that it is not speed but quality that will take you far. If you have the required patience, results should soon follow. In my own case, the success of my book made me aware of another area that mythology writers should look into: TV writing. With its three principal aspects of story, screenplay, and dialogues, TV writing is clearly a promising income generation platform for writers of mythology. But it comes with its own set of challenges, because writing for television is vastly different from writing a book.

Now one may argue that the "story" aspect of a mythological show is already there, since these shows are based on our epics and puranas. Yet while the broad framework may be in place, every show will have their own interpretation of it.

This is even true for the epics themselves. The sage Valmiki's Ramayana is the fountainhead, so to speak. However, over the years other versions have been written in various languages, and each has added its own interpretation to the original work. Some have tried to humanise the principal antagonist, Ravana; others have found back stories to supplement their line of thought.

The most notable deviations can be found in the retelling of the epic by Tulsidas. For instance, there is no mention of the Lakshmana Rekha[1] in the sage Valmiki's version. It was added by Tulsidas. And in the original work, the protagonist, Lord Rama, is not depicted as a god, a Vishnu avatar, but as the ideal king and ideal man.

But the biggest deviation is that in the original Ramayana, Lord Hanuman is not depicted as a monkey. He is a Vanar, which is a combination of *Van*, i.e., "forest" and *Nar*, i.e., "man", meaning a forest dweller. Such revelations can be disturbing, because they challenge what you thought you knew. If Lord Hanuman wasn't a monkey, how do we envisage him? And how do we handle this

---

1 The protective line in the soil that Lakshmana draws around their dwelling to protect Sita in his and Rama's absence.

in the visual medium? What kind of a furore would there be if Hanuman is not shown as a monkey or if the Lakshmana Rekha is omitted from the screen version?

I remember a conversation that I had while working on a book with the affable and unassuming Moti Sagar, son of the legendary film-maker Ramanand Sagar, and someone who himself played a key role in the making of a grand epic TV show, *Ramayan*, along with his illustrious father. He informed me that during the initial phase of the show someone at Doordarshan[2] had recommended a visit to an aged gentleman in Pune who was possibly one of the biggest authorities on the Ramayana at that time, to discuss how the show could be made more authentic. What the aged gentleman told the senior Mr Sagar confounded him. He was of the opinion that society back in the day did not see breasts as sexual objects and so both men and women roamed bare-chested. However true this may or may not have been, there was no way one could depict this in the show, and Mr Sagar conveyed as much to the TV channel's officials, who soon realised that some tweaks and modifications are always needed so as to be in sync with the times and, more importantly, not hurt the sensibilities of devotees.

Sometimes, however, a film-maker or director will make a deviation purposely. Actor and film-maker Sanjay Khan told me that in his show *Jai Hanuman* he had shown Lord Rama shooting an arrow at Bali from the *front*, and not from behind as the story usually goes. This invited the ire of certain communities, who were unhappy with the deviation. Mr Khan was invited for a discussion, and he was able to win over his detractors by stating that the deviation had been deliberate, since he was of the opinion that a man as pure, honourable and brave as Lord Rama should never be shown killing an adversary from the shadows rather than

---

2 India's public broadcasting organisation, providing TV, radio, and other services.

defeating him fair and square. This impressed the aggrieved parties so much that they no longer pursed the matter.

The genesis for *The Hunt for Rama's Bow* came from a conversation at a literary festival where a panellist said that today's generation might be more familiar with The Avengers than with Hindu mythology. That struck a chord with me, and I decided to do something that would make mythology more relevant to young people today. I set the book in 2020. How would we react if a mythical monster arrived on a modern college campus?

Another goal was to integrate less well-known but fascinating information from the epic and convey it in a seamless manner. Now a general belief is that Lord Rama was from India and Ravana from Sri Lanka. Forget them being from different countries, they belonged to the same state! Lord Rama was from Ayodhya, which is in Uttar Pradesh, while Ravana's father's name was Visrava. His birthplace is claimed to be Bisrakh, a place that still exists, in present-day Greater Noida. Kuber was the ruler of Lanka. Ravana defeated Kuber and became the king of Lanka, but he wasn't an original inhabitant of the place. Ravana's wife Mandodri was from a place called Mayapuri, in Meerut, while in Jodhpur there is Ravan Ka Teela, believed to be where Ravana and Mandodri married each other.

Television writing does come with its own set of narratives. I worked with Siddhartha Kumar Tewary while he was in the initial days of setting up his shows *Shani*, *Radha Krishn*, and *Lav Kush*. Brainstorming on *Lav Kush*, we discussed how to tell the two brothers apart on screen. With two other writers also working on it, the end result was twofold. The first idea was to give the brothers different characteristics. If one was calm, the other was hot-headed. If one played by the book, the other didn't mind bending the rules. The second idea was to give them different weapons. Traditionally, Lav and Kush are both wielders of the bow, but to distinguish one from the other, one was given a bow and the other a sword. Storytelling in the visual medium is different from that of a book.

Writing mythological shows for television is highly lucrative. But be warned, television writing is exhausting, and involves multiple levels of writing and rewriting, especially at the nascent stage of pitching a show. Meetings may go on for months before a show is eventually green-lit, and a writer would only start getting their remuneration after that. If the show doesn't see the light of day, all the effort comes to a monetary naught.

We in India are sensitive about what is shown on screen, and anything in a film or on the internet may snowball into public interest litigation or defamation suits, as was seen recently when certain unsavoury dialogues made their way to Lord Hanuman's character in the film *Adipurush* (2023). TV, however, remains largely immune to it, downplaying such legal notices and letting their legal departments fight them while the production work blithely continues.

I remember showing the rerun of a show on Lord Krishna, originally aired by a sister channel before being aired on the channel I was working for. I remember my business head and I visiting one of my authors, an International Society for Krishna Consciousness guru, for a possible collaboration to impart life lessons from the Blue God's life at the end of every episode. While the meeting went off rather well, Prabhu called me a few days later after seeing an episode of the Kaliya Nag episode. He informed me that while the depictions from the show were extremely beautiful and eye-catching, the authenticity of the storyline (or rather the lack of it) would make it difficult for him to lend his name to it. While all of us in the office understood his dilemma, in retrospect I am so glad that he didn't take up the offer because all of us were stunned by the fact that the show depicted Radha and not Krishna eventually killing Krishna's evil uncle Kans. It was a tough pill to swallow then, and even now it amazes me how it could have been aired and continue its entire run, becoming a smash hit and yet with no one taking offence to it.

While there is plenty of cash to be made by writers of godly tales in the telly world, the same cannot be said for the largest film industry in the world, Bollywood. Producers, for some reason, are always shying away from making big budget mythological movies despite having the best repository of stories available and the ability to spend lavish budgets on their making. Despite everything going in its favour, the reason one barely sees mythological or mythological fantasy films in Bollywood is because most production companies get spooked by the budgets involved in the making: the sets, costumes, special effects, etc.

Which is why a *Brahmastra* is a one-off film in Bollywood, and several years in the making. Which is why one constantly hears of a Rajamouli making a *Mahabharata* or an Aamir Khan making a *Mahabharata* but nothing comes of it beyond such articles in the paper. Hollywood, on the other hand, constantly keeps on making movies inspired by myth and folklore, be it the Percy Jackson series or adaptations of *The Ten Commandments* or series like *Clash of the Titans*, *Wrath of the Titans*, and so on.

This is indeed surprising since pre-Independence, and for a few years after Independence, the Hindi film industry made several movies on mythological themes, for the first time giving avenues to writers to showcase characters in a larger-than-life manner for the masses, and on a pan-India level. In fact, the only film Mahatma Gandhi watched was also an adaptation of the Ramayana, titled *Ram Rajya*, that was released in 1943.

Most of what Bollywood asks its writers to dish out are mythological tales set in a contemporary period such as *Kalyug* or *Rajneeti*, both of which had the Mahabharata at their core, or *Hum Paanch* inspired by the Pandavas, Krishna and Kans, or even a modern-day interpretation of the Ramayana in Mani Ratnam's *Raavan*. In fact, the Bollywood espionage thriller *Naam Shabana* was also inspired by the Mahabharata. Its director, Neeraj Pandey, who had made the first movie in the series, *Baby*, felt that just as each character in the Mahabharata could have a standalone story delving into their past, their reasons, actions and motives for what they eventually come to signify, he could take a subsidiary character from *Baby* and produce a full-length movie on the same.

While these films are flashes in the pan, the important aspect that such films bring to the fore is the topic of interpretation. And interpretation is one area which gives an author ample scope to justify a character. A popular show on Epic called *Dharm Kshetra* was based on arguments and counterarguments that every major character from the Mahabharata has to face in the Heavens. We as a literary agency also try to bring about such narratives that make the reader aware of the compulsions of their protagonists. While we are currently working on the story of Princess Lakshmana (the daughter of Duryodhana, married into the Yadava family and torn in the battle of the two families), books on Duryodhana, Rukmini and Kunti titled *I, Duryodhana, Krishna's Consort* and *The Girl Who Loved the Sun*, respectively, have already found favour with Om Books International.

Each of these stories is broadly known. But why did Duryodhana believe that he was the rightful heir to the throne, what did Rukmini go through when, despite being Krishna's wife, she was overshadowed by his former lover, Radha, and what were the reasons behind the choices Kunti made before marrying Pandu? These form the narratives of the books and make the reader understand the vision of their authors, who themselves are getting into the shoes of a character to understand them better.

Staying with this topic, we also got Gufi Paintal, the casting director of B.R. Chopra's epic *Mahabharat*, to write a book in his capacity as casting director, but even more in his capacity as the actor playing one of the principal antagonists, Shakuni. He explains why Shakuni felt betrayed and takes the readers through the Mahabharata from the perspective of the man he immortalised on screen. This book, to be published by Om Books International, is a tribute to Mr Paintal, who unfortunately passed away before he could see the book in print.

There is a new criticism that may threaten the authors of mythological stories with an existential crisis. Of late, there has been a trend to label mythological stories as derived from Indian history, not myth, in a bid to give greater legitimacy to these characters and their glorious tales. And while I understand the rationale behind this, I must respectfully disagree, simply because what supporters of this theory fail to realise is that history has no gods. It only has great men and women. It is only mythology which has gods and goddesses. By claiming that these tales are historical, they are actually divesting gods like Rama and Krishna of their godly status, which is disappointing.

In essence, if you want to be a mythological author or writer, your path will be filled with opportunities but as many roadblocks too. From researching and reading books and scriptures to successfully navigating reader preferences, devotional attachment and possible criticisms, the life of someone writing mythology will be filled with ups and downs, but if you are really passionate about telling these amazing and legendary stories, do not hold back!

Your greatest reward will be appreciation. I remember my first meeting with Sanjay Khan, when I explained the premise of my *Vishnu Chronicles* series to him. I must have impressed him, because when I was leaving, Mr Khan decided to personally escort me, regardless of the fact that he was seventy-six years old. When I requested him to remain seated and not go to such trouble, he paused, looked into my eyes, and said in his baritone, "Son, the blood from the swords of a thousand soldiers cannot match the ink from the pen of one writer!"

Writing Historical Fiction

What It Might be Worthwhile to Keep in Mind before Embarking on This Adventure

Christoph Werner

Christoph Werner is a German novelist who was born and raised in the German Democratic Republic, i.e., in communist East Germany. Before his retirement, he taught at various universities in East and West Germany, working in the fields of technical English, translation, and English teacher training. Among his publications are short stories and novels, including several that have appeared in English: *Shadows of My Father: The Memoirs of Martin Luther's Son* (HarperLegend, 2017), *To Live in All Eternity: Caspar David Friedrich and Joseph Mallord William Turner* (tredition, 2019), and *Castle by the River: The Life and Death of Karl Friedrich Schinkel, Painter and Master Builder* (tredition, 2020); also, *Lifting the Iron Curtain* (tredition, 2019), a collection of reminiscences about life in East Germany. Christoph Werner lives in Weimar.

~

To begin with, we are not talking about historical fantasy or speculative fiction, though there are often no fixed boundaries between the genres. One could say that almost anything seems possible in the latter two, but they are not what we understand by historical fiction.

It is generally agreed that historical fiction is novels or narratives that take place in past times, conveniently more than fifty years before the author wrote them, since they might thus escape any accusations of libel, as all the persons appearing in the books would have passed on by then. Though beware of their descendants.

To be honest, I haven't amassed vast sums of money through my historical novels. The pittance my publisher paid me was just enough to cover the costs of the required travelling and research. So, anybody who wants both to write historical novels and to earn money from them should think twice, except, of course, if their name happens to be Hilary Mantel or Ken Follett.

I can, however, understand why people want to write books in general, or historical novels in particular: because they want to see them printed, or kept in the Library of Congress, or offered for sale in bookshops, or by Amazon and various other online booksellers.

Usually those who do so will manage to have well-meaning reviews published along with the books, reviews they have often written themselves or which were sent in by good friends or by their wives. Then, in return, they write approving critiques of other people's books, thereby making everyone happy.

Personally, I admit that I am not entirely free of such vanities, though on the other hand I do like to entertain people, because I think that they deserve a bit of fun, and if this means telling them something they didn't know before, or hadn't encountered in fiction in some palatable disguise, I believe that in itself is enough of a justification for writing historical novels.

I am not well read in Greek philosophy, but I more or less accidentally hit on something Aristotle is said to have written, namely, that the artistic representation of history was more scholarly and serious than exact historiography, since poetry went to the core and essence, while the exact account was only a series of details.[1] This convinced me immediately, because when reading history books I had often felt a kind of frustration: something seemed to be missing, something having to do with real, full-blooded life, and connected with a failure to scrupulously check the logic of the events.

The Bible says, in Matthew 18:20: "For where two or three are gathered together in my name, there am I in the midst of them." Applied to writing and publishing in general, that means that even though you may have only a small number of readers, perhaps a mere handful, made up of friends and acquaintances that you persuaded or blackmailed into buying your books, you are still doing humankind and the Holy Spirit of Literature a favour, small as it may appear.

My life so far, as a student of English and German, as a driving instructor, a schoolteacher, a university lecturer, an unemployed person, a freelance translator and a writer of sorts, not exactly a smooth career I reckon, has taught me to appreciate the little things and, more than that, to welcome any recognition by my fellow human beings.

The following account of some of my experiences in the field of book-writing, offered here for the benefit, I hope, of aspiring or would-be authors (or to discourage them, as I'm convinced there are too many of them!), is not noticeably well-ordered, but then art, literature, and fiction so often do defy law and order.

First of all, let us get rid of L.P. Hartley's notion that "the past is a foreign country: they do things differently there".[2] This is an annoying half-truth, as people in the past, though they possibly did do some things differently there, were mostly driven by the

---

1   Aristotle. "On the Art of Poetry." In: *Classical Literary Criticism*. Transl. T.S. Dorsch. Penguin, 1965, 43-44.
2   L.P. Hartley. *The Go-Between* (1953). Penguin, 1971, 7.

same desires, hopes, fears, bodily functions and other things as we people of today are.

You'll read about the probable and the improbable, the need to do your own research and use your own judgement, and, most importantly, the need to fill the gaps left by historians and the like out of a wrong sense of tradition, certain moral rules or what is usually regarded as decorum or propriety.

I'll start, in all modesty, with a book from my own pen, *Shadows of My Father* (2015), a novel built around one of Martin Luther's children, his youngest son, Paulus, who was a doctor and professor of medicine, an alchemist who sought the formula for creating gold, and the personal physician to a number of German princes.

In the book I describe the flight of Katharina von Bora, his mother, from life in the Cistercian monastery of Marienthron, in Nimbschen near Grimma in Saxony, to Wittenberg, where Martin Luther had started the Reformation a few years earlier. Katharina had become interested in the growing reform movement and increasingly dissatisfied with her life in the convent. Conspiring with several other nuns to flee in secrecy, she contacted Luther and begged for his assistance. Luther, who was a strong opponent of monastic life, particularly for girls, who "are forced to live a spiritual life before they can rightly know what flesh and blood is",[3] persuaded his friend the Torgau city councillor and merchant Leonard Koppe to send a covered wagon to the convent, a cart of the kind normally used to transport herrings to customers such as monasteries.

Nine nuns, still in their religious garments, hid themselves in the wagon, some behind the fish barrels, others even crouched inside them, "in each barrel a virgin".[4] When they arrived at their stopover, Torgau, they were said to have been received

---

3   Christoph Werner. *Shadows of My Father: The Memoirs of Martin Luther's Son. A Novel.* HarperLegend, 2017, 27.
4   *Shadows of My Father*, 28.

enthusiastically by the local citizens and immediately taken to church to thank the Almighty for their escape.

Can you believe that? I can't. The nuns had been huddled for hours in herring barrels and would surely have felt the need to relieve themselves, in both forms, as the journey took at least half a day. They must have emitted a truly formidable smell of fish and worse and would certainly have felt the urge to have a bath and a change of clothes before praising their Saviour and mingling closely with people in church, even if those people were hugely enthusiastic.

But no mention of this is made by historians or by other writers, which makes their accounts somewhat unsatisfactory.

Couldn't the wagon have stopped on the way to Torgau for the nuns to follow the call of nature? No, this would have been too dangerous. Nuns who fled from their convents were severely punished, like Florentina of Oberweimar, who was caught trying to escape from her monastery, brutally flogged after first being divested of her clothes and gleefully ogled by the men who did the flogging, and then incarcerated. People who helped nuns escape were generally doomed when caught. For example, there was Heinrich Keller from Mittweida in Saxony, ordered by Duke George of Saxony to be beheaded because he had helped a nun flee from the cloister of Sornzig. Such executions were quite legal at the time, since they were carried out in accordance with ecclesiastical and secular law, which called for the death penalty in such cases.

Likewise, something interesting is missing in the descriptions of Katharina's and Martin Luther's romance and final marriage. Luther was not keen on getting married and did not, as he said, suffer under the monk's vow of chastity. "With women I had nothing to do other than a few times in the confession, and there I did not look at them. And other than the natural discharge at night, I was not troubled by sexual lust."[5] We can therefore deduce

---

5   Ibid. 30.

that when he married Katharina von Bora he had had no sexual experience, at least not with women. At that time, in 1525, he was forty-one years of age. Katharina, a lively and communicative woman, was twenty-six.

When she was five years old, in 1504, her father had sent her to a Benedictine cloister for education. At the age of nine she moved to the Cistercian monastery of Marienthron, as mentioned above, and possibly became a Bride of Christ, though we don't know anything about a "bodily embrace of Christ", i.e., a mystical wedding. We can be sure that the girls would have talked among themselves about life outside the convent, about living with a man and about what it meant to get married and lose your virginity on the wedding night. Besides, it was not uncommon at a time when the monastic system was in general decline, and even before that, for unchaste nuns to be impregnated by monks from other monasteries, while others, the more chaste ones, might be fingered by their confessors or even persuaded to sin with them, as it was their duty to obey the priests, who were Christ's or God's vicars on earth. The girls would certainly have exchanged confidences about their experiences, and very likely been physically intimate with each other.

Now imagine the scene when the Luther couple, after having been wedded, were conducted, fully clothed, to the bridal bed by friends and guests. Although only symbolic, this process and what followed in the solitude of the bedchamber must have caused them great embarrassment, chaste and untrained as they were in the things of the flesh. It is quite conceivable that Katharina, drawing on her experiences in the monastery, lent her husband a guiding hand and thereby initiated the conception of their eldest son, Johannes.

Why are these heart-rending and at the same time touching details left out by so many authors? Don't they have sufficient imagination or are they so stuck in traditional writing or morals that they even bend the truth to the detriment of the story? Don't follow their example, should you decide to start writing!

My second point relates to the description of military affairs in history, and I'll start way back, with the Carthaginian general Hannibal (247–183 BC).

When Hannibal reached the banks of the Rhône on his way to Italy, his army probably consisted of no more than 38,000 foot soldiers and 8,000 horses, with an undetermined number of elephants, some sources say there were thirty-seven of them.[6]

Though obviously a good deal of supplies could be obtained by foraging, purchase or fighting as the case might be, the army still had to carry supplies with it, involving large numbers of supply wagons, pack horses, mules and so on; water supplies would be vital for such a multitude. In particular, thought would have to be given to the elephants, which formed such a vital part of the army. Their speed was not more than around 4.8 km an hour, not much quicker than the normal walking speed of 4.5 km per hour. The daily distance they could cover was therefore about 24 to 32 km. War elephants were probably used as baggage animals on the march, and if so, could certainly manage a load of up to 400 kg. But an elephant needs to be watered twice a day, at least, and their daily drinking capacity is approximately 114 litres (a normal bathtub holds about 150 litres), while their daily food ration is in the region of 7 kg of grain and 90 kg of dry fodder. Elephants have very sensitive skins, cannot stand extremes of hot or cold, and, if cold and wet, easily catch chills; while their feet are not up to prolonged marches on wet or rocky ground. Similar problems applied to the unshod cavalry horses, whose so-called hipposandals, made of soft materials like leather, had to be renewed constantly. The foot soldiers also needed extra footwear. All this had to be in sufficient supply, either carried by pack animals or on wagons or partly by the soldiers themselves.

---

6 See Tony Bath (1981). *Hannibal's Campaigns: The story of one of the greatest military commanders of all time*. Barnes & Noble, 1992.

When the Carthaginian army finally stood on Italian soil, it could muster no more than 12,000 African foot soldiers, 8,000 Spaniards and 6,000 horses. The passage of the mountains had been as costly as a severe defeat.

For a Roman legion in action, the total grain requirement for soldiers, horses and mules was around 18.4 t per day. An army consisting of eight legions therefore required 147.2 t of grain per day, not including the green fodder for the animals.[7] Hannibal's army, forgetting about the elephants for the moment, would thus have needed about 1,325 t (1,325,000 kg) of food for the nine days that it took them to cross the Alps.

Of course, we assume with this that there was enough potable water on the march, of which one soldier needs 5 litres and a horse 30 litres a day, particularly when marching over 2,400-m-high passes.

Clearly, I'm not in a position to question the numbers that have come down to us from the old days, but I only ask the writers of fiction to look more closely into the probability and trustworthiness of the data found in history books.

My next example is the famous Battle of Culloden (1746), of which some astonishing things have been handed down to us, even by such a renowned source as the *Encyclopaedia Britannica*, which tells us that some 1,000 of the Young Pretender's army of 5,000 weak and starving Highlanders were killed by the 9,000 Redcoats.

Weak and starving Highlanders? Carrying heavy muskets and some of them shields and swords and charging the English over a distance of several hundred yards over boggy ground? When I visited the battlefield a few years ago, the guide, very nice in his kilt and with his Scottish accent, told me with a tragic mien that the Scots hadn't eaten for three days before the battle, and he almost shed tears when he said that brother fought against brother, referring to

---

7 *Römische Legion*. At https://de.wikipedia.org/wiki/R%C3%B6mische_Legion#cite_ref-sb_21-1>

the Scots that fought on the English side and the English on the Scottish side. He wasn't happy when I expressed some doubts that one could fight effectively after not having eaten for three days. He said that was the way Scots were, and still are, constituted. I was impressed that after almost 300 years the tragedy of Culloden was still so much alive in my Scotsman. I secretly apologised for my doubts, which turned out to be premature after he told me that his own clan hadn't taken part in the battle. Instead, they had gone poaching while their countrymen died on the battlefield.

Let us take a further example of the supplies that an army needs: Kutuzov's Russian army of 120,000 soldiers and 40,000 horses pursuing Napoleon's no longer Grand Army in the winter of 1812. To feed such numbers just for one day, 850 fully loaded supply wagons would be needed. Of course, the draught animals, at least four to a wagon, and the 850 drivers also had to be fed, so that when the supply distances became longer and longer with the advance of the army, the supply troops used up a large part of the food intended for the fighting soldiers.[8]

For even more recent times, let us look at Hitler's Wehrmacht invading the Soviet Union in 1941. The three huge army groups (north, centre and south) were each about one million soldiers strong at the beginning, and seventy-five freight trains, a number hardly ever reached and diminishing quickly in the course of the fighting, were needed, daily, to supply them with weapons, equipment and food.

There is, by the way, a persisting myth in the historical memory of many Germans that the Wehrmacht was predominantly motorised. Far from it. The invasion of Russia started with 750,000 horses used as draught animals, riding beasts and for other purposes. Sixty per cent of transport behind the front was managed by animals. Before the Battle of Stalingrad, some

---

8 See Dominic Lieven. *Russia against Napoleon: The Battle for Europe, 1807-1814*. Allen Lane/Penguin Books, 2009.

150,000 horses, as well as a number of oxen and even camels, had been accumulated between the Don and the Volga. The troops of the Sixth Army, encircled at Stalingrad, and especially the vast majority of its artillery and medical units, depended almost entirely on horses for their mobility.[9] The majority of horses had been withdrawn behind the front to the west because of lack of fodder at the beginning of the winter of 1942. The remaining several thousand starving beasts were slaughtered and eaten by the equally starving soldiers in the Stalingrad Pocket around Christmas 1942.

Incidentally, I have long wondered why the Wehrmacht has so frequently been praised for its military efficiency in British publications on World War II and in war museums, when in reality it made one blunder after another, particularly in blindly or cravenly following Hitler's paranoid belief in the superiority of the German race and, consequently, of its soldierhood and acumen. The biggest blunder of course was the invasion of the Soviet Union, carried out in the misguided underestimation of its patriotic response, narrowly followed by the catastrophic undervaluing of the ability of the British to rally to their country's cause in a time of national danger.

Some of that praise of the Wehrmacht's efficiency seems to have come from the old tradition that says that the more you praise your enemy's strength, the greater your glory must be in defeating him.

Speeches to armies before battles are also a favourite theme of gullible or uncritical storytellers. Among the innumerable examples let us take just two: Napoleon's words allegedly spoken to his troops before the Battle of the Pyramids in 1798, and Elizabeth I's Tilbury speech.

Napoleon is said to have told his army: "Remember that forty centuries look down upon you from these monuments!"[10]

---

9 See Antony Beevor (1998). *Stalingrad*. Penguin, 2017.
10 A quotation that has interestingly survived in multiple versions, e.g.,
    "*Soldats! Du haut de ces monuments, quarante siècles vous regardent*",

The looking-down-upon might have been somewhat difficult because the pyramids were 15 km away. More importantly, how could Napoleon have made himself understood to 20,000 soldiers deployed for the battle? Had he sent mounted adjutants to spread his words to each company, of which there were at least 130? Unthinkable. Here we are again: Beware of generals, or kings for that matter, who are said to have spoken to their armies, be it Alexander the Great, Frederick the Great or Elizabeth I, who on the eve of the Spanish Armada spoke "to her troops" assembled at Tilbury Camp to defend the country against a Spanish invasion. Again, how could she have done that? She must have had a giant's voice or had her speech delivered to the army by members of her retinue.

As for Napoleon, we should not forget that the source of his speech was memories transcribed many years later during his exile on St Helena.

Not just speeches, prayers were also said to have been delivered by great men. The praiseworthy Robert Graves, see below, obviously drawing on some antique historian, describes in his novel *Claudius the God and His Wife Messalina* how, before reaching Marseille on his way to conquer Britain, the Emperor Claudius was caught in a life-threatening storm and started to pray "to every God in the Pantheon" for rescue from the impending calamity. It seems to have helped, the five ships landed at Marseille safely, and the sailors and guards "swore that it was the most beautiful praying that they had ever heard in their lives and that it gave them new hope".[11]

Now what was that again? A storm is raging through the sails, driving seawater over the railing and into the faces of everyone on

---

alternatively, "*Allez, et pensez que du haut de ces monuments quarante siècles vous observent.*" Alan Moorehead. *The White Nile* (revised edition, 1972). Penguin, 1983, 98.

11 Robert Graves. *Claudius the God and His Wife Messalina* (1934). Penguin, 2006, 243.

deck, yet they could still hear the emperor pray? And were able to appreciate the aesthetic beauty of the prayer? Had Neptune reinforced his voice? Or had the court scribblers put down the story afterwards?

Logistics in general seems to be the most underestimated part of warfare and consequently plays either no or only a minor part in writers' narratives. The same is true for what an army on the march leaves behind with regard to garbage and, yes, let's be blunt about it, shit.

It is a biological fact that a man, or woman for that matter, on an average excretes 150 g of stool per day (we'll forget about the amount of urine for now).

Fifteen thousand soldiers under General Ernst von Rüchel marched from Weimar to join battle near Jena on 14 October 1806. Let us assume that each of the 15,000 produced 150 g of stool on that day, which they left behind in their camp in Weimar or on the march to Jena. That amounts to roughly two-and-a-half tons of excrement, nicely distributed on both sides of the road, where the soldiers, leaving their unit, would have had to run to relieve themselves. Then they had to hurry back to rejoin their unit. And what, pray, did they wipe their behinds with? Nobody knows for sure whether they cleaned themselves at all. And the little river Ilm was not near enough to be of help. In fact, there was and still is hardly any suitable source of water on the road to Jena. And what about the more than a hundred thousand troops that Napoleon led into the battle at Jena? There must have been a horrible and persistent stink for days in Weimar and around Jena and Auerstedt. And let us not forget the peasants and farmhands who had to work the fields and meadows and fruit trees beside the roads. And the rats and other vermin feeding on the garbage, and the diseases they spread. Hardly any mention of this is made in the stories set in that time. If you believe them, everything was clean, hygienic, orderly, everybody was healthy; no sick or wounded soldiers were transported on the baggage wagons or left behind in the pitiful care of peasants; nobody died on the march.

When you read about the Battle of Leipzig in 1812, it is much the same. For the most part, the slaughter is glorified. Yet during and after the battle thousands of the wounded and the dying were carried into the churches of Leipzig, which had been transformed into military hospitals. There they fell into the hands of surgeons who sawed, hacked, cut and cauterised them. The wounded moaned and screamed, pinned down by their comrades or medical helpers on makeshift operating tables constructed from church benches. Within these hospitals, fever raged so fiercely that very few succeeded in coming out alive. The dead, robbed of their clothes, were thrown out of the windows on to the streets every day, and large rack wagons were filled to the brim with corpses. The wagoners stepped on the dead bodies while stacking them and worked with rolled-up sleeves as though they were handling wooden logs. Often, soldiers refused to be taken to the hospitals because they believed they would certainly die there. They preferred to crouch on a street corner or on the stairs of a house in the dim hope of survival.

Talking of Napoleon brings us to the German poet, statesman and natural scientist Goethe, who met Bonaparte in the Thuringian city of Erfurt in October 1808. Tradition has it that Napoleon, when he caught sight of Goethe and before he started to talk to him during an audience at which a large number of people were present, said something like *vous êtes un homme* or *voilà un homme*, which Goethe himself wanted to be interpreted as a kind of *ecce homo* paraphrase in the sense of "Look, what a man!" My objection here is that our only source for this high praise of Goethe by one of the mightiest princes of the time is Goethe himself, someone never accused of being overly modest. Perhaps Napoleon, beleaguered as he was by so many who wanted his ear, just meant, oh God, *another* of these tiresome Germans, and Goethe, we will give him the benefit of the doubt, simply misheard or misunderstood him.

Let us turn to a gentler, more digestible, topic, that of language. Here almost anything goes, as is shown by what many reputable writers of the past and present have produced.

There is no recipe that I can suggest, just that you should avoid anything that makes you lose the reader.

And what might that be? Certainly phrases from everyday language that weren't used at the time of your heroes, like *okay* or *Hi!* Or *Hello!*, which didn't come into use until the second half of the nineteenth century. Also, anything that is derived from technical innovations of modern times would probably irritate the reader, like *to text somebody*, to *give somebody a bell*, or even words like *nerd*, *movie*, *meme*, *vibe*, and a hundred others.

There are also treacherous words like *gas*. This word didn't exist before Jan Baptist van Helmont in the seventeenth century called the haze rising from cold water "gas". "In the absence of a name, I have taken the liberty of calling this haze gas, as it differs little from the chaos of the old."[12] That is to say, it is derived from the Greek word *chaos*.

On the other hand, it might surprise some people to read a historical mystery novel about Sir Walter Scott in which a photo or photograph plays an important role. (Admittedly, that novel has not yet been written, but might be in the works, so to say.) The plot revolves around a photo, taken in the year of Scott's death in 1832, but then stolen from Abbotsford, the home of the writer, where it had been hidden for decades behind a painting, and recently offered by an anonymous person on the internet for a tremendous sum of money. The first recorded use of the word—in the form of the French *photographie*—was in 1834, i.e., two years after Scott's death, but the first photos were taken in the 1820s, so you wouldn't be lying to your reader if you used the word *photograph* two years prematurely, especially since there is no absolute proof of its first use in 1834. (It might have been earlier.)

---

12 Translated from *Gas*. At https://de.wikipedia.org/wiki/Gas

Well-known writers proceed differently in their novels with regard to language and still keep their readers in line.

In *I, Claudius*, written in the form of an autobiography of the Roman Emperor Claudius and first published in 1934, Robert Graves uses the English of his own time, the first half of the twentieth century, even when describing the Roman military. So you will find *division* for legion, *battalion* for cohort, *company* for maniple or century, *captain* for centurion, and so on. The foot soldiers in a legion—the legionaries—are here called *heavy infantry* (the term didn't come into use in English until the 1570s, and *infantryman* not before 1837).[13] *Field marshal* crops up, too (it in fact dates to the early Middle Ages, and originally referred to the keeper of the king's horses).

Returning to what I said above about the anachronistic use of very modern expressions like *hello*, Graves, when depicting a dispute between Arminius, chieftain of the Germanic Cherusci, and his brother Flavius, who served in the Roman army, allows one of them to greet the other with "hullo".[14] Emperor Tiberius addresses the Roman Senate as "my lords", the Roman province of Germania is called Germany (which didn't exist for another 800 years), and the Germanic tribes are called Germans. The Praetorian Guard are called the Guards, but now, hark, none of this has diminished in the least the success, trustworthiness and reputation of either the author or his book. In fact, in 1998, the *Modern Library* ranked *I, Claudius* fourteenth on its list of the 100 best English-language novels of the twentieth century, and in 2005 the novel was chosen by *Time* as one of the 100 best English-language novels from 1923 to the present.

How can this be explained? It is because of the ingenuity of the author in drawing the reader into the lives and characters of people of Roman times, whom he, with regard to their

---

13 *Infantry*. At https://en.wikipedia.org/wiki/Infantry#Etymology_and_terminology
14 Robert Graves. *I, Claudius* (1934). Penguin, 2006, 212.

feelings and ambitions and anxieties, credibly represents as our contemporaries. That is to say, we wouldn't have acted so very differently if, by means of a time machine, we had been transported back two thousand years and planted among the people who lived then.

This is not the only way to go about it, as you will soon realise if you read Margaret George's novel *The Autobiography of Henry VIII*, which was first published in 1986 and rightly became a great success, just like her other historical novels.

Margaret George chose a midway course, and her jumping between modern English and the language of the sixteenth century didn't disturb me as her reader in the least, particularly as it mostly involved syntax and hardly ever orthography or words no longer in use today. Especially in questions and negative sentences, she falls back on a kind of Shakespearian usage, as in the following selection of examples:

> When we suffer, Christ is speaking to us. But what does He say?
>
> I could not answer him honestly, for I knew not how I was able to think and attend to many things at once.
>
> The French have helped transport the gift. What say you to this? Shall we drink their wines?
>
> Think you we can transport it here to London without its expiring?
>
> Does he think I know not who prevented James from meeting me at York?
>
> ...the cooks fooled me not.[15]

Another interesting point in her novel is the form of address used for the King. Henry VIII started his reign being addressed as "Your

---

15 Margaret George. *The Autobiography of Henry VIII: With Notes by His Fool, Will Somers* (1986). Pan, 1988, 851, 831, 822, 816, 804, 786.

Grace" and then decided on something a little more majestic (which would set him above dukes and bishops, who were also addressed as "Your Grace"), after which "Your Majesty" became the appropriate form of address. So, gradually through the course of the plot "Your Majesty" replaces "Your Grace", which tells us how meticulous a writer Margaret George is (and therefore a good example to follow).

When writing *Shadows of My Father: The Memoirs of Martin Luther's Son*, I chose a different way to draw my readers into the time I was writing about. In the German version of the novel, which appeared before the English one, I used a kind of nineteenth-century German and inserted original letters, sermons, documents, medical reports and cooking recipes, which can still be understood by modern readers, though they might skip them if they find reading them too troublesome. (Judging from the feedback from some of my readers, they didn't mind.)

My final point is a recommendation not to be too punctilious, "more papal than the Pope".

For example, I don't think it sacrilegious to use modern calculations of the date alongside older ones, be they those of Roman times, the Middle Ages or the early modern era. In a historical novel about Sir Francis Bacon, Viscount Saint Albans, Baron of Verulam, philosopher and statesman, the writer might feel it appropriate to provide Bacon's life data, namely, 22 January 1561 to 9 April 1626. Within his lifetime fell the introduction of the Gregorian calendar, which replaced the Julian calendar used until then, so the date of birth of Francis Bacon is therefore usually given according to the Julian calendar, but the date of his death according to the Gregorian. In fact, his date of birth according to the Gregorian calendar—that is, according to today's time reckoning—would be 1 February 1561. It wouldn't be worthwhile, I think, to bother the reader with these intricacies.[16]

---

16 Though readers familiar with German can find out more about this

Of course, nobody today would think of giving the date of the Battle of Hastings other than according to the Julian calendar.

As for historical currency, try to convert it into today's or at least comprehensible values, as Robert Graves did in *I, Claudius* when he explained in an author's note that the "gold piece" that was the regular monetary standard at the time was the aureus, a coin worth 100 sestertii or twenty-five silver denarii; it could be thought of as worth roughly one pound sterling in the 1930s, when Graves's novel was published.

Or, should you choose to write about Richard of Cornwall, "the richest prince in Christendom" (1209-1272),[17] do your readers a favour by telling them that in his lifetime the pound sterling, the mark, and even the shilling were still only units of account: the only English coins in circulation were the silver penny and half-penny. A high-grade riding horse cost 10 pounds and a draught horse 10 to 20 shillings, a good cow cost 10 shillings and a pig 2 shillings. A master mason earned 4 pennies a day, and kitchen servants 2 to 4 shillings a year, amounting to roughly 0.15 pennies a day—which sounds like a pretty miserly wage, but as the servants could obviously live on it, it shows the value that the penny had at that time. (We can assume that they got their meals for free in the kitchens.)

For the modern reader it might be useful to be reminded that there were formerly 20 shillings to the pound sterling and 12 pence to the shilling, and thus 240 pence to the pound. This currency was in use in the United Kingdom until January 1971.

Historical novels, narratives and other forms of historical fiction deal with historical events and persons. Depending on the material chosen and the manner of representation, they may trace an individual biography or offer a broader historical perspective. This view of historical events may, as a consequence of the

---

fascinating man in Christoph Werner. *Francis Bacon: Empirist und Lordkanzler—Philosophie für unterwegs*. Mitteldeutscher Verlag, 2020.

17 See Noël Denholm-Young. *Richard of Cornwall*. Blackwell, 1947.

poetic freedom enjoyed by the author, not always be identical with the academically recognised one. Yet while intuitively felt, the account may still be credible, albeit rearranged according to aesthetic criteria.

However, these poetic liberties should not, at least in my opinion, lead to careless mistakes, or to errors made because of sheer laziness. These might sometimes seem trivial, but are not that at all, because they damage the general trustworthiness of the writer of historical fiction.

Let Goethe stand on the wrong side of Schiller on their monument in Weimar, as I read in one text, and you lose your reader's trust.

Believe Field Marshal Montgomery, Viscount Montgomery of Alamein, who in the German edition of his *History of Warfare* has an illustration caption that places the famous "Lange Kerls" ("Potsdam Giants") of Frederick William I of Prussia at his son's Battle of Leuthen (1757), and you will risk losing your reader's trust.[18] In fact, this regiment of giants never saw battle and was disbanded by Frederick the Great after he succeeded his father in 1740 (although a single battalion was retained under a different name, and did see action).

Let friends who visit the Prussian architect Carl Friedrich Schinkel on his sickbed in midsummer 1841 bring a bouquet of tulips, and you will lose the trust of attentive readers.

Let friends of the painter Caspar David Friedrich invite him for dinner and serve potatoes in May 1802 and you could anger your reader because at that time there was no way of keeping potatoes from harvest time through to late spring.

Letting the physician Paulus Luther, son of the reformer Martin Luther, treat shot wounds by pulling the lead shot out with his fingers, then cleaning the wound with boiled chamomile and

---

18 Feldmarschall Viscount Montgomery of Alamein. *Kriegsgeschichte: Weltgeschichte der Schlachten und Kriegszüge*. Translation of *A History of Warfare* (1968). Komet, 1999.

patching it up, instead of pouring boiling oil into the wound to clean it from the remains of powder and dirt, would be a mistake and again make you lose the respect of the historically well-informed reader. (The milder and more successful treatment, of which Paulus Luther hadn't heard, was first applied by Ambroise Paré, surgeon and physician to three French kings.)

The fate of Wilhelm von Grumbach, rebel against the Emperor and the Duke of Saxony, will serve to sum this up. Grumbach was caught, tortured and executed by dismemberment in Gotha in 1567. We read that, as he was being executed and his heart ripped from his body, he was heard to scream in a loud voice, "Gracious God, have mercy on me!" And when the executioner beat him on the mouth with the ripped-out heart, he is reported to have screamed long and horribly. Not only should historical novelists do their research properly; they should also use their common sense. Nobody can scream long and loud with their heart ripped out.

Writing historical novels is hard work, but it can be great fun, particularly if you take the fun seriously. Look at your sources with a critical eye—and then treat your readers to a vivid picture of the past.

Writing for Children
Paro Anand

Paro Anand is the author of thirty-three books for children and young adults, including plays, short stories, novellas, and novels. She has headed the National Centre for Children's Literature at the National Book Trust, India, won (among other awards) the National Sahitya Akademi Bal Sahitya Puraskar in 2017, and was an invitee to the India Conference at the Harvard Business School in 2018.

~

You don't know my nightmares. You don't see the dark shadows looming above my bed.
Or smell the whisky on his breath.
Or feel the weight of him as he presses against me, crushing my body as his hands roughly shut down my voice.
Sometimes I awake from non-sleep to find myself sweating.
I can't scream. For he has taken my voice from me. My screams are trapped in my chest, choking me, along with the hands. Those hands. Creepily soft and pudgy. But strong. Stronger than the whisky on his breath. The heat of him. The weight of him. And

I'm screaming again, deep inside my being, I'm screaming. My mouth, stretched wide. My throat hurting from silent screams that scratch me.

I dig deep into myself. If not for me, I have to be brave for Dad, for Mum, for Nana and Nani. It was their son who had done it. It was Mum's brother, it was Dad's brother-in-law with whom he played golf. So I have to be brave and face the world for them. I have to go back to school.

~

And now, the story from the father's point of view.
I watch as she leaves the safety of the car. The safety of my arms. I can see the tremble of her and for the first time I notice how thin she's become. I feel the stab of guilt again. It is a handy knife that stays near my gut and wounds me all the time. I should have kept my little daughter safe. How could I have let this happen? But he was my wife's brother, of course I trusted him. Who else would I trust? *No one*, whispers the knife, *trust no one...*

I watch her first tentative steps. She is literally learning to walk again. Like a little baby. She is my little baby girl. How could he? How could he?

~

For a moment, I want you, the reader, to close your eyes and think back to your own childhood. Think about a time when someone felt you up, grabbed you. Think it, remember it. Remember how it felt.

Did that feeling come back? Did your body remember that creeping, grabbing hand? For just a moment, did your blood run cold? Again?

Maybe you have kept it buried. You feel safe now that you're all grown up. But I want you to also recall if you talked to anyone about it. Did you? Could you? Were you told to just keep quiet? Remember that feeling of shame? As though you were at fault? Somehow.

I'm Paro Anand, and I write for children and teens.

Why would I write a story about rape for young readers? Why on earth? Why should they be reading this? Why should they even know the word "rape"? Certainly, when I was young, I don't think I had that word in my vocabulary. But truth time now. It's in your daughter's vocabulary already. She knows the word, she knows what it means. She knows about #MeToo, she knows about the constant drum roll of rape reports in the media. And we know she knows. But we fool ourselves into thinking that it's too difficult a subject to talk about. That this and subjects like assault, violence, terrorism, death, and discrimination are too difficult to talk about and should be sanitised for our young.

We—you and me—would rather our children didn't know. Of course, we would all prefer a perfect world.

But we also know that their world is not sanitised. I have interacted with almost half a million children, and believe me, they're already talking about all of these subjects. You may think, "Well, my son or daughter doesn't talk about this." Chances are that she does. She's just not talking to you about it.

Be brave, talk dirty to your kids

But can we really keep our children tightly closed in a cool dark place? Issues like rape, assault and violence are in the papers, in the news, on social media. Every single day. And yet we think that it's not going to happen to me, at least, not to my child. But truth time now. You know, deep down, it's your darkest fear. This is a monster that could come knocking on your door.

We, you and me, need to dig deep within ourselves and find the courage to give our children courage. Yes, we dread our kids asking us those difficult questions. We don't know how we are going to deal with it. But I urge you, be brave, talk dirty to your kids. Give them the tools to look that monster in the eye, face-to-face, and bring it down with courage. Take away the shame that the monster brings. Assure your child that being a victim does not have to define her.

So, yes, be brave, talk dirty to your kids. As a parent, grandparent, teacher. As a writer. As a creative person.

Because cotton-woolling is not going to keep her safe.

Blind eyes and deaf ears are dangerous even though it might be easier than having the courage to open up that conversation we as adults dread.

But how do we empower young people if we cannot empower ourselves to be truthful?

We have been taught to keep quiet. For generations we have been told *Ghar ki baat, ghar mein hi raine do*.[1] Let's break that cycle of shame and silence and speak out.

We may think my child is safe. This isn't going to happen to her. Fine, but what if she knows someone who is being bullied or worse? What then? Wouldn't we want her to speak up? Wouldn't we want her to be that voice of justice?

Because children are that voice. They have a strong sense of justice. Writer Shanta Gokhale reminded me of a wonderful example of this. The famous story of the Emperor's New Clothes. While the adults were too frightened to refute the emperor and praised his so-called new clothes, it was a child who shouted out and told the emperor that he was naked. Because children are born honest, born without hatred and fear. It's we who instill these traits in them.

Through writing for young people fearlessly and honestly, give parents the courage to accept what's happening. They have been conditioned to cover up. Break that mould of silence.

What do I mean when I say talk dirty to your kids? I mean talk to them about the things that they are already talking

---

1 Roughly: What happens at home, should *stay* at home.

about. Issues that are uncomfortable. Things that we wished they didn't know. But they do. And we need to admit to ourselves that they do.

And, like nits and lice, these questions itch at your child's young heart and mind. Some of those thoughts are too terrible to talk about. And yet, there they are. Who knew that one should talk about things like sexuality and assault with a child? When all she should be doing is playing.

But not talking about it doesn't make the issue go away. It doesn't resolve the complication, nor answer questions.

How?

As a writer and through my programme Literature in Action, through my work with children, especially those in difficult circumstances, I have had the chance to interact with a vast number of young people, and I have realised that stories are a safe space to talk about subjects like violence, divorce, death, bigotry, hatred and even, hold your breath, sexuality.

As a parent or guardian, read the same books your child is reading. Talk about the story, about what's happening. Pretty soon, you will be talking about the unresolved issues that itch at her. You aren't introducing the unknown. Rather, talking about the unexplained. And maybe even equipping her with the tools to resolve or at least come to grips with those issues.

I'll share some experiences.

Once, after I had told some stories, a girl asked me if the stories were true. I asked her what she thought, and she replied, "Of course the ghost story you told isn't, but the one about domestic violence is definitely true."

"How can you be so sure?" I probed.

She looked at me and said, "Because it happens in my house."

Other children joined in, many admitting to being witness to domestic violence in their own families or neighbourhoods. It was a shameful secret. One they had not talked about, at least not to an adult.

If I had asked them about the subject without the safety net of the story, of course all of them would have denied knowledge. But they empathised with the characters and were able to talk about their feelings of anger, revulsion and, most of all, helplessness. They felt that maybe they could do some of the things that the character had done in the story. The girls said they would refuse to be beaten when they were married. They would file complaints if it happened. And the boys? One boy summed it up, "When I get married, and if I'm mad at my wife, I'll fight with her. But I won't beat her. That's what I can do." The others nodded in agreement.

I don't know if they will. But if even one young man raises his hand in the future, then remembers this story and pulls that hand back, my *maqsad*, my purpose in life, will have been met.

Was it a one off?

Here's another experience that I treasure.

In a school, I had told a story about a girl who hates Muslims because her father was killed "by a Muslim bomb", as she puts it. But she befriends a classmate and later realises that he is Muslim. When they talk about her feelings, he says, "All Muslims are not terrorists, and bombs don't have a religion."

After the story was over, one young student put up his hand: "Ma'am, I'll agree with what you wrote in your story, all Muslims are not terrorists, but you will have to agree with me that almost all terrorists are Muslims, and what do you have to say about that?"

The child was twelve years old. He had obviously been hearing this. It was what I call "heard hatred". The kind we speak in the presence of our children, even as we hope that they are still reading fairy tales.

I replied, "Okay, let's forget religion for a moment and take up another issue. Let's talk about rape. Now of course, we can all agree that all men are not rapists. But, *beta*, you will have to agree with me that almost all rapists are men. So then, let's treat all men and boys as potential rapists. Which means, young man, I should treat you with suspicion and hatred too. Would you be okay with that?"

His fists clenched, his nostrils flared. I had just called him a potential rapist in front of everyone. But then, I saw the moment of understanding. It happened in a flash. Suddenly everyone was up on their feet, clapping. And the boy came up to me later and said, "Thank you, no one has ever explained this in a way I could really understand."

With both these topics, domestic violence and the terrorist bombers, it was the safety net of story, of fiction, that brought clarity to their very muddied reality.[2]

When I first started working with children as a twenty-something girl, I was a drama teacher. I found no playscripts in the Indian context that were contemporary and relevant to our children. There were either Western plays or ones that retold myths and legends. And that is how I began writing. My initial forays were cute, safe stories. It was what I thought children's literature should be. But these were more or less cookie-cutter stories from the West with Indian names.

It was when I later headed the National Centre for Children's Literature and met children from villages, from areas of conflict, that I realised my stories were just as irrelevant. And so I started to write stories about "real" children. Reality fiction that represented them. I wrote *No Guns at My Son's Funeral* (Roli Books IndiaInk,

---

[2] It doesn't have to be all doom and gloom, of course. I was so amused when my own son, as a little kid in Class Four, was hauled up by his teacher. She asked him, "Why were you and Pulkit talking about diapers?" He said, "Ma'am we weren't talking about diapers." She accused him again and again he refuted it. Finally, he said, "No, ma'am, we were talking about sanitary pads, it's what girls use when they get their period." At home he asked me, "Sonia ma'am is a girl, how come she doesn't know about sanitary pads?" Surely he was wiser than Sonia ma'am, and surely she would have been better off had she taken them aside and explained any misconception they may have had as children in the fourth standard.

2005). It was the first book of its kind for young people. Fifteen years later, it is still one of the most widely read by children. But at that time, some schools were wary of such a title for children, such a subject. In fact, we almost changed the title to "sanitise" it. I am so glad I didn't. Because when I talk about my books at any interaction and then ask the children which one they want to hear me perform, 100/100 times this is the book they want. Because of the title. And then the content leads to a very fruitful discussion on the senselessness of violence and the vulnerability of young people in conflict zones.

My book *Being Gandhi* (HarperCollins, 2019) presents Gandhi to children in a way that brings his teachings more within reach of their own lives and actions. Rather than talk about Gandhi the man, or the historical events around him, I talk about how relevant his teachings are even today. How we can find our own inner Gandhi and put him into action even now.

Through my writing, I hope to raise awareness and create empathetic human beings. I hope that my stories are not just stories for children, because a good story can be a call to action.

Who else if not our young will be the flagbearers of a better tomorrow, a more tolerant today? And how do we get them to be that change? Not through lectures and books on moral values that you and I would reject. But rather, through sensitive stories that create empathy and fight apathy. Stories that empower and drive them to positive action.

There has to be a light at the end of a dark tunnel. And we can story our children to not only see that light, and believe in that light, but be that light.

Losing Higher Ground

The Short Story Today

Anjum Hasan

Anjum Hasan is the author of the novels *Lunatic in My Head* (Penguin Zubaan, 2007), *Neti, Neti* (India Ink Roli, 2009), *The Cosmopolitans* (Hamish Hamilton, 2015), and *History's Angel* (Bloomsbury 2023), the book of poems *Street on the Hill* (Sahitya Akademi, 2007), and the short story collections *Difficult Pleasures* (Penguin Viking, 2012) and *A Day in the Life* (Penguin, 2018). Her books have been shortlisted for the Sahitya Akademi, Hindu Best Fiction and Crossword Fiction awards, and longlisted for the Man Asian Literary Prize and the DSC Prize for Literature. She is currently a New India Foundation Fellow and lives in Bangalore. She is married to the author Zac O'Yeah.

~

The first short story that bothered me was Anton Chekhov's "The Bet".[1] Till then, I believed that narrative resolution meant happy

---
1 Anton Chekhov. *The Bet: Short Story*. Harper Perennial Classics, 2015.

endings. Rip van Winkle might find, when he wakes up, that twenty years have passed, or Sinbad will see that his only hope of survival after the shipwreck is to hang on for dear life to the giant roc, but these disruptions are only delicious means to redress. Whereas all the dark prefiguring of "The Bet" ends in nothing. The hero simply vanishes on the last page.

Chekhov's story asks which is the worse punishment for a crime—life imprisonment or the death penalty? The young lawyer who stakes fifteen years of his life to prove his point does not emerge triumphant from the cell where he has been living out his self-imposed solitude. He decides—following on a decade and a half of the most voracious bibliomania, hundreds of books consumed and discarded—that human concerns don't matter one whit, and then he slips out of the garden gate and disappears. To where? And why does he forgo all that money, two million roubles, that he is to get for winning the bet? As a ten- or eleven-year-old, immune to irony, this tortured man's strange renunciation and sudden disappearance, not to speak of that unclaimed cash, bothered me. Chekhov, master of enigmatic endings, provides no answer. I had to learn to live with my discomfort, accept the slippery nature of the modern short story, understand that its author might open a wide window on time and then leave it ajar for all eternity.

The realism of Chekhov's nineteenth-century Russia is so precise that it has been said his fiction can be used as a sociological source. But his moral code is never obvious, unless one takes all of this to itself add up to an ethic: the extraordinarily vivid, quicksilver detailing; the ironic yet often loving focus on character traits; the way individuals appear so set *in their time* and yet often seeking a higher perspective on it. Around the same time as I read "The Bet", I came across other stories, staples of the school reader, which were, in their recognition of and refusal to redeem earthly loss, similarly tragic: Rabindranath Tagore's "Kabuliwala" about the unlikely friendship between a vagrant man and a radiant child that can, once time has passed, never be recovered—no matter that the author, unlike Chekhov, does provide recompense in the form of a few banknotes to temper our sadness with. Or D.H. Lawrence's "The Rocking-Horse Winner", in which money itself is the object of lust and there's never enough. Yet indulge too avidly in this passion and it can turn against you.

Like most children I was also drawn to stories that worked in the opposite way—their various morals were clearly grasped but they were not pitched exclusively in any time and place. Aesop's fables, Sufi parables, the tales of Hans Christian Andersen and the more allegorical ones by the Grimm Brothers, even Jesus and his miracles, or courtly intrigues from the Hindu epics—all these had the roundedness so dear to a child, who is rarely bothered by their lack of realism. And yet this hunger for realism inevitably takes over and one soon stops craving this other sort of spiritual satisfaction.

The Hindi writer S.H. Vatsyayan (who went by the better-known penname Agyeya) writes in his philosophical and literary exploration of the temporal, *A Sense of Time*, about some of these traditional narratives:

> One might object that they sought to present moral truths, not reality: but the moral truths were the root and substance of reality—to the audience as well as the storyteller of that time. What happened in the story was true, that is why it was endlessly being used to illustrate and demonstrate what was true: the story was an audial model of the structure of truth and reality.[2]

A Sanskrit drama opens with the good-natured ribbing of Krishna by Satyabhama for coming home late, followed by the playwright's invocation to the very same Krishna, "thus vanquished

---

2   S.H. Vatsyayan ("Agyeya"). *A Sense of Time: An Exploration of Time in Theory, Experience and Art.* Oxford University Press, 1981, 37.

in repartee", that he protect us. Agyeya draws attention to the dual time operating here—the exchange between the gods occurs in a timeless *out there*, while the appeal to them is set in the mortal *here and now*. His book is partly a lament for the loss of the imagination—thanks to the Western belief in time as money, time as linear, time as the source of endless change—that once allowed us to recognise these two realities and live simultaneously in both.

Out of this earlier realm of absolute truth appear those early signposts of mutable, subjective truths—Nikolay Gogol's "The Overcoat", Premchand's "Kafan", O. Henry's "Gift of the Magi", Edgar Allan Poe's "The Black Cat", Guy De Maupassant's "The Necklace"—marked not by age-old familiarity but modern surprise, accident, chance, coincidence, and circumstance. Leaving behind its origins in myths and fables, the short story grows into the ultimate temporal—and secular—form. There are no earlier incarnations and no hereafter. *Now* is the sum total of the aeons and *this* is all there is to the expanse. Anything in the present can be the subject and substance of a story. I'm always charmed by that anecdote about the feverishly productive Saadat Hasan Manto boasting that no subject was too strange for him. Someone knocked at the door of his office when he worked at All India Radio, Delhi, and asked "May I come in?" Manto was challenged to write a play by that name, which he promptly turned out.

But this carpe diem spirit does not imply that the short story has lacked inherent value; in its microscopic focus on a person or a handful of people lies the conviction that the individual counts for more than the mass and yet without sympathy, he or she counts for nothing. The harassed clerk's timorous appeal in "The Overcoat"—*I am your brother*—has come to be regarded by some as an implicit slogan for the modern short story.

In most Indian languages the break from the literature of the past resulted in the flowering not just of the short story but literary movements around it—ranging from the Nayi Kahani writers in Hindi and their championing of interior life, to the hard-boiled urbanism of the Manikodi group in Tamil Nadu. Amitav Ghosh explores its genesis in the essay "The Indian Story": the start with Tagore in the late nineteenth century and the high point reached with the "new writing" movements of the 1960s. He writes that "the story was the chosen instrument of the subcontinent in the spring time of its nationhood".[3] (This compares interestingly with the United States, where the form became so popular, a hundred years previously, with writers like Washington Irving, and then Poe and Nathaniel Hawthorne, that it came to be seen as a quintessentially American one.)

Ghosh's essay, which was published in the mid-1990s, suggests that the short story is no longer our weapon of choice in India, and it seems to have had its day. But in most Indian languages, though the novel has gained ground as a form, it did not edge out the short story, except in English—at the close of the previous century, the English language novel had in terms of prestige, appeal and reach very much overtaken the short story. In the past couple of decades, the story has seen a modest comeback. It has not displaced the novel but given a new constraint—shortened attention spans—the market has made space again for the form. In fact, stories are very much more than a literary genre—they are now, by definition, everyone's and can give form to virtually anything. Every one of us has a story and are routinely urged to tell it. To seek a political voice or to campaign for our sexual or religious or ethnic identities is to try and make space for our story. Marketing mantra or advertising shtick tries ennobling itself by taking the shape of stories. And everyone—corporate trainers, behavioural therapists, gamers, activists, academics, educators—is potentially a storyteller; stories are the most fatuously ubiquitous tools of twenty-first-century professional life. Meanwhile, stories themselves—that is, stories as contemporary fiction—are

---

3 Amitav Ghosh. "The Indian Story: Notes on Some Preliminaries". In: *Civil Lines 1: New Writing from India*. Ravi Dayal, 1994, 48.

increasingly sought out as the basis of popular entertainment or that ugly portmanteau, infotainment.

As a writer of stories, I am often being told that I'm a potential supplier of content—that is, plot lines—for web series or films. The relationship between film and literature is well-established; several leading modern writers of short stories also worked in the industry (Ashokamitran), wrote screenplays (Manto), and directed films (Premendra Mitra), and it is impossible to read them without noticing the pacing, the image-making, the compression that comes from cinema. Cinematic techniques—the freeze frame or the slow motion—became literary ones, while literature—the sensibilities of specific writers—influenced any number of auteurs. What cinema materialised was a changed experience of time, writes Agyeya:

> It was not that the new awareness of time—awareness of the fragmentation, distortion, deviation, reversal or multidimensional scattering of time—was reflected only in the fictional form of the novel or the short story; it was reflected also in the graphic and even the plastic arts. Surrealism in art had its counterpart in the surrealist novel and the surrealist cinema: there was continuous interaction between these several art-forms.[4]

Doubtless this interaction lives on in subtle ways but today's obsession with content that can be streamed as online entertainment is a market obsession. By seeing stories as composed of a series of tangible events those who sell them create in the consumer an urgent need to know what happens next, which can only be sated with more story, that is, story in the sense of narrative propelled by an insistent forward movement. This view of narrative, as that which entertains through propulsion, makes no space for any other

---

4   S.H. Vatsyayan ("Agyeya"), 1981, 55.

possible reckoning with time, and especially not the much more fluid manner—both expansive and compressed, looking both to the future and to the past—in which we actually experience time in human consciousness. In the first volume of Proust's *Remembrance of Things Past*, which itself is a monumental attempt to reconstruct life through such a freely associative engagement with time, the narrator recalls the novels of a writer named Bergotte who,

> if he had hit upon some great truth, or upon the name of an historic cathedral, he would break off his narrative, and in an invocation, an apostrophe, a lengthy prayer, would give a free outlet to that effluence which, in the earlier volumes, remained buried beneath the form of his prose, discernible only in a rippling of its surface, and perhaps even more delightful, more harmonious when it was thus veiled from the eye, when the reader could give no precise indication of where the murmur of the current began, or of where it died away. These passages in which he delighted were our favourites also. For my own part I knew all of them by heart. I felt even disappointed when he resumed the thread of his narrative.[5]

This is one view of narrative—as that which acquires appeal through digression because in doing so it mimics the nature of remembering itself. (And it's worth mentioning that a precursor in the psychological novel genre, *Tristram Shandy*,[6] is constructed out of a series of digressions and reflections on time.)

Then there is the form associated with modernists like Virginia Woolf—lyric fiction—which is as much poetry as plot, and in which the obligatory hallmarks of realism are done away

---

5   Marcel Proust. *Remembrance of Things Past*. Vol. 1: *Swann's Way*. Transl. C.K. Scott Moncrieff. Henry Holt, 1922, 127.
6   Laurence Sterne. *The Life and Opinions of Tristram Shandy, Gentleman*, 1759-67.

with, what she called "the plausible and preposterous formulas which are supposed to represent the whole of our human adventure". Should the novelist dare to cut adrift from these "the story might wobble; the plot might crumble; ruin might seize upon the characters. The novel, in short, might become a work of art."[7] Such a work of art was imagined as closer to the short story than the stately and capacious nineteenth-century European novel; modernists such as Woolf, James Joyce, Joseph Conrad and Henry James moved between stories and novels. Amit Chaudhuri, himself a writer of both, quotes Irish short story writer Frank O'Connor to the effect that

> *Ulysses* was not so much a novel as a very long story, for the novel records the effects of the passing of time on its characters, and Joyce's novel only covers a single day. In this comment lies a key to the poetic paradox of key modernist novels like *Ulysses* and *Mrs. Dalloway*; at their heart lies the epiphanic moment, which, magnified and augmented into twelve or twenty-four hours, seems to contain everything in it, and is still fleeting, temporal, fragmentary, incomplete. The novel, then, becomes a poetic act of perception on a large scale […][8]

~

So the short story—that "epiphanic moment" and that signal token of individuality—now, increasingly, is a source for the sedative of unremitting plot. This comes out of the growing identification of "telling of a story" with "storytelling"—not all writers of the short story are aiming to be campfire entertainers, but the tag of storyteller

---

7   Virginia Woolf. "The Art of Fiction". In: *The Moment and Other Essays*. The Hogarth Press, 1952.
8   Amit Chaudhuri. *Clearing a Space: Reflections on India, Literature and Culture*. Peter Lang, 2008, 158.

is today hard to escape. Storytelling in this contemporary sense has little to do with the modern fragmentation that Chaudhuri and Agyeya describe above, which has been foundational to at least one prominent stream of modern fiction.

I can see this increasing fragmentation in our own lives taking two very different forms as far as short stories go, both tendencies driven by peculiarly twenty-first-century anxieties. One preoccupation is with how to keep the consumer hooked to stories, or at least distract her for a short while from her now permanent state of juvenile distractedness. Artists, certainly writers, are of little account here. The charge falls to creative entrepreneurs who search frantically for newness, not so much in content, which is really fodder, as in form, i.e., the latest iteration of digital media that can be passed off as new. Newness is a prerequisite; these "products" must be pitched to prospective investors as original. Entrepreneur Anushka Shetty has recently developed a new storytelling platform and describes it thus in an article:

> As someone who has been voicing the need for innovation in publishing and content consumption for the past two years, I'm certain that a certain section of readers has been expanding its horizon to newer forms of content for some time now, and the pandemic has only accelerated the move. That's why we have built Plop Stories, with a sharp focus on re-inventing story-telling to make it mobile-first, immersive and interactive. Audio, video, simulations, decision trees, and many more immersive elements promise a fun, engaging experience, where you not only read the story but also become a part of it. These stories are not created by us, but by a plethora of creators around the globe who publish interactive fiction in the "Plop" format and monetise it.[9]

---

9   Anushka Shetty. "The pandemic is showing us the opportunities that

This is what Italo Calvino once called, much before the digital takeover of our lives, a "literature machine". Anticipating today's bots that produce Shakespearean sonnets, he asks, following on developments in cybernetics that break down and recombine language as per mathematical formulas, if such a machine will soon replace the writer. He is unruffled by the prospective death of the author, that "anachronistic personage", but his essay does not end with this Barthian conclusion. The machine may churn out endless combinations of language, may even be able to mimic the subjective personality of the writer, but what makes these permutations interesting is their potential for unexpected meaning or unforeseen effects. Just as puns or slips of the tongue are funny because they call up preconscious ideas or patterns, so myth is the realm of the buried and the unsayable, and the story or fable, straining to break out of language, to say what cannot be said, has the power to evoke the unexpressed myth, and thus rescue itself from the machine.

> Literature can work in a critical vein or to confirm things as they are and as we know them to be. The boundary is not always clearly marked, and I would say that on this score the spirit in which one reads is decisive: it is up to the reader to see to it that literature exerts its critical force, and this can occur independently of the author's intentions.[10]

What Shetty describes is merely yet another sexed-up version of the combinatorial game; the question is, what of the reader alert to the hidden meanings with the aid of which she can find her way

---

publishers have beyond the traditional book." In: *Scroll.in*, 23 June 2020. At https://scroll.in/article/965365/the-pandemic-is-showing-us-the-opportunities-that-publishers-have-beyond-the-traditional-book

10 Italo Calvino. "Cybernetics and Ghosts". In: *The Uses of Literature: Essays*. Transl. Patrick Creagh. Harcourt Brace, 1986, 26.

out of, to use Calvino's metaphor, the labyrinth? A certain quality of solipsism in contemporary short fiction reveals that the writer is not quite confident of getting across to such a reader. David Foster Wallace and Lydia Davis are two of America's best-known short-story writers, and the fiction of both has a terminal quality. Davis's are a play on the question: What makes a story? The answer is not just Manto's *anything* but—*everything*. "Observations" is one critic's word for such writing. A snatch of overheard conversation, a dream, an advertisement, slogan or piece of advice, stray passing thoughts while passing through life, the experience of travelling or being in public places, formal letters, informal exchanges, recollections of family life and friendships—all of these and more are stories in Davis's sense. Their not being easily slottable into this or that literary genus is usually what occupies her readers, but what's more interesting is the philosophical position this variousness suggests. Her collection *Can't and Won't* features two tiny pieces called "Contingency (vs Necessity)" and "Contingency (vs Necessity) 2: On Vacation". The first consists of three lines: "He could be our dog. / But he is not our dog. / So he barks at us." And the second, only slightly longer story goes: "He could be my husband. / But he is not my husband. / He is her husband. / And so he takes her picture (not mine) as she stands in her flowered beach outfit in front of the old fortress."[11]

This feeling that contingency intrudes on necessity, making it seem somehow unnecessary—or the other way around: the contingent appearing necessary—goes to the heart of contemporary short fiction, which does not have to bother with even the minimal narrative scaffolding a novel requires. Why single out detail x when y is just as interesting or, equally, just as banal? This might sound like a recipe for nihilism and in fact some of Davis's longer pieces with reflective narrators draw close to that problem, such as "The Letter to the Foundation", in which a college professor gets a two-

---

11 Lydia Davis. *Can't and Won't*. Penguin, 2015, 18 and 20.

year research grant. The story takes the form of a letter she writes, years later, to the foundation that gave her the award, recalling how her life changed, or did not change, because of it. She has found it painfully difficult to be a teacher (her description of this dislike is utterly despairing and funny) and was relieved that the money freed her of teaching. "Now a strange thing was happening. I sometimes felt removed from my life, as though I were floating above it or maybe a little to the side of it," she writes. And later, "There was also a greater clarity of vision [...] It seemed that it wasn't I who had changed but everything around me. Everything was sharper, clearer, and closer [...]"[12]

So, getting money and recognition can be clarifying but what should you do with the freedom they bring? Davis's story asks this in a practical way, but the question eventually becomes an existential one. What should one do as someone with human agency *in general* and not only when relieved of the pressures of earning a living? Isn't everything quite provisional and random— one's very existence, in fact, entirely unnecessary?

> Sometimes I did exactly what I wanted to do all day [...] and then the most terrifying sort of despair would descend on me: the very freedom I was enjoying seemed to say that what I did in my day was arbitrary, and that therefore my whole life and how I spent it was arbitrary.[13]

Davis shows in her fiction that this arbitrariness can be creative but also a route to terror.

David Foster Wallace's stories concern individuals who are as much unmoored from society as Chekhov's characters are rooted, even if often unhappily, in it. Their brutal individualism, their chronic inability to fit in makes them, paradoxically, lose

---

12 Ibid. 186.
13 Ibid. 205.

all distinctiveness; they have little by way of those conventional biographies and personalities that have come to seem indispensable to characters in realist fiction. In the collection *Brief Interviews with Hideous Men*, many are not dignified with names but have generic descriptors such as "the depressed person", "hideous men", "the mother-to-be", or just empty pronouns: I, he, she, you. These stories are not driven by event or even the modernist turn towards heightened perception, though they have their roots in the latter; they are plangent accounts, often written as monologues, of those so socially dysfunctional they are losing all sense of selfhood, an anomie they express either through casual violence, power play in sexual relations, or cries in the dark.

"The depressed person", for instance, in a story of that name, is both certain she cannot communicate the extraordinary and yet everyday horror of her depression and at the same time feels incapable of caring for anyone but herself.

In "Suicide as a Sort of Present" an unnamed girl grows up loathing herself, feels an enormous internal pressure to be perfect, and can never measure up—all owing to some "very heavy psychic shit laid on her as a little girl".[14] As a mother she feels the same deep antipathy for her son when he falls short, but she cannot, as a good, a model mother, express it. So the child becomes increasingly loathsome and his mother ever more loving and forgiving outwardly and ever more despairing and hating inwardly. This is the sense in which these stories are terminal—the characters' psychological conundrums are described clinically, often with terms taken from psychoanalysis, which is more narrative than panacea, however.

One of the "hideous men" is terrified he could be a psychopath because he repeatedly initiates loving relationships with women, then cries off, constitutionally unable to commit. The diagnosis seems more important than the cure—characters over and over

---

14 David Foster Wallace. *Brief Interviews with Hideous Men*. Little, Brown, 1999, 241.

again seek to tell their unspeaking interlocutors what they're like or urgently demand a characterisation from them, and with this judgement the story closes. The move from the novel of action to the psychological novel seems to have ended in this—the stasis of self-knowledge.

There is a similar feeling of arrested movement in Davis's stories. One of her inspirations is Flaubert, whom she has translated and in whose voice she sometimes speaks. Several pieces in *Can't and Won't* are tagged "story from Flaubert". But if Flaubert discovered the lyrical possibilities of the quotidian, in Davis we are repeatedly presented with the scenario that *everything goes*. The quotidian has reached its limit, exhausted its meanings and Davis's writing both illustrates as well as helps us—through her careful, almost decorous gaze on it—bear, sometimes even be moved by, this sense of surfeit.

Philip Roth once said, comparing his situation to Milan Kundera's, that in the United States everything goes and nothing is important, while in Czechoslovakia nothing goes and everything is important. The word I've used above, "terminal", is also one that Kundera uses in his *The Art of the Novel*, talking of the "terminal paradoxes" of the European novel, of which Kafka's fiction is representative. With novelists like Kafka "all existential categories suddenly change their meaning":[15] the self no longer has the weight it had for Proust, the distinction between public and private has collapsed because K. even in his bedroom is watched by emissaries from the Castle, and so on. If the self in Kafka's fiction is post-Proustian, the self in Wallace's fiction is post-Kafkaesque. In Kafka, the enemy, History, is at the door; the characters' actions are severely limited, and their thoughts taken only with making sense of and finding release from their situations. In Wallace, the enemy is so insidiously within that even

---

15 Milan Kundera. *The Art of the Novel* [*L'art du Roman*, 1968]. Transl. Linda Asher. Grove Press, 1988, 12.

the most rudimentary action can come to seem not just worthless but suicidal.

In a Chekhov story called "The Black Monk", a young university professor lives in a state of impossible exuberance and chats with visions, a condition that today would inevitably be described as schizophrenic. Yet this liminal existence is a joyful, productive one; the black monk of Kovrin's hallucination convinces him that his intellectual work has immortal worth, that there is eternal life, and that he, Kovrin, is one of God's chosen ones who will lead mankind into it. This is a sickness, agree Kovrin and the monk, but an exalted one. His family, when they notice his madness, bundle him off to a doctor, and Kovrin gets well, but this wellness, this sensible, stolid state, reveals to him the mediocrity of his own life and the tedium of others' good intentions. "How fortunate Buddha, Mahomed, and Shakespeare were that their kind relations and doctors did not cure them of their ecstasy and their inspiration,"[16] he says as spiritual emptiness takes over, his marriage breaks down, and his health weakens till, experiencing one final revelation, he dies.

This glimpse of another, richer, untainted life, this hope for the fulfilment of human potential, recurs in Chekhov's stories. Volodya, seventeen years old, kills himself out of despair over his own social awkwardness and the soullessness of others, while believing that "somewhere in the world, among some people, there was a pure, honourable, warm, refined life, full of love, affection, gaiety, and serenity..."[17] A dejected landscape artist believes that human spiritual energy is being wasted on temporary, passing needs, drawing us further and further from the essential truths, and that there is no point painting "for the entertainment for a predatory, unclean animal".[18] Such beliefs may even be misplaced

---

16 Anton Chekhov. "The Black Monk". In: *The Lady with the Dog and Other Stories*. Transl. Constance Garnett. Willey, 1917, 142.
17 Chekhov. "Volodya". In: *The Lady with the Dog and Other Stories*, 170.
18 Chekhov. "The House with the Mansard". In: *Selected Works*. Transl. Ivy

but no less passionate for that. Anna Sergeyevna married young because she was "devoured by curiosity, I wanted something higher. I told myself that there must be a different kind of life. I wanted to live, to live..."[19] This urge leads to the love affair she seems to regret.

So the timeless is fervently yearned for and sometimes glimpsed, but the story cannot pin it down. The larger purpose is just over the horizon, like the skyline on which the black monk first appears, but the author's sights are firmly set closer home. He cannot follow the hero of "The Bet" when he runs away from his cell. His writ runs only in the temporal arena, but one of the things that gives his stories their great power is exactly this: the recognition that there is always something else.

Agyeya declares, "Man needs the timeless order of experience if he is not to disintegrate under commodity time."[20] How, then, to make metaphysics modern? Tagore's writings provide one answer: by drawing on the creative excess, the abundant superfluity inherent in life, in one's making of literature or art. Life—or the life force—tends to exceed a purely functional purpose, and so the artist's identification with this fecundity is the ideal way to live in a state of grace and harmony. A couple of decades after Tagore's death, short stories that emerged during the post-Independence literary movements mentioned above present a much darker view of things and one which revealed, as poet Adil Jussawalla wrote in his introduction to the 1974 anthology *New Writing in India*:

> the petty bourgeoisie's inability to break through to a higher level of consciousness and action. Even the traditional ways through God and sex are less used. [...] This is the writing of a bourgeoisie at a dead end.[21]

Litvinov. Raduga, 1973, 81.
19 Chekhov. "The Lady with the Dog". In: *Selected Works*, 137.
20 S.H. Vatsyayan ("Agyeya"), 1981, 32.
21 *New Writing in India*. Ed. Adil Jussawalla. Penguin, 1974, 34.

He added, however, that "[w]ithin the limits of bourgeois writing" the literature has some virtues; among other things it shows "a conscious attempt to rework traditional myths and symbols in a modern context".

Today that reworking continues in many genres—including poetry—but in some varieties of fiction it has acquired a decidedly nationalist colour. Many popular mythological retellings are informed less by a hunger of the spirit or a tussling with the metaphorical import of myth, and more by just the desire to hark back to what is seen as quintessentially Indian and ancient. The forms these stories often take—the rendering of Hindu gods as superheroes, for instance—fit neatly into the contemporary demands of the entertainment industry, rendering mythology just one more source of narrative.

And what meanwhile of those failed attempts to reach a "higher level of consciousness"? In a creative writing class that I sometimes teach, I once prescribed, as reading, "The Overcoat" and Hindi writer Uday Prakash's much longer but equally harrowing "Mohandas".[22] While Gogol dramatises all the inequities of Tsarist Russia in the humble and succinct story of one clerk, Prakash's account of humiliation and powerlessness is almost ninety pages long in translation. The forces that slowly and comprehensively crush a dirt-poor man, who just happens to share a name with the Father of the Nation, operate in deeply insidious ways, and it is a moral necessity, Prakash appears to be saying, to describe their workings in detail, as much as the light-heartedness and hope the so-called oppressed can also feel each living day.

One of the students wrote in before the class to say the stories were "too much misery porn for a single evening's reading pleasure" and that she was now "ready to slash my wrists and die". She wished the texts had been more balanced—"one humour/

---

22 Uday Prakash. "Mohandas". In: *The Walls of Delhi*. Transl. Jason Grunebaum. Hachette, 2013.

mystery/etc." and the other "realistic fiction". She said she was "an empath who also suffers from a stress triggered autoimmune disorder, so I tend to avoid certain topics unless absolutely required". There were many perverse things about this response—the idea of misery in fiction as pornographic, which I took to mean gratuitous, the equating of realism with misery, the idea that misery was a "topic" one can choose to ignore, and that stories had "topics", a view which negated the possibility that they could be, and the best were, about many things at once. But what struck me as most perverse was her argument that because she tended to feel too much—as an empath—she had to shield herself from feeling too much. This word and this understanding of empathy were new to me—it seemed to use the very idea against itself. Discussing the stories in class, I saw that while her response might have been the most extreme, the broad consensus was the same: suffering in fiction was hard to take and ought to be rationed.

David Foster Wallace has written about the difficulty of teaching Kafka to American undergraduates, describing how they don't get Kafka's humour because it does not take the form of the essentially adolescent, risible comicality that makes for popular humour in America. It is not too rarefied for his students but too serious a humour: a "religious humour [...] a harrowing spirituality".[23] What can make the short story feel terminal today is just this: in writing without any recourse to this harrowing spirituality—because it no longer cuts ice—our stories become increasingly literal reflections of the monstrous realities they are describing, and this literality too puts off readers who see in it only a pornographic impulse. They are losing that critical element which Calvino called myth, and which Agyeya calls the timeless order, and which Chekhov hints at in story after story. This is as much true of Uday Prakash as of Wallace.

---

23 David Foster Wallace. "Laughing with Kafka". In: *Harper's Magazine*, July 1998, 26.

And so any breaking through to a reader's genuine interest feels like an act of subterfuge. Prakash's translator Jason Grunebaum writes in an afterword that following the publication of his story Prakash received postcards scrawled with the words "I am Mohandas".[24] Of the small minority in my class who were moved by it, one student said she realised that the area in central India where the story is set is exactly where her family comes from. The next time she visited there, she had decided, she would try to find Mohandas.

---

24 In: Uday Prakash. *The Walls of Delhi*, 218.

On Your Fingertips

Writing for Television

Gajra Kottary

Gajra Kottary is one of the most successful writers in Indian television, with cult and award-winning shows like *Astitva: Ek Prem Kahani* and *Balika Vadhu* among others to her credit which have run for thousands of episodes. She is also a novelist and short-story writer. Her published works include the novels *Broken Melodies*, *Once Upon a Star* and *Girls Don't Cry*, and a volume of collected short fiction, *Autumn Blossoms*.

~

When I went to journalism school after graduation, it was dinned into us that facts were sacred. Imagination was something to be avoided at all costs in reportage.

I was, however, drawn to imagining, extrapolating and analysing events and even psycho-analysing characters. So within the ambit of journalism, I did the next best thing to reporting—feature writing—and met with reasonable success.

One thing led to another, and soon after I began writing fiction. I published a collection of short stories centred around women. That collection got me my first offer to write for television. I must confess that I was not too enthused initially, as I believed that the medium was replete with saas-bahu[1] sagas and I did not relate to any of that.

But my first producer Soni Razdan, also the wife of well-known film-maker Mahesh Bhatt, was more than an emancipated woman and did not want any of the saas-bahu stuff. Together we believed that we could tell stories of another kind which would appeal to a larger audience. Our collaboration resulted in *Humare Tumhare*, my first series for television. It was about two estranged sisters who come together, for the sake of the children, when one of them is detected with cancer.

In my own idealistic way, with *Humare Tumhare*, I proved that one could still tell quality stories around women through such a powerful medium. It really was so much more powerful in those pre-OTT (streaming) days. I felt heartened that the days of *Hum Log* and *Buniyaad*, pioneering works of Indian television, long-running serials that I used to watch in my college years, were perhaps not over.

My first daily soap *Astitva* helped reinforce this belief. Amazingly for TV it was a subject that the channel agreed to try out as an experiment. It was the story of a gynecologist, a committed career woman who falls in love and marries a man ten years younger than her. The writing team and the channel felt that we would just enjoy doing something different; we all believed that it wouldn't last beyond six months anyway. However, it ran for three-and-a-half years! The experience was heartening. It also taught me the rigours of TV writing for daily soaps: No waiting for inspiration to strike, it's all about creative perspiration. It was a tough grind. Like a labourer who has no choice but to go to work,

---

1 Mother-in-law–daughter-in-law

we kept at it, fingertips ever ready to work and rework episodes on our laptops.

The post-workout thrill of course is when you see your work literally come alive and watched on screens across the land. Books may sell in thousands, if one is a best-selling author. But television shows have audiences[2] running into millions. Now, to get your story out to those millions, however, there are a lot of challenges.

The key to television writing is to realise that it is a numbers game. And that most often it is the channel providing you with the idea. So, you are writing to a given brief. If you are among the fortunate few who have been given a free hand to come up with your own idea, right at the start, the choice of a subject is critical. It has to have mass appeal, and be aspirational and relatable at the same time. You have to keep in mind that your audience largely comprises women/housewives from the not-so-affluent class. The storyline therefore has to be women-centric to make it appeal to that demographic. For it is they who decide what their entertainment staple, and its sensibilities, ought to be. Hence, we have to choose our stories wisely: ones that are laden with emotion and drama. Despite these limitations, an author's voice trying to make a point is a bonus worth aspiring for.

In the volatile mix of high drama and teary emotion, the key factor to remember is longevity. The story should have the potential—should the combustible mix become popular—to go on and on and on. This aspect is vital as a lot is invested behind the scenes in making a serial take off; both in terms of money and creative endeavour. Hence the business model is to maximise returns on any successful story.

Longevity necessitates many strategies. For example, there ought to be many hit-and-miss chances in the narrative; scenes in which the hero and heroine come so close to finding each other, but are yet so far. There could be instances of mistaken identities, mistaken

---

[2] An average of over 50 million for a moderately successful show.

beliefs which get corrected, time leaps and even reincarnations to keep the story going on. In the case of *Balika Vadhu*, which ran for eight long years, we took two generation leaps!

Over the years, television has put its writers through hoops of stress and strain. Soaps began on a weekly basis, but some channels now air them seven days a week. The median is at least five episodes a week. So spiking stress levels and early burnouts are par for the course. Actors routinely fall sick and the script needs to be changed at the last minute. Ever so often, important characters take up other shows on the side, so the script has to accommodate their absences as well. If you have to be on your toes in other professions, scriptwriters in this business have to be on their fingertips!

Coming back to the audience, one of the triggers is to make the characters, and themes, relatable. "Make them enter the houses and kitchens of our audience," is the refrain of television channel executives to the writers. And when they enter your hearts, millions start identifying themselves with the characters. The costumes are copied and the jewellery becomes sought after accoutrements at social events. Forms of greeting, such as the Rajasthani *Khamma Ghani*,[3] became a fashion during the long spell of *Balika Vadhu*.

When the characters become larger than life, thanks to social media, you get a hundred unsolicited suggestions every day on how to move the story forward. And, if word is leaked that you are plotting an end to a popular character, the writer even receives death threats, as I once did, when social media leaked the fact that the writers were intending to kill "Shiv", the popular character who was the beloved husband of our protagonist Anandi in *Balika Vadhu*. His fans told me to desist from what we intended.

Another guideline to follow is that the story has to be aspirational in its appeal to the audience. Hence the protagonist, usually a female, has to be morally upright through the vicissitudes

---

3   Literally, lots of greetings.

she is going through. There can be no shades of grey in her, even though she may be hounded by assorted antagonists. The shades of grey, which are so essential to a story, can be injected by the subsidiary characters who will give the serial its conflict points. They ironically become the repositories of the more gritty stories within a show, with more interesting tracks than the main track.

Such speed-breakers may limit the creativity of the writers, but they can take comfort in the fact that they aspire to a higher ideal in terms of the telling of a moral story which influences millions. There is also the aspect of battling social evils and trying to shape a social cause through a popular serial. We did it in *Balika Vadhu* where we took on the issue of child marriage head-on. I am gratified to say that we did receive feedback in terms of several child marriages which got cancelled due to our clear stand in the serial's story.

Writing for serials, films and OTT (streaming) platforms in India is distinctly different from practices in the West. Here, the writing is compartmentalised. More often than not, there is the team of writers who will create the story, then the screenplay writers take over and finally the dialogue writers step in and add words to the script. In the West, all these departments are helmed by just one team of writers. At times one feels that the process of compartmentalisation dilutes the vision of the prime writer. On the other hand, the involvement of three distinct groups in the creative process fosters team spirit and adds to the quality of the final product. Dialogues, for example, have a lot of weightage in the Indian scenario. Our soaps are verbose, and they need to be so for the benefit of our predominantly female audience, who are busy cooking in the kitchen during prime-time telecasts from 7 p.m. to 10 p.m.!

Again, the screenplay for serials has to be production- and budget-friendly. Unlike in films, and to some extent in OTT platforms, which may be mounted on a lavish scale, the production budgets for soaps tend to be sparse. Hence the need to control costs is paramount. So, scale down your imagination to the budget you are given, cut your coat according to your cloth. There is also the imperative to shoot at least twenty minutes of the story every day for telecast. So it is important to have total directorial control on the day's shoot and that can only happen if the screenplay is tightly written. And yes, there is the all-important hook, a cliffhanger that motivates the audience to come back the next day. As the desperation for numbers increases, the drop points or freezes, as they are currently being called, have often become desperate and contrived, but they are a necessary evil in a series.

Potential television scriptwriters must realise that the route to getting to the goalpost is nothing if not arduous. There are too many people whose opinions have to be considered. First off, the production house has its creatives—people who are involved in the creative side, as opposed to the operational side. They will give some inputs to the writer, which might be valuable given their constant exposure to the business. Then, the production house pitches the story to the television channel and there too the story has to run the tiered gauntlet of creatives.

At the same time, the feedback might be so vague or so outlandish as to make the writer tear her hair in frustration. But you have to get used to these and script your writing to any feedback coming from the production house or the channel while trying to keep to your creative conviction. It is usually manageable, but there are times when it's one against the other. I still remember the tremendous pressure on us from channel executives, who in turn were pressured by a particularly emotional group of fans. The fans wanted the grown-up child bride (in *Balika Vadhu*) to forgive her repentant adult and adulterous husband as they now seemed perfectly mature and matched. But if we bowed to popular sentiment, wouldn't we be sending out the message that it was okay to marry as kids, that there would be a few hiccups and then all will be well again? The writers' team stood its ground and Anandi refused to get back with Jagdish.

And when the story is finally green lit and gets to be telecast, there will always be pulls and pressures emanating from the audience which is armed with the all-powerful remote. Their deciding to stay on the show or flick the switch to watch another channel will decide your ratings. Nowadays, ratings are available on a minute-by-minute basis. So you can ascertain whether the romantic scene between the protagonists was a greater lure than the comic interlude or the villain's track. You are then expected to tailor your story accordingly in the quest for popularity and longevity.

Another major angst that a TV writer deals with is that unlike the classic three-act structure of any good story that has a beginning, middle and end, a TV series in India usually has a clear beginning, a chewing-gum-like stretchable middle and, often, a hurried end, where the tracks are wound up quickly as platforms decide that running the show is no longer viable. So very often logic goes for a toss as tracks are wrapped up with speed.

A few years ago I worked on a very moving story of an old mother who after the death of her husband gets shunted around from one of her three sons' homes to another, until she takes a decision to live on her own with dignity. The last bit was the punch, with a lot of the meat of the story being her experiences at each of the sons' homes before she reaches that stage.

When she reached her third son's home on screen and was figuring out the dynamics of this home, the channel decided to pull the plug on the show. So we only got to see how unhappy she was with the son here, and how she bonded with her grandson, and had no time to see what happened thereafter. I am sure viewers wondered, justifiably so, what the point of the entire story had been?

With all the deference to inputs from the serried ranks of channel executives to get to the audience, and then to comply with audience tastes, you might wonder if it is worth the chase. But when you hear your soap's signature tune wafting across the neighbourhood every night, it's music to your ears and makes up for all the cacophony of the day.

Writing for the Stage

Francis Jarman

Dramatists are not like other writers. Not for playwrights the lonely anguish of the poet, or the long brutal hours of brooding and rewriting that create the novel. You are never alone if you write for the stage, although, especially at the beginning, there will have to be moments of deep concentration, probably somewhere where you *are* on your own and will be undisturbed. It need not be in a room. Two of my plays were conceived, and their plots and main characters outlined in my imagination, as I walked along a beach in Greece (on separate occasions, years apart). The beach wasn't clean, on both days it was cold and windy, and there were few people about (it was winter). How the inspiration came, under such uninspiring circumstances, I have never wholly understood, but being able to concentrate, without many distractions, may have helped.

Some thinking and writing may be done in noisy, crowded places. The first good dramatic scene that I ever wrote, one that, years later, I am still proud of, was jotted down on a notepad in a slow train, trundling along on the way back from an academic conference. Sitting opposite me was a bulky lady with a tiny, hyperactive dog, which (with no discouragement from its owner) repeatedly scrabbled on to the table and over my notepad, smearing the writing from my pen.

Even if you are in a quiet room, though, with your pen poised (or your fingers twitching over the keyboard) and an empty piece of paper (or blank screen) in front of you, you will not be alone. Several different spirits may be hovering behind your shoulder—less metaphorically: at the outer edges of your consciousness—jostling to make their contribution to the creative process.

First, whether playwright, poet or novelist, you will at some point be inspired by your *muse*.

The film *Shakespeare in Love* has been responsible for encouraging a whole range of misconceptions—of theatre in general, of Late Elizabethan theatre more specifically, of Shakespeare, and of the way in which writers work—one of these being that once a suitably exciting love object has flashed on to the playwright's emotional radar the inspiration will flow and flow: light will break through windows, nightingales and larks will go for it, and there will be much inappropriate use of balconies, etc. Unfortunately, it isn't quite like that, otherwise writers wouldn't need to do much more than stagger about with their tongues hanging out, looking for The One.

(By the way, I've just broken one of the cardinal rules for writers, which is that you never, ever, however indirectly, compare yourself with Shakespeare. In a moment, I'm going to break the rule again.)

Muses are probably an essential, because when you write you are normally writing not only for your own critical intelligence but for someone else too, either a real someone or a someone in your mind's eye: to impress or seduce them, to restore their good opinion of you, to make up for past rejections or humiliations. The muse can be your mother or father, your ex-girlfriend, your former schoolmates (all those bullies who used to push you around), or friends and family who have long marked you down as a loser. Well, then, you say, look at my smash hit, my literary prize, my rave reviews, my fancy publication, *and show some respect!* The writer may even have internalised this and be unaware of the origins of their motivation. Not that I exclude the idea of a writer Doing It for the Good of Literature. (Though here I visualise someone who looks more like a bank manager, a T.S. Eliot clone, maybe.) However, the peculiar, strenuous and (in most cases) extrinsically unrewarding nature of literary writing would suggest that there must be a strong personal reason why anyone should choose to indulge in it.

Lorca, the Spanish poet and playwright, was less than enthusiastic about the muse, who "dictates and sometimes prompts", but "can do relatively little, for she is distant". She "awakens the intelligence" but comes "from outside us".

It is probably healthier for the muse to remain distant, too. The history of writing is littered with damaged wives and girlfriends who were cajoled into becoming the emotional, often practical, support team for an immature, egocentric, self-declared "genius". In an interview, Polly Sansom commented acerbically on her relationship with the manic playwright Heathcote Williams:

> I think a man who needs a muse is a man who basically needs … well why not replace the word "muse" with "mummy" or "parent"? What is a parent's job? It is to give nourishing food to your child, make sure that your child has all the right crayons, a lovely place to do their homework and then to admire their work and encourage them to do more of it.[1]

---

1 Andrew Billen. "Polly Sansom: 'A man who needs a muse basically needs a mummy'." In: *The Times*, 8 April 2020. At https://www.thetimes.co.uk/edition/times2/polly-samson-a-man-who-needs-a-muse-basically-needs-a-mummy-hj7j3d2np

Then, according to Lorca, there is the *angel*, who "dazzles, [...] shedding his grace", giving "lights", just as the muse gives "forms".[2]

But the third member of Lorca's trinity of artistic inspiration is the most interesting: the *duende*, a dark, sudden, Dionysiac inspiration that emerges from sources too deep to be grasped logically. When the duende rides you, there is magic and danger, and—for a true artist of course—no possibility of compromise. The duende will not approach at all, declares Lorca, "unless he sees that death is possible. [...] the duende enjoys fighting the creator on the very rim of the well. Angel and muse escape with violin, meter and compass; the duende wounds."[3] Put more prosaically, the duende is there at those creative moments where everything is risked. Non-writers don't understand this, nor do writers who always have a safety-net, but poets know it, and great performers know it best of all.

This is incomparably true of theatre, too (but not of film). Words and movements conceived in thoughtfulness, perhaps with just an inkling of their potential magic, are transformed by fine acting into passion and heartbreak. Film can merely fossilise this, recording it as a memory: Brando in the "I coulda been a contender" scene in *On the Waterfront*; Helena Bonham Carter in *A Room with a View*, teetering on a hillside outside Florence, caught between joy and panic; Daniel Auteuil as Henri of Navarre in the French film *La Reine Margot*, trapped, frightened, but defiant; Halle Berry in *Monster's Ball*; Innokenty Smoktunovsky in the Russian *Hamlet*. Everyone will have their own list—but the actors onstage can not only hold the audience in their grip, they can also thrust the knife in, and turn it, and do it differently every time. The audience waits for such moments, and there is a

---

2 Federico García Lorca. "Play and Theory of the Duende" (1933). Transl. Christopher Maurer. In: F. García Lorca, *In Search of Duende*. New Directions, 1998, 50, 51.

3 Ibid. 58.

communion, an event of shared excitement. In the words of the playwright Terrence McNally:

> When a play is going well, the audience breathes as one. They stop breathing. They breathe together because they're getting this from other live people … People are in the theatre for one reason: to hear this story and meet the people in it. That's a human need.[4]

For all its beauty, the same scene in a film is just a dead thing. This is a reason why so many film actors return again and again to the stage, despite the financial sacrifices this entails, because of the magic that theatre can create.

For the playwright watching rehearsals, there comes a tipping point when the actors stop reading or reciting their lines and slip into the characters. That moment is deeply thrilling, as is the "birth" of the play on the stage (either in dress rehearsal or on the opening night, and sometimes on both occasions). There is nothing like this for the novelist—holding the first copy of your new book is a fine moment, but it's not magical. On the other hand, it is sad to write a play and never see it performed. I can't agree with Dr Samuel Johnson's dictum that "A play read affects the mind like a play acted."[5] However beautiful or witty it may be, a play that has never been staged is like an airplane that has never flown.

I shall never forget the moments of duende I experienced in the theatre, beginning with the treacherous killing of Hector in Shakespeare's *Troilus and Cressida* in a London production that I went to see as a schoolboy. Achilles enters swiftly with his team of killers. Catching Hector unarmed, he gloats over his enemy's helplessness:

---

4 "Terrence McNally Obituary". In: *The Times*, 25 March 2020.
5 *Dr Johnson on Shakespeare.* Ed. W.K. Wimsatt (1960). Penguin, 1969, 72.

> *Achilles.* Look, Hector, how the sun begins to set,
> How ugly night comes breathing at his heels.
> Even with the vail and dark'ning of the sun,
> To close the day up, Hector's life is done.[6]

It was terrifying, and the temperature in the theatre seemed to plummet. What made it so exciting? The way the actors moved, the lighting, the intonation of the lines—and the text, of course.

I remember, too, the scene in a fine production of Schiller's *Maria Stuart* where the author, with a cavalier disregard for the historical facts but with psychological acumen, brings together the two rival queens, Elizabeth of England and Mary Queen of Scots. Elizabeth patronises and sneers at the captive Mary, until Mary can stand it no longer:

> *Mary.* The throne of England's sullied with a bastard.
> The noble-hearted British [*sic*] are betrayed,
> By a sly trickster.
> —If right prevailed, *you* would lie here before me,
> Here in the dust, for *I'm* the rightful Queen![7]

"Bastard" was not merely an insult. In the eyes of Mary's Catholic adherents, she was indeed the rightful Queen of England: Henry VIII's marriage to Catherine of Aragon had never been legally dissolved, and so Elizabeth, daughter of the interloper Ann Boleyn, was illegitimate and thereby without proper claim to the throne. On this issue, Elizabeth was insecure and vulnerable, as Mary well knew. Schiller's imagined catfight between the two queens is a gift for actresses, and in this production they gave it everything, with thrilling effect.

---

6   William Shakespeare. *Troilus and Cressida*, Act V, Scene 8, 5-8.
7   Friedrich Schiller. *Maria Stuart* (1800), Act III, Scene 4, 2447-49, my translation.

The most frightening final scene of any major drama is perhaps that of *Ghosts*, Ibsen's notorious play about family guilt, hypocrisy, and the horrors of syphilis. Osvald Alving has inherited the disease from his father. Nursed by his mother, he is waiting for the return of the terrible symptoms. There is a powerful nighttime scene between mother and son, in which Osvald reveals his dread of the inevitable coming regression into infantilism and the "softening of the brain". He shows his mother some tablets he has secreted and begs her to give him "a helping hand" when the time comes. Mrs Alving tries to comfort him but is unwilling to face up to the situation. For the moment, though, the crisis seems to be over. Then the dawn breaks:

[She goes to the table and puts out the lamp. The sun rises; the glaciers and the peaks in the distance glow in the morning light.]
Osvald *[sitting in the armchair with his back to the view, suddenly speaks without moving].* Mother, give me the sun.[8]

The actor's timing was perfect—and I was surely not the only person in the audience whose blood ran cold.

When I turned my own hand to playwriting, the first play I wrote, *A Star Fell* (1998), about the so-called Indian Mutiny, contained a lot of violence. My template—though I wasn't aware of it at first—may have been Peter Shaffer's *The Royal Hunt of the Sun*, a ponderous and gloomy epic that had had great theatrical success in the 1960s, and which I had seen in its maiden production. My own play had not one, but two massacres, but what turned out to be the most poignant moment was no more than a vignette.

---

8   Henrik Ibsen. *Ghosts* (1881). Transl. Peter Watts. In: H. Ibsen. *Ghosts and Other Plays*. Penguin, 1964, 101.

The British garrison is being besieged by the mutineers. Their situation is hopeless. A message arrives from the leader of the rebels (the "Peshwa"), offering the British an honourable withdrawal. The message—which is intended to lure them into a trap—is carried by one of the rebels' British captives, Mrs Jacobi, whose children are being held as surety for her return to the rebel camp. Mrs Jacobi, a minor character in the play, is in a desperate physical and emotional condition, but at first General Wheeler and his daughter Ulrica barely notice her, so interested are they in the message she has brought. Then Wheeler instructs her:

> *Wheeler.* Mrs Jacobi, you must take my reply to the ... to the Peshwa.
> *Ulrica.* Can't she stay here, Daddy? Can't we send someone else with the message?
> *Mrs Jacobi.* I have to go back. They have my children.
> *Wheeler [suddenly noticing her ears]* Poor woman, your ears are torn!
> *Mrs Jacobi [tired and sad, touching her hands to her ears].* They wanted my earrings.
> *[Fade to black. Exeunt.]*[9]

My intention here was that Mrs Jacobi's whispered understatement should *evoke* rather than show her abuse and humiliation at the hands of her captors, and the effect was brilliantly achieved. The actor playing General Wheeler lowered his voice and slowed his delivery, and there was a deep hush of emotional concentration as Mrs Jacobi replied, and the audience *felt* the pain and despair contained in her words "They wanted my earrings."

Less is often more. In modern stage productions and films almost everything is shown, including acts of the grossest kind.

---

9   Francis Jarman. *A Star Fell: A Play* (1998). Third, revised edition. Borgo, 2009, 67-68.

Even Shakespeare didn't spare his audience the blinding of Gloucester in *King Lear*: "Fellows, hold the chair. / Upon these eyes of thine I'll set my foot. [...] Out, vile jelly! / Where is thy lustre now?" (perhaps the most horrific lines that he ever wrote).[10] But Shakespeare's audiences were used to being entertained with "slasher movie" horrors in real life, at the places of public execution. As Dr Johnson sagely observed, "let it be remembered that our author well knew what would please the audience for which he wrote".[11]

Whether the blood is real or only ketchup, the repeated viewing of cruelty will make us indifferent—I have caught myself laughing out loud at poorly executed, clichéd acts of violence in television films—whereas our imaginations hold a reservoir of nightmarish thoughts and images more terrifying to us than anything we can be shown. The great Greek tragedians sensibly kept most acts of violence offstage, although it has been debated whether they did this because they were obliged to by "the small number of actors employed" and the "practical limitations of realistic staging and acting".[12] In his *Ars Poetica*, the Roman poet Horace argued that although the mind

> is less actively stimulated by what it takes in through the ear than by what is presented to it through the trustworthy agency of the eyes [...] you will not bring on to the stage anything that ought properly to be taking place behind the scenes, and you will keep out of sight many episodes that are to be described later by the eloquent tongue of

---

10 William Shakespeare. *King Lear*, Act III, Scene 7, 66-67, 82-83.
11 *Dr Johnson on Shakespeare*, 126.
12 Philip Whaley Harsh. *A Handbook of Classical Drama*. Stanford University Press, 1944, 33. For a different view, see R. Sri Pathmanathan. "Death in Greek Tragedy". In: *Greece & Rome*, Vol. 12, No.1, April 1965, 2-14, who dismisses these "external factors" and argues that there are usually "good dramatic reasons" for the deaths to take place offstage.

a narrator. Medea must not butcher her children in the presence of the audience [...] I shall turn in disgust from anything of this kind that you show me.[13]

The "practical limitations of realistic [...] acting" apply when the actors are incompetent, as I was when I played Cassius in a school production of Shakespeare's *Julius Caesar*. Every night I had to kill myself on stage; every night I fell awkwardly and unrealistically, bashing my head and genuinely hurting myself; and every night, adding insult to my injury, someone in the audience laughed.

To do justice to its subject matter, *A Star Fell* had to be brutal. There is a scene in which Mrs Jacobi and Lady Wheeler are shown being verbally abused, kicked, and humiliated by their captors, and another scene in which the wicked Sultana's servant strikes Lady Wheeler. But the "earrings" vignette, with its quiet horror, proved to be more effective as theatre than either of these. As for the more substantial acts of violence: the play's two massacres invite, and were given, a "stylised" treatment; there is also a rape, but this takes place offstage.

The applause at the end of each performance was deeply gratifying, but the comments made to me by members of the audience were more interesting. One gentleman confided in me how impressed he had been by the actress who played the Sultana. She prowled the stage like a tigress, graceful (in her Indian sari) but threatening, spitting out hatred and (verbally) flashing her claws. The gentleman from the audience was obviously fascinated.

So, for the record, was I. I can understand how directors and playwrights can fall in love with "their" leading lady—though not so much with her as a person, as with what she is bringing to life—at least for the duration of the production. I had the pleasure

---

13 Horace. "On the Art of Poetry". In: *Classical Literary Criticism*. Transl. T.S. Dorsch. Penguin, 1965, 85.

of standing in for a missing actor at one of the rehearsals and experiencing, close up, how good the actress playing the Sultana was. Her gentleman admirer noted how cunningly the Sultana manipulated those around her, but he was frustrated that she didn't receive her comeuppance at the end of the play. Instead, as so often happens—and as indeed happened to the historical figure that my character is based upon—she got away with it (and with the money, too). He told me that he'd wanted to jump on to the stage and strangle the witch! A great compliment to the whole production, I told myself, but good that he didn't do it.[14]

More disturbingly, I received an email from another member of the audience, who expressed his admiration for my courage in revealing myself in public in such a manner: "A play like this is a kind of diary in which personal experiences and thoughts are indirectly, or perhaps sometimes directly, presented to the audience."

No such thing! Writers have *plot* ideas, which they put into practice using the invented figures that we call *characters*. Even a historical figure must be reinvented by the author—playwrights are not biographers. And none of my plays is about me; none of my characters represents me in any way.

I was so open to other people's views and inputs when writing *A Star Fell* that it was originally intended to be a workshop production, in which I would develop a plot and flesh it out together with the members of the cast. There followed hours of wasted rehearsal time as stances were adopted, positions clarified, egos given free rein, and my text suggestions messed around with. For some, my take on the Indian Mutiny wasn't politically acceptable, i.e., I wasn't portraying the Indian rebels as Third

---

14 Rita, the working-class protagonist of Willy Russell's play *Educating Rita* (1980), is similarly tempted, during a performance of Shakespeare's *Macbeth*. She wants to shout out and warn Macbeth that he is in danger, but she doesn't: "Nah. Y' can't do that in a theatre, can y'?" (Longman, 2000, 60).

World freedom fighters and the colonial British as nineteenth-century Nazis. One of the actors objected to there being several non-white characters who were plainly villainous.

Under pressure, I therefore agreed to modify the figure of Azimullah Khan, making him more complex and "torn". On the urging of the director, we finally closed the discussion and agreed that my text, as it now stood, would be our script. Years later I researched Azimullah Khan and published a short biography.[15] I can assert with confidence that, though he was multifaceted and interesting, he was also wicked and spiteful, in short, a much nastier piece of work than the Azimullah Khan of *A Star Fell*. But I have no intention of further changing my play, which is neither history nor biography, but a drama.

What I learned from this is that actors should be discouraged from messing around with the text. And they should be dealt with firmly if they try to "improve" their lines or come up with rewrites of whole scenes or even "new ideas that need to be developed". I agree completely with Hollywood screenwriter Joe Eszterhas when he recommends: "Don't be open to too many ideas about changing your script." And why not? Because: "*You're* the writer; *they're* not. Plus this: Most of their ideas will be asinine. Believe me: I've heard thirty years of asinine ideas." The actors may be persistent. Actors may have become actors precisely *because* of their obsessive need to be noticed. Eszterhas therefore advises (in the spirit of *A Clockwork Orange*): "If they mess with you, give them a little taste of the old ultraviolence."[16]

Teamwork is necessary, but a play production is not an exercise in grassroots democracy, any more than an airline flight or a surgical operation is. The director needs to keep a tight grip

---

15 Francis Jarman. "Azimullah Khan—A Reappraisal of One of the Major Figures of the Revolt of 1857". In: *South Asia: Journal of South Asian Studies*, Vol. XXXI, No.3, December 2008, 419-49.
16 Joe Eszterhas. *The Devil's Guide to Hollywood: The Screenwriter as God!* St. Martin's Press, 2006, 212.

on his production if he is going to bring it to market. Alfred Hitchcock understood this well:

> I was once quoted as saying that actors are cattle. My actor friends know I would never be capable of such a thoughtless, rude, and unfeeling remark; that I would never call them cattle ... What I probably said was that actors should be *treated* like cattle.[17]

Which means they should be gently herded in the right direction.

Actors can be shameless. I was once approached by one with the request that I add a romantic interlude between her character and the character played by one of her male colleagues. There should be lots of kissing, she said. The audience would love it! "But why should there be a love scene between them?" I asked her, racking my brains to think whether I'd missed some significant emotional involvement between the characters, and expecting her to tell me what I'd overlooked (after all, they'd been rehearsing the play for weeks, and she might indeed have spotted some intriguing possibility). "Oh, he's just *too cute*," she said—but it was the actor she meant, and not my character.

The director is a different matter altogether. Unlike many of the actors, he or she probably knows what they are doing, and what they are talking about. There is a well-established, pragmatic tradition that plays can be edited, cut, adapted, adjusted, reorganised and so on to meet the circumstances and needs of the production. Within reason, the director must be allowed to do this. (The writer probably won't be able to stop it from happening anyway.) The director carries the artistic responsibility for the production. If things go pear-shaped, the writer can slip away from the awfulness, but the director must stay with his troops. The

---

17 *Hitchcock on Hitchcock: Selected Writings and Interviews*. Ed. Sidney Gottlieb. University of California Press, paperback edition 1997, 56.

director may ask for lines to be changed or scenes to be rewritten. The director understands better than the writer does what the actors can do and what they can't. The director may unilaterally change the text in small, sensible ways.

Yet I draw the line at "creative" directors who think they know more about the play than the writer does. At its most extreme—for instance in German *Regietheater* ("director's theatre", i.e., theatre in which the input of the director is more important than anything else)—the director upstages even his own actors, making himself the true star of the production, by doing "interesting" things with the play.

Some spurious credibility for this has been sought with the argument that older plays must be made "relevant" (more accessible? easier to digest? or simply: easier?) for a modern audience. If this is the price that must be paid for keeping such plays in the repertoire, so be it, but let the "relevance" (please!) not be in the form of gags and stunts. The trapezes, boxes and climbing frames, the actors bellowing and leaping about like a caricature of asylum inmates, the addition of gratuitous, exhibitionistic nudity or provocative anachronisms (I once saw a production of Puccini's opera *Turandot* in which the action was transposed from a mythical China to the Beijing of Chairman Mao): unless the text was intended all along to be a flimsy vehicle for such experiments, the gimmicks should not be allowed to distract attention from the substance of the play.

Matching an older play to the taste of the times is nothing new. Nahum Tate won approval for his "happy ending" version of *King Lear*, in which Lear regains his kingdom and Cordelia doesn't die, so much so that this "improvement" on Shakespeare held the stage from 1681 until 1823, when Edmund Kean restored the tragic ending. In his notes on the play, Dr Samuel Johnson remarked on the popularity of Tate's adaptation ("the public has decided"). Adding his personal "sensations" to "the general suffrage", he revealed that he had been so shocked by

Cordelia's death that he had long refrained from rereading the closing scenes of the play.[18]

On the subject of "directorial improvements to Shakespeare", we might give the playwright George Bernard Shaw the last word. Shaw watched a spectacular but brutally edited version of *Hamlet* directed by and starring the actor-producer John Barrymore (1925). He published a crushing letter to him:

> Shakespear [sic], with all his shortcomings, was a very great playwright; and the actor who undertakes to improve his plays undertakes thereby to excel to an extraordinary degree in two professions in both of which the highest success is extremely rare. Shakespear himself, though by no means a modest man, did not pretend to be able to play Hamlet as well as write it; he was content to do a recitation in the dark as the ghost. But you have ventured not only to act Hamlet, but to discard about a third of Shakespear's script and substitute stuff of your own [...].[19]

He advises Barrymore to "concentrate on acting"—a profession in which the American was undoubtedly brilliant—"rather than on authorship, at which, believe me, Shakespear can write your head off."[20]

As well as actors and directors, there are other figures with whom playwrights may have problems. Wherever serious money is involved—we're talking Broadway and London's West End, but also the mainstream theatres in other cities—producers, theatre company directors and managers, and theatrical agents start to be important. The financial constraints in commercial theatre tend to

---

18 *Dr Johnson on Shakespeare*, 126.
19 George Bernard Shaw. "A Letter to John Barrymore". In: *Shakespeare's Tragedies: An Anthology of Modern Criticism*. Ed. Laurence Lerner (1963). Penguin, 1968, 87.
20 Ibid. 88.

make "unknown" writers the victims of the vicious circle of fame: they won't do your plays unless you're famous, but you won't become famous if they don't do your plays. It's hard for an outsider to break into the world of the theatre, and it's not surprising that many modern playwrights were originally professional actors (who knew how to use their contacts).

There are only a limited number of types of play that are commercially relevant, some of the obvious ones being (a) musicals (overwhelmingly so), (b) farces and boulevard comedies (those reliable standbys of the middle-class, middle-aged theatre-goer), (c) "alternative", left-wing theatre (mostly in university towns, with a numerically restricted but loyal clientele), (d) experimental, "art" theatre (ditto), and (e) the classics (strongly patronised by busloads of schoolchildren and tourists). Which means that it's rather awkward if, as a playwright, you're (a) unmusical, (b) serious-minded, (c) not stridently "progressive", (d) happy to let others push the envelope, and (e) still alive.

Anyone who writes plays for local theatre groups, university drama clubs, and other enthusiastic amateurs will find that they are expected to write for large casts, often with a high percentage of women and only a handful of people who can act. Plays like this are seldom commercially viable. As one agent wrote to me, he couldn't take my play to the appropriate people "because of the cost", i.e., they would not consider a play with such a large cast by an unknown author, because of the financial risk. This was an honest reaction, even though it revealed more about the commercial concerns of the agent than about his artistic commitment. Commoner is the agent's rejection slip that simply states that "due to an enormous workload we are unable to offer to take on any new clients at the moment". What this apparent lack of entrepreneurial curiosity really conceals is the vicious circle that I have already described.

I sent my musical *Girls Will Be Girls* to the office of a world-famous composer and producer of musicals. A reply eventually came, from the "assistant to the Head of Production", politely declining the play, thanking me, rather solipsistically, for my interest in their company (I had been hoping for *their* interest in *me*), and explaining that they felt this was "not something for development by [their] organisation". It was a short-sighted view, because at the time their "organisation" was going through a mediocre phase, serving up unconvincing productions with weak musical numbers. *Girls Will Be Girls* is full of great songs (I can allow myself to praise the music, since I didn't write any of it), and I believe they could have done worse than take a closer look at it. But, in any case, writers don't want to be developed; they want to be discovered.

Surely the critics, at least, should be willing to place artistic considerations in the foreground? The relations between creative artists and critics (who themselves may be failed or timid would-be artists) have seldom been easy. Asked what they think of the critics, artists will tend to say things like: "why not ask a lamp-post how it feels about dogs?", or: "critics think they know the way, but they just can't drive the car", or: "like eunuchs in a harem, they know what to do, but they haven't got the equipment to do it", or: "they're the gadflies that hinder the oxen from ploughing" or "the lice that crawl on literature", or even: "people who piss into a river and say, oh look, what a big stream I made!"[21] What many artists have found galling is being judged, not by their peers, but by those lacking comparable practical experience in what they are criticising; or, as Lord Byron put it (in 1809):

> A man must serve his time to every trade
> Save censure—critics all are ready made.[22]

---

21 Opinions on critics attributed to the playwright Christopher Hampton, the critic (!) Kenneth Tynan, and the writers Brendan Behan, Chekhov, Hemingway and Robert Frost.
22 "English Bards and Scotch Reviewers". In: *Selected Poems of Lord Byron*. Wordsworth, 2006, 700.

The reviews of my own plays have always been positive, but they've never been very perceptive (compared with the comments of my friends, which were sometimes the opposite in both cases!). I would recommend ignoring reviews, and certainly not replying to them directly, as the composer Max Reger is claimed to have done, writing to the author of a negative review: "I am sitting in the smallest room of my house. I have your review before me. In a moment it will be behind me."[23]

Finally: I haven't really explained yet "how it's done"—how plays get written. In my own case, it helped me considerably to be able to work for a drama group, writing scripts for a team whose resources, possibilities, and weaknesses I was broadly aware of. The downside of this (apart from producing plays that aren't seen as commercially viable) is that there are things I can't expect the actors to be able to do, and so I don't write them. There are exceptions. Because I knew that we had an outstanding actor to play the wicked Sultana in *A Star Fell*, I took the risk of giving her a passionate dramatic monologue, in which she not only parodies a dialogue between two of the other characters but concludes with a poetic and emotional peroration. It was ambitious, but the actor carried it off.

Beginnings and endings are of great importance. Productions by the drama group I worked with tended to open quietly, with a masque, tableau, or single talking head, before exploding into action with a crowd scene or a song-and-dance number. Some plays are famous for their spectacular opening scenes. One of my favourites is *The Revenger's Tragedy* (1607), the Jacobean shocker probably written by Thomas Middleton. The revenger himself, Vindice, enters "carrying a skull". Then "the Duke, Duchess, Lussurioso her Son, Spurio the Bastard, with a train, pass over the Stage with Torch-light", and Vindice hurls his hatred and scorn at them:

---

23 Quoted in *Modernism and Music: An Anthology of Sources*. Ed. Daniel Albright. University of Chicago Press, 2004, 147.

> *Vindice.* Duke, royal lecher! Go, grey-haired adultery,
> And thou his son, as impious steeped as he:
> And thou his bastard, true-begot in evil:
> And thou his Duchess, that will do with Devil,
> Four ex'lent characters—[24]

For a dramatic opening, that is hard to beat! And as a bonus it conveniently introduces several of the main characters right from the start. (Curiously, the 2002 film version by Alex Cox failed to do much with this scene.)

The playwright can also make the opening of the play lyrically memorable, as Shakespeare does in *Twelfth Night* ("If music be the food of love, play on") and *Richard III* ("Now is the winter of our discontent").

More conventionally, he can use a dramatic Chorus to introduce the story, as in *Romeo and Juliet* ("Two households, both alike in dignity"), *Troilus and Cressida* ("In Troy, there lies the scene") and *Henry V* ("O for a Muse of fire, that would ascend / The brightest heaven of invention").

Or he can go for a shock effect, like the Witches in *Macbeth* ("When shall we three meet again / In thunder, lightning, or in rain?") or the (for a Late Tudor audience) disturbing sight of a king *in extremis* in *1 Henry IV* ("So shaken as we are, so wan with care").

The plots of stage comedies tend to be driven by stubborn misunderstandings, and end with (and through) their resolution. In the final scenes of the play, rivals, enemies, and estranged friends are reconciled, those who belong together come together, and the world is a happier and better integrated place than it was before. There may be engagements or weddings. My own play *Girls Will Be Girls* (2000) ends, after many plot confusions and complications, with five happy couples (one of them a lesbian pair) on the stage—not quite a world record, I know (think *Seven*

---

24 Thomas Middleton. *The Revenger's Tragedy*, Act I, Scene 1, 1-5.

Brides for Seven Brothers), but difficult to organise plot-wise—and nobody is excluded from the celebratory circle of reconciliation.

> *Allan [looking at the reconciled couples].* Is this what they call a happy ending?
> *Sammie.* Perhaps...[25]

Yet some comedies are darker. In Shakespeare's *Twelfth Night*, Malvolio famously excludes himself: "I'll be reveng'd on the whole pack of you!" (he is perhaps not irredeemably lost, since the Duke calls for someone to "Pursue him, and entreat him to a peace").[26]

A play that makes any claim to being about serious matters in the real world cannot pretend that that world contains no evil. My second comedy, *Lip Service* (2001), which is about power struggles and sexual and ideological conflicts at a feminist cosmetics company, ends with the exclusion of the two "villains", the tyrannical chief executive Bella and the ultra-egotist and preening would-be Casanova Bill Bullock ("BAM! That's my company. Bullocks's Active Marketing. I'm Bullock!").[27] After Bella's reign of terror has been ended by a staff revolt, she storms out, taking Bill Bullock, whose services are also no longer required by the company, with her. It is hardly true love, but Bill and Bella deserve each other, and here too a kind of comedic "coming together" takes place:

> *Bella [half-heartedly].* Come along, Bullock, I've got a business proposal for you.
> *Bill.* That's the spirit! Think positive, baby. Think constructive. Think *big*. There are big things we can do

---

25 Francis Jarman. *Girls Will Be Girls: A Play* (2000). Second edition. Borgo, 2007, 112.
26 William Shakespeare. *Twelfth Night*, Act V, Scene 1, 377, 379.
27 Francis Jarman. *Lip Service: A Play* (2001). Second edition. Borgo, 2007, 42.

together. "Bill and Bella's Active Marketing"—BABAM! That has a ring to it! *[On their way out]* You and I will make a great team. There are new worlds to conquer! Let's get our heads together over a drink. I know a fantastic little place, just round the corner from here… *[Exeunt Bella and Bill]*[28]

Bill has already been thwarted in three attempts to lure female members of the company staff to his favourite restaurant, or back to his apartment, "for drinkies by candle-light".[29] It seems that with Bella he has finally hit gold (she will eat him alive, of course, but he's too stupid to realise that).

My other male chauvinist is the rock music agent Ronnie de Silver in *Girls Will Be Girls*. In his very first scene, Ronnie manages to offend each of the women on the stage, including his former girlfriend, Elaine. The salacious "joke" that he makes about her not only always raised a laugh from theatre audiences, but has even gained a certain notoriety in other circles:

> *Rickie [with heavy sarcasm]*. You're so charming, Ronnie.
> *Ronnie [bowing]*. It's the company I keep.
> *Elaine.* While we're on the subject, don't you think, *at your age*, that it's rather tasteless…?
> *Ronnie.* Funny you should say that. Because you know what *you* remind me of, Elaine?
> *Elaine.* No?
> *Ronnie.* The British Museum.
> *Elaine [suspicious]*. How come?
> *Ronnie.* It's got lots of interesting things to do and see, but everything's so *old*.
> *Sammie [unnecessarily]*. Yeah, fossils and old bones.

---

28 Ibid. 109.
29 Ibid. 79.

Sally. Ha, ha, look who's talking.
Ronnie. No, that's a different museum. What I'm trying to say is: everyone's already *been there*. *[Leeringly]* If you know what I mean by that. They don't charge admission. People just go in and out as they please.
Elaine [very angry]. You bastard![30]

When the British Library (a sister organisation to the British Museum, and once housed under its roof) acquired a copy of *Girls Will Be Girls* for their national copyright collection, the Head of the Modern English section wrote to me, "I notice the British Museum gets a mention!"

My "serious" plays, *A Star Fell* and *Invictus* (2006), both of which are based on historical events, end with the future fates of the main characters being revealed. (A device well-known from films and television series.)

In *A Star Fell*, the different "villains" are dragged before a British military court to be sentenced. Azimullah Khan as Chorus describes what is going to happen to each of them, and the play then ends (as it also began) with his words.

Invictus, a play about the Roman emperor Constantine, likewise begins and ends with monologues addressed directly to the audience, in this case by the Machiavellian court chamberlain and eunuch Euphratas. In the final scene of the play, he invites the main characters to each "have their own last word", before revealing to the audience that he himself "was given many honours, and lived to be old. May you too die peacefully in your bed, as I did."[31]

This is as far as I have been prepared to go in the direction of actor-audience interaction. In the past, such interaction was often spontaneous, when actors hurled back the rotten cabbages that had been thrown on to the stage, or when the actor George

---

30 *Girls Will Be Girls*, 53-54.
31 Francis Jarman. *Invictus: A Play*. Borgo, 2006, 103.

Frederick Cooke, booed in 1772 for a poor performance in the slave-trading port of Liverpool, told the theatre audience, "I have not come here to be insulted by a set of wretches, every brick in whose infernal town is cemented with the blood of an African!"[32] For the most part, though, it remains an essential of realistic acting "that the actor should never seem to notice the audience".[33] In my experience, going to the other extreme usually has unfortunate results, with exaggerated Brechtian "distancing" and "alienation" making the performance unbearably didactic, and the audience participation indulged in by many experimental theatre groups leading to chaos and embarrassment.

Openings and endings may be important, but a lot must still be done in-between. What is served up to the audience needs to have *some* quality, if only as a matter of politeness. It's easy for someone to toss a novel aside, or switch channels on the television, but very few people have the courage to get up and walk out of a theatre performance. Once in their seats, the audience are committed to the play (at least until the interval), and they should be given something in return for that commitment, and for the money they paid.

The plot is a road map taking its characters from the opening scene to the final one, and it should make sense. Although they are not real people with existences outside the play, the characters should be so convincing (and the things that they do so plausible) that you could imagine that they *might* be real. "He goes off at the end of scene 3," you tell yourself, "to make room for the intimate scene between B and C, but I need him again for scene 5 (with B), so how do I motivate his return (and engineer C's departure from the stage), and then get him off at the end of the scene, before bringing him back for scene 8? How about: 'Oh, I think I'll go off and make myself a coffee'? And: 'Hello again, I was wondering

---

32 Quoted in Adam Hochschild. *Bury the Chains: The British Struggle to Abolish Slavery* (2005). Pan Macmillan, 2012, 117.
33 W.H. Auden. "The World of Opera". In: *Secondary Worlds*. Faber, 1968, 88.

where you were'?" Naturally, you can't have your characters drifting off the stage in search of a coffee in every second scene.

Clumsy entrance lines can quickly become clichés ("Anyone for tennis?"), far-fetched coincidences and deus ex machina effects should be used sparingly, and an imaginative stage direction like the notorious "Exit, pursued by a bear" (in Shakespeare's *The Winter's Tale*) can only ever be used once! To avoid mistakes, I worked out the intricacies of the plot continuity of *Girls Will Be Girls* with a board representing the stage and my little daughter's Lego figures standing in for the characters.

And yet—what matters most in a fast-moving play is what the audience *perceives* (rather than what they deduce), and what is plausible to them during the performance. One of my plays was only days away from dress rehearsal when one of the actors pointed out that "*this* character coming on at *this* moment, and for *these* reasons, isn't logical!" The director quickly replied that if no one in the cast had noticed it for weeks it was unlikely that anyone in the audience would notice it during the two hours of the stage performance. He was right, too. (And does anyone watching Shakespeare's *Othello*—as opposed to scholars analysing it—ever worry about how silly the plot is? It's still a marvellous play.)

The magic is what counts, and when the magic of the performance works, a play will reward its author with more joy and satisfaction than any other form of writing.

Follow Your Nose
(Why Playwrights Write)[1]

Ramu Ramanathan

Ramu Ramanathan is a well-known playwright, director, and poet. He has written *Cotton 56, Polyester 84*; *Jazz*; *Comrade Kumbhakarna*; and *Mahadevbhai*. His book *3, Sakina Manzil and Other Plays* (Orient Blackswan, 2012) is a collection of eight plays. He has also penned a book of poems, *My Encounters with a Peacock* (i write imprint, 2017), and *To Sit on a Stone and Other Shorts* (Red River, 2020), and co-edited *Babri Masjid, 25 Years On* (Kalpaz, 2017), with Sameena Dalwai and Irfan Engineer. He is the editor of *PrintWeek* and *WhatPackaging?* and has been associated with the printing industry for thirty years.

~

Theatrewallahs seek the High and Mighty Nose. This is because we live in a day and age where perfect nonsense goes on in the world, and sometimes there is no plausibility at all.

---

[1] The following talk was given at an award ceremony in Pune.

I

Congratulations to the Five Fellowshippers for being selected for Tendulkar-Dubey Fellowships in the Performing Arts in 2019.[2]

Thank you, Ashok Kulkarni (Managing Trustee, Sahitya Rangabhoomi Pratishthan) and Satish Alekar, for inviting me to speak. I have penned my thoughts; and so, I seek your permission to read the words of these pages.

Also, I flashed back in time, and I asked myself, what wise advice would old me (in 2019) have for a young me (in 1989)?

So, dear Five Fellowshippers: let me start at the beginning.

One of the all-time great playwrights according to me is Sophocles.

And *Oedipus Rex* by Sophocles remains the best murder mystery of all time. Because in the end, the detective discovers that he, Oedipus—the king—is the murderer.

Aristotle in his *Poetics* selected Oedipus as the most exemplary of tragedies.

And yet, the play was a runner-up in a drama competition.

There are two morals to this story:

a) Never trust drama competitions.

b) It's an extraordinary piece of writing, and I think all the Five Fellowshippers must read the play tonight.

While reading the play, they must keep in mind one thing, probably the only thing, I learnt from Satyadev Dubey.

How does the play smell, yaar?

Believe me, every play has a smell.

I learnt that very early in my life. That the olfactory nerves in my nostrils are pretty good.

---

[2] "The fellowships, which pay homage to the late playwright Vijay Tendulkar and theatre director Satyadev Dubey, were instituted by Sahitya Rangabhoomi Pratishthan fourteen years ago. They are accorded to five young, experimental, and talented artistes each year" (*Pune Mirror*).

All of us are familiar with the smell of the lobby of a five-star hotel or the smell of an airplane ready to take off or the smell of making love to someone who is not there the next morning.

Plays are similar. They have a scent or an odour or a lingering something that stays with you.

This scent or odour is not like the smell or odour of an auditorium. Bal Gandharva auditorium has one; so does Sudarshan. Likewise, Prithvi and Kamani.

But this is different.

You have to develop it. Please ensure the olfactory nerves in both your nostrils classify each and every play that you read or see or rehearse.

Does it pass the ABCDEF test?

What is the ABCDEF test?

A for Alekar.[3]

B for Beckett.

C for Chekhov and Chandralekha.[4]

D for Dickens and Dostoyevsky (neither of whom are playwrights, but I learnt my best lessons about the theatre from them).

E for Euripides, and for Elkunchwar[5] (who was very brave in Nagpur, two days ago, at the Marathi Natya Parishad Sammelan).[6]

F for Fosse. Jon Fosse.[7] Now Mr Fosse is a Nobel laureate...

G for Girish Karnad,[8] and for Gajvee[9] (who was very brave in Nagpur, two days ago, at the Marathi Natya Parishad Sammelan, when he spoke in the presence of the chief minister).

And so on.

---

3   Satish Vasant Alekar (b. 1949): Marathi man of the theatre.
4   Chandralekha Prabhudas Patel (1928–2006): A renowned Indian dancer and choreographer.
5   Mahesh Elkunchwar (b. 1939): Indian playwright and screenwriter.
6   Annual Marathi theatre meet.
7   Jon Fosse (b. 1959): Norwegian dramatist.
8   Girish Karnad (1938–2019): Indian actor, film director, and playwright.
9   Premanand Gajvee (or Gajvi) (b. 1947): Marathi playwright and poet.

II

Remember—even if playwrights and theatrewallahs do *not* talk to each other, plays talk to each other.

That's why theatre has dialogue.

These are the dialogues of the million and one plays that have never, ever been performed on a stage. But they are the backbone of our civilisation.

So, did Satyadev Dubey say this to me?

Nope.

But I inferred.

Like every time I see the Uruguayan football team kick an opponent on his shins or bite an opponent's earlobe off, I think of Juan Carlos Onetti, one of the greatest novelists I know, and I forgive the Uruguayan football players for their thuggery. I infer that if this nation gave birth to Onetti it did something that Uruguayan noses can be proud of!

Like every time someone says they have *not* read or *cannot* read Gabriel García Márquez's *Chronicle of a Death Foretold* (over and above looking very hurt) I request them to watch Francesco Rosi's 1987 film that is based on the novel. When someone says the movie was even more incomprehensible than the book, I have one of those days that I call: Today I lost all faith in humankind, for the nth time.

Why is Rosi important? Of course, he directed innumerable important films in the 1960s and '70s, in the heyday of Italian cinema. Today, in the day and age of gaming and Netflix, Rosi may be considered "dated". But the lesson I inferred from him was: his film scripts can be the script of life. Imagine: a day in your mother's life, or a day in your maid's life. Now imagine this day looking like a Rosi film script.

This is called inferring. And for this you need a nose.

At this point of time, I request all of you, including the Fellowshippers, to please touch the tip of your nose.

What does your nose say? Is it nosey or is it not nosey?

Let us now flashback many centuries.

Mr Abhinavagupta[10] was certainly very, very nosey.

He said three things about the *Natyashastra*, thousands of years ago. He said: you need to master three elements if you want a nose like mine.

1. *Vastu*, the plot.
2. *Neta*, the characterisation.
3. *Rasa*, the impact of the play in performance.

Then he said something as an aside. And my advice to all Fellowshippers is: always pay heed to the aside, asides are the important things in our lives, onstage and offstage. Anyway, Mr Abhinavagupta said one, two, and three are not important.

He said: What is truly important is narrative (*itivritta*), which has to be revealed slowly and has to sustain the interest of the people.

Because in the ultimate analysis, itivritta is what you infer.

And it is this itivritta that has triggered my imagination. And the imagination of this imagi-Nation.

We theatrewallahs need to use our imaginations a bit more—because they who are watching us are always tinkering with the narrative. Which is why we need newer avatars of imaginations before they conjure newer ten-headed forms of the narrative.

Remember Mr Abhinavagupta's mantra: bros and sisters—your inferring needs to be better than their inferring.

Question: Why so?

Answer: We live in a day and age of ideological putrification and demonisation of the imagination, where one and only one dominant thought has swallowed all the other 1.4 billion thoughts.

Theatrewallahs—be it directors, playwrights, actors, and those new beasts called creators and theatre-makers—need new tactics.

Unfortunately, Amazon and Flipkart do not deliver tactics.

There are no Union Budget announcements for tactics.

---

10 Abhinavagupta (ca. 950–1016): Indian philosopher and polymath who wrote a commentary on the *Natyashastra*, an ancient Sanskrit text on the performing arts.

There is no TV show or WhatsApp group for tactics.

And so we need to seek our own tactics.

Tactics could be borrowed from Krishen Khanna and V.S. Gaitonde and Francis N. Souza and Gaganendranath Tagore at the NGMA.[11]

Or a tactic could be borrowed from Manmohan Desai.[12] One reason I say Manmohan Desai is that his cinema (no matter how critical we are of his populism), for example, *Amar Akbar Anthony*, has been consumed by a lot more people than the plays we stage. How do we resolve this conundrum?

As the legendary Narayan Surve[13] said, when shall we write plays whose dialogues will be mouthed by rickshaw drivers, road diggers, koli women selling fresh fish, nurses in hospitals, *doodhwallahs*[14] and *isstriwallahs*[15] and *paanwallahs*[16] and the newspaper vendors who distribute the newspapers to each of our homes but do *not* read them.

All of them consume cinema. But do they consume plays? If not, why not!

I shared this with a friend. She said, why is this important?

Perhaps it is not.

This is the time to remember a man with a very fine nose: Gabriel García Márquez. I nominate him for one of the finest pairs of nostrils of the twentieth century. Márquez and M.K. Gandhi and Lenin and Agarkar[17] (although technically Agarkar is nineteenth century) and Kosambi[18] and Bob Dylan.

---

11 Major Indian artists; the NGMA is the National Gallery of Modern Art.
12 Manmohan Desai (1937–94): Indian film director, many of whose films were popular hits.
13 Narayan Gangaram Surve (1926–2010): An important Marathi poet.
14 Milk-sellers.
15 Isstriwallahs iron clothes for a living.
16 Vendors of paan, a preparation of betel chewed as a digestive stimulant and narcotic.
17 Gopal Ganesh Agarkar (1856–96): Indian social reformer and educationist.
18 D.D. Kosambi (1907–66): Indian intellectual and polymath.

In fact, Nobel laureate Bob Dylan had such a fine nose that he decided to sing through it.

So be it!

When Gabriel García Márquez (GGM) writes a book like *One Hundred Years of Solitude* he is saying many things. One, he is telling us the story of Macondo village. But what my nose inferred is that an entire nation and its people and their voice plus their noses have been forgotten for a hundred years.

And mankind cannot afford to do that again.

Yet. There are many more voices that need to be heard.

Which is why we need many more noses that should be permitted to infer.

The other day I had to explain "what is an Indian village" to young children in a school. These were privileged children who had never seen a village. I started to do so.

After a few minutes I realised I was talking about Maryganj in Phanishwar Nath Renu's *Maila Aanchal*; Gangoli in Rahi Masoom Raza's *Aadha Gaon*; Shivpalganj in Shreelal Shukla's *Raga Durbari*; Manohar Shyam Joshi's *Kasap*; and the village in Munshi Premchand's novel *Godaan*. These five milestone books in Hindi had shaped my nose's understanding of a village.

Life was imitating art!

Dear Fellowshippers and theatrewallahs, please ask yourself to think about that one nose whose inference impresses you. It can be the nose of Sophocles, or the noses of Renu and Raza and Shukla and Joshi.

Or it can be the noses that blow their phlegm and snot on the streets of Shaniwar Peth or Koregaon Park.[19] The local colloquialisms, the gaalis,[20] the sound effects, the sentences without verbs, the hotchpotch of two languages clashing into each other. The Marathi of the Peshwas clashing with the Marathi

---

19 Localities in Pune.
20 Terms of abuse.

of the Kunbis.[21] The Marathi of Khandesh mingling with the Marathi of Konkan.[22]

III

I request the Five Fellowshippers to touch the tips of their noses yet again.
Ask your nose these questions!
Can you narrate your story on stage with someone else's words?
Will you be able to watch the drama unfold from the wings?
In 2050—if this planet is still going round and round the sun—will you be able to tolerate your creation?
These are the questions all of us need to ask our noses.
It is called the *Naak Mein Dum*[23] Test.
But don't fret.
Creating is simple. Don't complicate it.
The eighteenth-century poet and playwright Schiller kept a bunch of rotting apples in his drawer. He said they sparked creativity.
Schiller would stick his feet in tubs of cold water.
Contrariwise: Vijay Tendulkar wrote anywhere and everywhere. Neither noise nor voice could deter him. When in doubt, he would not be intimidated by his nose. Instead, he would start picking his nose.
Márquez aka GGM kept yellow roses in his house, on his table. Always yellow roses. He felt nothing awful would happen to him if those flowers were around. He had to be surrounded by yellow roses and he had to be surrounded by women.
There were writers who listened to music while writing and then these writers wrote sentences the way Beethoven wrote musical scores or Chick Correa improvised his jazz notations.

---

21 Peshwas ... Kunbis: In effect, the "princes" and the "peasants".
22 Khandesh, Konkan: Different areas of Maharashtra.
23 Botheration.

Some created while sitting, others imitated the master painters—and created while standing.

And so Ernest Hemingway, Charles Dickens, Virginia Woolf and Lewis Carroll wrote their best works standing up.

Tendulkar wrote vertically, horizontally, semi-vertically, and semi-horizontally.

My grandfather (a Sanskrit professor from Lahore) introduced me to three great writers: Gurdial Singh,[24] Kedarnath Singh,[25] and Faiz.[26] Papaji (my grandfather) told me that Khushwant Singh[27] started writing each of his new books with the most expensive pen in the market. Also, he wrote only on yellow, ruled pads. These pads were imported from a single, very fancy shop in Paris.

Speaking of poshness and taste.

What *is* taste?

One, as aforementioned, please have a good pedigree nose.

Two, do not pick the good pedigree nose when you are receiving the Sangeet Natak Akademi[28] (if you ever get it by fluke). On that day, please ensure your nose behaves in front of the President.

Three, ask your nose questions. For example, if your nose claims to be a proud Marathi nose, ask your nose, *Naak Bhau*,[29] have you heard of the six theorists in Marathi literature? Ra Bha Patankar and Sudhir Rasal and Ra Ga Jadhav and Da Ga Godse and Ma Su Patil and the Dadaist Ashok Shahane?[30]

If your nose is dangling in the air, change the subject.

---

24 Gurdial Singh Rahi (1933–2016): Punjabi writer.
25 Kedarnath Singh (1934–2018): Hindi poet.
26 Faiz Ahmad Faiz (1911–84): Urdu poet.
27 Khushwant Singh (1915–2014): Prominent Indian novelist, historian, journalist, diplomat, and politician.
28 An award, the highest national recognition given in India to practising artists, teachers, and scholars.
29 Mister Nose.
30 R.B. Patankar, etc.: Eminent writers and critics.

Ask the following questions.

Why does Kedarnath Singh reciting his poems have only 234 views on YouTube?

Why does the playwright Tom Stoppard delivering a lecture on good theatre have 4321 views on YouTube?

And why do three songs choreographed by Prabhu Deva for Hrithik Roshan, Dhanush and Arjuna have more than one billion views, each?

Is this the nature of the beast?

Will theatre always remain a minority art?

If your nose is unable to answer these questions, *aapki naak katt gayi, samajh lo*.[31]

Unless, we ensure through feng shui and vaastu[32] that bad taste and bad art have bad karma. For starters, imagine what would happen if middle-class people stopped purchasing plastic flowers, those wooden birds on living room walls, those hideous curtains, those Nilkamal chairs, those scene-scenerywallah bedsheets.

But is this the only way to alter people's bad taste? Ask your Left Nostril this question.

Question: Why Left Nostril?

Answer: According to the Latest Nostril and Nose Survey Index commissioned by Nikoloi Gogol,[33] *the Left Nostril is much more amenable to radical ideas than the Right Nostril.*

So, scare the perpetrators of bad taste like they scare you about how a copy of the Mahabharata inside your home will ensure the battle of Kurukshetra in your living room. Similarly, we (theatrewallahs) should spread rumours that if you watch a bad TV soap, your mobile phone will be auto-locked for thirteen days; or if you pick up a floral dress in seven gaudy colours, your banker will run away with your fixed deposit.

---

31 "Your nose got cut, understand!" (a great insult).
32 Traditional Indian theory of architecture and design.
33 Nikolai Gogol (1809–52): Russian author who wrote the satirical short story *The Nose*.

Instead, we must convince them to own a copy of one great play by each of the great playwrights.

Start with A for Aristophanes.

Brekekekekex koax[34]—in my view, this is the best piece of dialogue writing, ever. This is from Aristophanes's play *The Frogs* (penned in 405 BC).

Speaking of great playwrights, it's bizarre how we reduce every great writer to one play.

And so Bhartendu Harishchandra[35] is known for *Andher Nagri*.

Bhuvneshwar[36] for *Tambe Ke Keede*.

Swadesh Deepak[37] for *Court Martial*.

Dharamvir Bharati[38] for *Andha Yug*.

The point is, don't reduce the greats to one work.

The point also is: don't reduce your creation to one thing.

Don't reduce your own work to one theme, and one grand idea.

Yes, you have one nose.

But that apparatus breathes a million times in your lifetime.

And each breath of air is a life saver.

---

34 From the famous Chorus of the Frogs in Aristophanes's play.
35 Bhartendu Harishchandra (1850–85): Major Indian poet, dramatist, and prose-writer. *Andher Nagri* was not his only play.
36 Bhuvneshwar Prasad (1911–57): His *Tambe Ke Keede* (1946), penned around the time of Samuel Beckett's *Waiting for Godot*, is the Hindi play that shaped Indian theatre most in the twentieth century. A tormented genius about whom not much is known (which is the reason why I am extra fond of him).
37 Swadesh Deepak (b. 1943): Indian playwright. *Court Martial* (1991) is his best-known play, but (according to Deepak himself) not his best.
38 Dharamvir Bharati (1926–97): Distinguished Hindi writer. His play *Andha Yug* (1953) is regarded as a classic.

IV

We live in an age where everyone else's nose will want your nose to create a town that is engulfed with the smell of chikoos,[39] or a town that you can only walk into with your nose covered because of the stench of hydrogen sulphide from the factories.

In the good old days, the high and mighty noses wanted theatrewallahs to create socialist noses, or communist noses, or mythological noses, or folklorish noses. Basically, the idea of a committed nose and a nose that stood for social protest. And you have had legendary theatrewallahs who have been accused of having noses that practised politics, or nose activists who felt the need to dictate to theatrewallahs what was right or wrong or, to be dialectically proper, Left or Right. And if your nose didn't know how to create works in a particular way, your nose was a reactionary nose.

As you can imagine, there is a massive Nose Industry that drives our planet.

So dear Five Fellowshippers—what is the duty of your nose? What about your nose's revolutionary duty? What is your nose's creative duty?

When Tendulkar Saab was asked this question: first and foremost, he scratched his nose. Then he said, I think the question is interesting. But the basic idea is to create theatre that is alive and kicking and not create plays in a premeditated way.

I see some of you are getting restless.

Your noses are twitching.

Some of your noses want to sneeze.

Some of your noses want to know if something is going on under your nose.

So, let me be brief from hereon, and try to wrap this up with three final things.

---

39 A type of fruit-tree common in Maharashtra.

Point 1

Some of you know me as a person who researches. Is that good or bad? It is good. Everyone must research. The problem arises when the research shows. The ideal situation is for your work to be like a magic act. Like an exemplary magician, you must reveal nothing. Like a magician, you do the trick, but the audience must never know how the trick is done. Like a magician, you will pour a lot of energy into research, the technique, the science, and R&D, and riyaz,[40] and rehearsals. But ultimately, it's all for that Aha! moment. There is *no* escaping research.

Let me explain. I recall looking at a black and white photograph online. It was of a library. When I looked at it, I knew that it was a writer's library or a professional journalist's library. Because when I zoomed into the photograph, I saw ten to twenty books about vast and myriad topics. There was the history of Aztec bones, a book on assassinated world leaders, a book on how to crack jokes with a straight face, eleven tips on how to make your own cigarettes, a map of the moon's surface, etc.

I was right. It was a photograph of Ernest Hemingway's library in Cuba. He was researching for a short story.

Point 2

I recall some fun banter with Namdeo Dhasal.[41] He said that the best place for a writer like me to live in was—a brothel.

Why? I asked him.

He said: Millions of great conversations, all kinds of characters, every night there's a party. Plus, all kinds of people: businessmen, politicians from Mantralaya, Kamathipura construction workers, taxiwallahs, and you have a very good relationship with the police because they are present 24/7.

---

40 Music practice.
41 Namdeo Laxman Dhasal (1949–2014): Marathi poet, writer, and Dalit activist.

When I looked at him, a bit sceptical, Dhasal added that a brothel offers the best hours for a writer to work, which is the morning time. Mornings in a hotel are always the most peaceful and tranquil, and there is that edgy smell of sex, booze and gaanja[42] in the atmosphere.

Of course, Dhasal was making fun of gentrified middle-class writers. But the larger point he wanted to make was: stay connected with life.

Let me explain.

A decade or so ago, I was on a tour through Uttar Pradesh. It was for a project for a major newspaper. It meant travelling from Mathura to Gorakhpur. On an average one town per day. On one occasion I met a Bahubali.[43] At that time, he reigned supreme. Later, they locked him up. Then he contested elections and was elected as an MP with a thumping majority. His ops: a hundred murders, plus a crime network involving opium, borewell scams, and money laundering.

When he formed a political party he was under surveillance. One of Bahubali's strategies to distract the intelligence agents was faking conversations on telephone lines. He had a battalion of young boys who worked for him. On cue, one of these innocuous, illiterate kids would enter an STD booth and make a telephone call to one of the numbers that were under surveillance. These boys would conjure up the most surreal and absurd conversations on the phone. The idea was that the CBI or CID or whoever was monitoring these conversations would be totally confused.

Please understand. At any point in time there were hundreds of plays being enacted on these malfunctioning telephone lines from UP to Delhi. Now think about the predicament of the trained professionals in their suits-and-boots who were listening to these conversations.

---

42 Hashish.
43 A strongman.

Please note that this is not exclusively a UP phenomenon.

Let me introduce you to another gent with a mighty fine nose. He does not live in Awadh or Bundelkhand. He lives in San Francisco. His name is David Streitfeld. He is a scribe for the *New York Times*. He was part of a team that bagged the 2013 Pulitzer Prize for Explanatory Reporting on how the economy was being reshaped by Apple with their factory that manufactured fake reviews.

More power to Mr Streitfeld's nose.

But the question my nose asks me, in the era of fake news, is, if what Mr Streitfeld says is true, what is real, and what is unreal? What is not fake, and what is a lie? What is life, and what is play?

Point 3

Since I have mentioned Márquez aka GGM, let me conclude with a short story of his, "Sleeping Beauty and the Airplane". Like most of GGM, the story is about many things. But the plot is this: there's a passenger who notices a Sleeping Beauty, a very, very beautiful woman. The passenger sighs, and he asks the attendant at the ticket counter whether she believes in love at first sight. The clerk responds: Is there any other kind of love? Because the other kinds are so impossible to handle.

I deployed this line in a play of mine called *3 Sakina Manzil*. A play that got a pat on the back from both Tendulkar Saab and Dubey Saab, on the same day.

Those are the days you live for. If you are a theatrewallah. A pat on the back.

That's also the time I realised it's *only* one day, out of 11,680 days of doing theatre.

A percentage of 0.00856.

That's it.

Dear Five Fellowshippers: That's why we theatrewallahs exist, I guess. For a pat on the back from someone whose nose we look up to.

So, Five Fellowshippers, besides keeping your noses clean and doing hot-water fomentation with eucalyptus oil, please do ensure that those who watch your work or see your work fall in love with it, in a few seconds.

Question: What is art?
Answer: 0.00856
That's art.
To make someone fall in love at first sight.

Don't think about commas and semicolons and full stops and adverbs.

Also, don't think about dates and theatre festivals and box office and petty politics and reviews and previews.

Think about your face—and, more importantly, the nose on that face—printed on a postage stamp.

Don't think about how millions of people will be licking the postage stamp, and how the postage stamp will be lying around in nooks and corners with cockroaches and centipedes trampling on your nose.

Just think how your stamp will ensure a twenty-first-century Romeo and Laila or Juliet and Majnu in Muzaffarpur or Una will pen the most beautiful love letters to each other. And then they will put your stamp on the envelope to cement their love.

That's the moment your nose will twinkle like a star in the sky.

I think that's it. Those are the points I wanted to share with you. I hope they are useful.

All the best to all of you—and indeed all of us.

Theatre zindabad.

Long live your nose.

Long live our nose.

Many Ways to Make a Play
Shanta Gokhale

Shanta Gokhale is a Mumbai-based writer, translator, theatre critic, and cultural columnist. She has been a lecturer in English, a public relations executive, and arts editor of *The Times of India*, Mumbai, and has written two award-winning novels in Marathi and three plays, staged in Mumbai and elsewhere. She has authored a critical history of Marathi drama, edited three books on theatre, and translated various works from Marathi into English and vice-versa. She won the Sangeet Natak Akademi award (2016) for overall contribution to the performing arts, the Balshastri Jambhekar Award (2016) for translation, the Ooty Literary Festival Lifetime Achievement Award (2018), Theatre Group Thespo's Lifetime Achievement Award (2018), the Maharashtra Foundation's Lifetime Achievement Award (2019), the Tata Literature Live! Lifetime Achievement Award (2019), and a Sahitya Akademi award for translation (2021).

~

Harold Pinter has said,

> I have often been asked how my plays come about. I cannot say. Nor can I ever sum up my plays, except to say that this is what happened. That is what they said. That is what they did.[1]

One of Pinter's plays, *The Homecoming* (1965), started with the line, "What have you done with the scissors?"[2] When the line came into his head, he did not know who was going to say it to whom. All he had was a line that could start a conversation. He would call the characters in the conversation A, B and C till they put on enough flesh and blood in the course of writing to acquire names.

In contrast to Pinter, Vijay Tendulkar:[3]

> I could not proceed to write a play unless I saw my characters as real-life people, unless I could see them moving, doing things by themselves, unless I heard them emoting, talking to each other. I was never able to begin writing my play only with an idea or a theme in mind.[4]

Now here's Simon McBurney of Complicité. He has read G.H. Hardy's *A Mathematician's Apology* and wants to make a theatrical piece based on it. So he calls his team together, they toss ideas and scenes around, and a few weeks down the

---

1 Harold Pinter. "Art, Truth and Politics". Acceptance lecture on receiving the 2005 Nobel Prize for Literature. At https://www.nobelprize.org/prizes/literature/2005/pinter/25621-harold-pinter-nobel-lecture-2005/
2 Harold Pinter. *The Homecoming* (1965). Faber, 1999, 3.
3 Vijay Tendulkar (1928–2008): Influential playwright, film and television writer, essayist, political journalist, and social commentator who wrote primarily in Marathi.
4 Vijay Tendulkar. *The Play is the Thing*. Sri Ram Memorial Lecture X. Sri Ram Centre for Performing Arts, 1997, 15.

line, they have devised the stunning piece of theatre called *A Disappearing Number*.[5]

I will now dare to insert myself into this august company. I am an old-fashioned playwright. By which I mean that I sit in front of my computer and write for days together in total isolation. What comes out at the end is something I consider, at that point, to be a complete play, ready for the stage. Whether it makes it there or not is another matter.

The question that writers get asked most frequently about their work, whether they write novels, plays or short stories is, "Where do your ideas come from?" I have quoted Pinter's and Tendulkar's contrasting answers to the question. Mine is a third way of coming to a play. I feel compelled to write a play when happenings around me throw up disquieting questions. Writing a play is my way of arriving at some answers.

My first play, *Avinash*,[6] grew out of a sense of dejection over our attitudes towards mental illness. Several instances had been piling up in my mind over the years.

A neighbour had married off his mentally disturbed son to "cure" him of his condition.

My Master of Social Work colleague and her UK-educated husband had had their mentally challenged daughter exorcised of the "evil eye".

An old school friend had invited me to tea. In the middle of our cheerful conversation I heard an agonised cry from an inner room. I stopped mid-sentence, shocked. My friend said with equanimity, "Don't worry. It's only my sister. She's retarded so we keep her tied up."

Then I heard that a friend's middle-class, upper-caste landlord had thrown his wife out of the house because she had "gone mad".

---

5   Simon McBurney (Theatre Complicité). *A Disappearing Number*. Oberon, 2008.
6   Seagull, 1993.

This was the tipping point. I simply had to write a play to sort this thing out. I allowed some time to elapse to distance myself from the immediate event. I did not want details from real stories to creep into my play. Those stories were at the foundation of my play; but the structure had to be a work of imagination.

Gradually a situation, a family, the dramatic event around which it would reveal its attitudes began to take shape in my mind. The protagonist was to be called Avinash. He was to throw up his job and lie in bed all day drinking, occasionally letting out a cry of frustration. The big question was how to put such a disruptive force on stage in the midst of his family. Would it not lead to a play of mutual recriminations, screaming and shouting? A loud melodrama in fact? That was not the play I wanted to write. My interest was in exploring how this middle-class family responded to the stress of having a person like Avinash in their midst. How they negotiated their love, fear, and impatience to arrive at answers based on their beliefs. One day it struck me that I could choose not to have Avinash on the stage at all. In his state of depression, he would confine himself to his partitioned room. But that partition would cast its long shadow, literally and metaphorically, over the whole play. Avinash's very absence would turn into a dark, looming presence.

Often, all you require is a theatrical device to set you free to write the play you want to write. The actual writing is a matter of time and craft. It took me roughly ten days to write *Avinash*. Magically, six weeks after it was written, it was on the stage, directed by Satyadev Dubey.[7] His stature being what it was, this was like an ISI mark[8] on the play. His production in the original language, Marathi, was followed by productions in Hindi, Kannada, Malayalam and, years later, in Assamese.

---

7   Satyadev Dubey (1936–2011): Major figure in Indian theatre as director, actor, and playwright, also a film screenwriter, actor, and director.
8   Certification of quality by the Bureau of Indian Standards (formerly the Indian Standards Institution).

I wrote my next play, *Dip and Dop*, in English in the late 1980s. As a liberal who believed reason to be a better guide to human action than emotion, I was disturbed to see the growing power of Hindutva, the right-wing political ideology, which constantly harked back to a selectively imagined "glorious past" to whip up false pride and gain control over people's minds. The play that emerged from the situation was a wacky *pas de deux* between two sisters. Its light-hearted absurdity clearly indicated that I was not unduly worried about this lurking beast swallowing up the world as I knew it. In my play, Dip the older sister is a dedicated homemaker who cooks the same brinjal[9] curry every day but with renewed fervour, believing it to be the best in the world. Dop, the younger sister, is an aspiring writer who, although she barricades herself behind books, is still under Big Sister's constant watch. Her fictional characters, however, escape in the night to romp around freely while Big Sister is sleeping. The performance space was confined within counters holding huge cooking vessels and other household equipment. In one corner stood an immense vat of pickles made by MOTHER before she died. Dop complains mildly of its stink, and the mould that is gathering on it. Dip asks how Dop can say such things about MOTHER'S PICKLES! The only way Dop can survive and grow as a writer is to escape this claustrophobic atmosphere. Finally she does, leaving Dop feeling that she and MOTHER have been betrayed.

Zubin Driver, who writes and directs edgy, way-out plays, was rehearsing *Dip and Dop* for a full-fledged production. Dolly Thakore was to play Dip and Deepika Roy, Dop. Then someone fell ill or had to go abroad or something, and the play ended as a reading.

A freelance playwright's life is as vivid an illustration as you can get of the many slips that occur 'twixt the cup and the lip.

---

9   Brinjal: Eggplant, or aubergine.

I wrote my next play in Marathi. Osho[10] had died mysteriously in 1990, suspected of having been poisoned by his confidantes. He was one of a train of prominent gurus and godmen in India who wielded unimaginable power over people's minds and lives. The most powerful of them lived unabashedly flamboyant lives. Dhirendra Brahmachari had been one such in the 1970s and '80s, suspected of brokering defence deals. The closeness of gurus to political power centres granted them immunity from scrutiny, allowing them to use their sprawling ashrams as facades for their unsavoury activities. So-called spirituality, political power and shady business deals made a murky nexus that undermined the country's interests in unseen ways. I had to write a play to explore this ugly underbelly of our society.

What excites me most when I start contemplating writing a play about a contemporary issue is converting it into a compelling human situation. To do this, I allow fleeting ideas to gather in my mind undisturbed. While I go about life, my subconscious is at work absorbing and sifting experiences, mixing them with dreams and long-lost memories till suddenly one day it sends something floating up—a situation or a character or relationships that I can forge a play with. In the present case I had all of them, but no form to carry the load. I knew my godman was going to be an innocent dispenser of spiritual counsel who was to be trapped later into providing a face for a wayward son's gunrunning business. The godman was soon to be murdered and his death announced as the result of natural causes. But his wife would find out the truth, landing her in a dangerous situation. So she would stitch up her lips till such time as an opportunity presented itself to expose the truth. I even had a title for the play. *Why Are You Mum, Mrs P?*

I waited patiently for the form to turn up

---

10 Chandra Mohan Jain (1931–90), also known as "Rajneesh" or "Bhagwan".

One day it happened—the eureka moment. A memory returned of the afternoon I had watched a Ras Lila[11] performance in Imphal and been deeply moved. The dancers had performed in a circular space with the audience sitting all around. Presiding over the performance was the *sabhapati* (father of the performance), whose costume and demeanour carried spiritual force. His role was to indicate by the subtlest of gestures that somebody, a dancer or a member of the audience, was transgressing *auchitya*, the principle of aesthetic propriety, by a show of excessive emotion.

I had my form. My actors would be artisanal. They would trundle on to the stage the tall ladder seat on which the sabhapati would sit. They would draw the circle that marked the performance space. They would sit on the stage watching the performance. They would rise on cue, and as they entered the circular space, the audience would see them transform themselves from actors into characters. The sabhapati would set the play going by reminding the actors of the ancient art of which they were practitioners. What they did in the performance space had to be worthy of that tradition. The main narrative was to be enacted in the circle and the two tributary narratives on its periphery. The space for the *sutradhar* (narrator) and *vidushak* (clown), the latter played against tradition by a female actor, would lie outside both. This pair would address the audience directly.

Why Are You Mum, Mrs P? went through four drafts, each prompted by my theatre instincts and comments made by theatre groups and friends to whom I read the play. Had somebody shown an interest in directing it, it would have gone through further changes. Rehearsals are an unfailing test of how a play will flow in performance. There is only so much that the writer can visualise sitting at her desk. If the director and actors are to make the play

---

11 The Manipuri Ras Lila is a formal dance celebrating the divine love of Lord Krishna and his devotee Radha. Five forms of Ras Lila are performed in three different styles in the front courtyards of temples. The chief temple for the dance is the Sri Govindaji temple in Imphal.

their own, they will ask for changes. Dubey asked for a different ending for *Avinash*. He wanted a statement that would close the open end I had written. So I wrote a long speech for him, but later changed it to something like the previous ending. Sunil Shanbag, who directed the Hindi translation of the play, liked what I wrote and kept it in his production.

Why Are You Mum, Mrs P? was never performed. One reason was its huge cast. By the mid-1990s, the economy had been fully liberalised, making it difficult for fringe groups to do theatre on shoestring budgets. Satellite TV had entered our lives in a big way, bleeding theatre of its writing and acting talent. Bowing to circumstances outside her control, Mrs P left the scene and has been sitting mum in my file ever since, not unstageable in theory, but unstaged in practice.

In November 2008, Prithvi Theatre, an intimate space in Juhu, Mumbai's northern suburb, celebrated Satyadev Dubey's work with a massive exhibition. The director of Prithvi, Sanjna Kapoor, asked if I could write a script for an inaugural show that would bring memories of his ways and plays back to the stage. It was a one-off show that I was very happy to write. I knew Dubey's work well and he was a dear friend too. Sunil Shanbag directed the show. This led to his asking me many months later to consider writing a play about censorship, with Vijay Tendulkar's *Sakharam Binder* at its centre.

Tendulkar had written the play in the 1970s, a decade in which singers, writers, playwrights, and students were challenging the establishment, questioning the moth-eaten morality of the middle-class, and declaring, with Bob Dylan, that "The times they are a-changing". Three plays written by Tendulkar in that decade had set the official and street censors on his tail. *Sakharam Binder* was one of them. The official censor board had asked for some thirty-five cuts in it, enough to destroy the play. The producer and director had taken their fight against this unreasonable stipulation to court. I had translated the play into English for the benefit of non-Marathi-speaking lawyers and judges involved in the case. The case was fought and won. However, even after the play was granted legal permission for performance, groups belonging to the Hindu right made life miserable for everybody involved in it. I interspersed in my play those scenes from *Sakharam Binder* that had invited their most violent wrath. The narrators of the play, which Sunil had titled *Sex, Morality and Censorship*, were a *shahir*[12] and *lavni*[13] dancer from the traditional *tamasha*[14] form of Maharashtra. Tamasha had been an early victim of moralistic sanitisation by the government, so they had a natural place in the play.

Sex, Morality and Censorship was first performed in 2009, and has had a long and successful run.

The seed for my next play was sown around 2010, when Irom Chanu Sharmila, a frail young peace activist from Imphal, Manipur, completed ten years of a Gandhian hunger strike she had undertaken to demand the abolition of the Armed Forces Special Powers Act (AFSPA), 1958. Manipur had been declared a "disturbed area" and AFSPA had been enacted by Parliament to allow the army a free hand to shoot and kill anybody they suspected of being an insurgent. The army was not expected to rape, but they did that as well. Sharmila had started her fast three days after she witnessed what came to be known as the Malom massacre, when soldiers had shot and killed ten innocent civilians standing at a bus-stop.

I became interested in her fight when I realised that ten years of fasting had brought her no nearer to her goal than she had been when she started. I had to write a play about what was going on. I began collecting every piece of material I could lay my hands on about Sharmila and her battle. I did not want to write an activist play to inform an audience of the events of her life and chivvy it

---

12 The "poet-composer" in the role of narrator.
13 A song-dance combination popular in Maharashtra.
14 A lively, traditional Marathi folk art form, often with singing and dancing, frequently presented by local or travelling performers.

into sympathy for her and her cause. What I was interested in doing was to see her in the larger context of war, violence and the eternal battle between the individual and the state (Anouilh's *Antigone* leapt to mind).

While these ideas were becoming crystallised in my mind, serendipity landed a gift in my lap. I saw an Indian production of Richard Shannon's *The Lady of Burma*. There were distinct parallels between Aung San Suu Kyi's imprisonment by the junta in Myanmar and Sharmila's hospital imprisonment in Imphal. But Shannon did not address the questions that interested me. His approach to Suu Kyi's story was simple. The actor who played Suu Kyi would sit in the prison of her home, recalling the most painful events of her life—her mother's illness and death, her brother's accidental death, her husband's death in England by cancer—interspersing them with accounts of the political events she had been part of. At the end of the play, I found myself agreeing with the British critic who had remarked that it might just as well have been a radio play.

Shannon's play became a negative pointer. I decided to keep Sharmila off the stage. On stage I had another protagonist called Woman who goes through a nightmarish experience. Woken from her afternoon siesta by a gunshot, she finds her neat middle-class home invaded by a storyteller, his group of musicians and other assorted people floating in and out. Their stories and the pictures they display in her picture window of Sharmila in hospital and the violence in Manipur, a window that otherwise opens on to a pretty patch of garden, gradually change her attitude to Sharmila from indifference and scepticism to awe and respect.

The Fair One, as I called the long one-acter, was done and ready for the stage. It was read, appreciated, but not performed.

Then the story changed. Sixteen years into her fast, Sharmila gave it up. She decided to stand for elections. She received a drubbing. She was rejected by her people for betraying the cause. Her family turned their backs on her because she had fallen in love with an "outsider" and planned to marry him. Suddenly she had no home to go to except the very hospital where she had been incarcerated for sixteen years. It was a uniquely painful situation that needed to be written about as a second act to my play. Documentary material of this phase of Sharmila's life was meagre and scrappy. But that worked very well for me. Out of those scraps I wrote a second act in which I imagined the effects on her of being force-fed for sixteen years, of being rejected by her people and of now facing two clear choices for the future. Which would she choose?

The well-known playwright-director Mahesh Dattani, who had recently relaunched his old theatre group Playpen, asked if he could do the play. I was hardly going to say no. They did two preparatory readings before small audiences to feel their way into the play. Then they did a run of six shows. The production had to be crowd-funded. No producer would touch it, despite Dattani's clout in the field, because of its political content. He called the play *Mengoubi, The Fair One*.[15] It was a sensitive, beautifully performed and sung production.

In 2014, a radical political transformation took place in India. We saw a new kind of political game being played, a new kind of politician taking the stage, a new ideology being promoted and greedily devoured by the public. It was a deeply troubling situation for people who believed in democracy and the Constitution. I began to feel the push to write a play examining what makes a ruthlessly ambitious politician. I read analyses of democracy. I read about Adivasis whose exploitation I was going to depict. I read articles about the liberating but also dangerous impact of the new media, particularly WhatsApp, on our politics and people. As I read and thought, my protagonist began to gain shape. He came from a background of humanist ideals but lost

---

15 Shanta Gokhale. *Mengoubi, The Fair One*. Dhauli, 2019.

his moral compass on his way to the top. A bhajan[16] that my mother had been taught by her guru, written by a comparatively unknown Hindi poet but set to a haunting tune, returned to me. I made it the theme song of the play because it traced the protagonist's moral decline perfectly.

> How shall I come before you my Lord in this stained shawl? It was pristine when you sent me down to earth. But my deeds have stained it. How shall I come before you wearing it?

I called the play *Maili Chadar—The Stained Shawl*.

Maili Chadar was read at Studio Tamaasha under Irawati Karnik's direction. This was Sunil Shanbag and Sapan Saran's sixty-seater space in Versova, a northern suburb of Mumbai. It took three-and-a-half hours to read. Sunil said afterwards that it was a powerful play but too risky to perform in these times.

To me theatre is nothing if not risky. However, if a playwright chooses to write such plays, she must not expect to see them performed. She can't have her cake and eat it too.

---

16 Devotional song.

Poems Matter Because They Have Holes

Making Peace with Language and Myself

Arundhathi Subramaniam

Arundhathi Subramaniam has been described as "one of the finest poets writing in India today". She is the author of thirteen books, including five volumes of poetry. Widely translated and anthologised, *When God is a Traveller* (HarperCollins, 2014) was the Season Choice of the Poetry Book Society and was shortlisted for the T.S. Eliot Prize. It also won the Sahitya Akademi Award in 2020. *Love Without a Story* was published in India (Context, 2019) and the United Kingdom (Bloodaxe, 2020). As editor, her most recent book is an acclaimed anthology of medieval Indian sacred poetry, *Eating God* (Penguin Ananda, 2014). Other works include *The Book of Buddha* (Penguin Viking, 2005); the bestselling biography of a contemporary mystic, *Sadhguru: More Than a Life* (Penguin Ananda, 2010); and, most recently, *Adiyogi: The Source of Yoga* (Element, 2017, co-authored with Sadhguru). She is the recipient of various Indian and international awards and fellowships, including the inaugural Khushwant Singh Prize, the Raza Award for Poetry, the Zee Women's Award for Literature, the International Piero Bigongiari Prize in Italy, the Mystic Kalinga award, and the Charles Wallace, Visiting Arts and Homi Bhabha Fellowships, among others.

~

It fits like soul-skin sometimes. And it takes one hell of a lot of nip and tuck and darn at others. We've had a long and interesting courtship, with all the fear and mistrust that goes with intimacy.

That's English for me.

It was Thomas à Kempis who said he'd rather experience "contrition" than know how to define it. I commiserate with that. I don't know how to define English, and I don't know whether it's good for my health, my moral fibre, my politics, or my inner well-being. But it is the language I know.

It's the language I fight in, wonder in—on occasion, dream in. The language I wear closest to my skin. Pyjama language, in a manner of speaking.

It's the language I write poetry in as well, which makes it endoderm language. Or more. The language *under* my skin. The language I breathe in. Well, almost.

Let me just say I'm comfortable enough with it to laugh at the snobberies of my "English-medium" education. And comfortable enough to enjoy words like "archipelago" and "palimpsest" and "peripatetic" without apology for my polysyllabic fascinations.

Belonging doesn't come easy, though. There will always be bits of the self that stick out, that stay obstinately unmapped. Belonging nowhere, belonging everywhere—both seem to take negotiation.

There are some places I know I don't belong to, however. I don't belong to the tribe that sees English as a sign of Western contamination, or to that which sees it as a passport (along with fairness creams and smartphones) to the Great Indian Dream. I don't belong to the tribe that seeks to consciously "sully" it, or to that which believes it must be cleansed.

I am an amateur. A diehard amateur. An unlicensed practitioner. A non-card-carrying lover of English. A language upstart. That is the only way I can enter this space, the only way that empowers me, the only way that makes sense to me—particularly with a language that has its battalions of experts on everything, from its anatomy to its geopolitics, from its chemistry to its palmistry, from its rhyme to its reason.

> …No, we don't serve up
> neat styrofoamed verse.
> We sprawl, we lumber, we stain.
> We love like everyone else,
> with the thick odour of pathology.
>
> We are ink and syrup
> and virulent acid.
> We are the midgets
> who turn in three strides
> into lords of the universe.
> We are here to restore order,
> to put the voices—of books, lovers,
> teachers, customs officials—
> in their places.
>
> We are the upstarts,
> ready finally to take up space,
> demand time,
> settle down on the page.
>
> —"Claim"

Upstart-ness, I've found, doesn't entail *trying* to be mutinous. I don't have to split my infinitives or roughen my cadences to prove my distance from a colonial history. I don't have to write about caste violence and communal genocide, tsunamis and Himalayan yogis, to establish my cultural credentials. I don't have to pepper my work with Tamil phrases or Sanskrit aphorisms to underscore my rootedness. In short, I don't have to try to be idiosyncratic. I don't have to try to be a cultural oddball, to prove that I am different or contemporary or cutting edge. I don't have to try to be *anti*-English to prove I'm politically kosher.

There are multiple ways to question, to critique, to examine a heritage, without denying, severing or feigning amnesia over it. I don't feel the need to amputate my history; I merely don't want to be a puppet of it.

My journey through language is about my journey to become *me*.

It is a journey that seems to call for relentless, interminable subtraction. But subtraction isn't just pain; it is also elation. Outsider-ness isn't just about feeling evicted, lost, homeless. It is about growing lighter, less encumbered, about finding sudden exhilarating vantage points and deeper views of the canyon of cultural memory than ever before. The outsider can be a fugitive. The outsider can also be a guest, even a welcome visitor.

> Give me a home
> that isn't mine,
> where I can slip in and out of rooms
> without a trace,
> never worrying
> about the plumbing,
> the colour of the curtains,
> the cacophony of books by the bedside.
>
> A home that I can wear lightly,
> where the rooms aren't clogged
> with yesterday's conversations,

where the self doesn't bloat
to fill in the crevices.

A home, like this body,
so alien when I try to belong,
so hospitable
when I decide I'm just visiting.

—"Home"

~

A journey from English to english sounds facetious. But it's not far from the truth. "There are fewer capital letters / than we supposed" I wrote in a poem some years ago. This is a tale about coming to terms with language as a lower-case affair—emphatically not about capital letters. This is also a tale about coming to terms with language as a substance riddled with holes. (English to english to en_lish, one might say, if one were being coyly graphic.)

English has meant resource and refuge, scalpel, scimitar, and sanctuary over the years. Increasingly, it is a process, an unfolding, potholed and uncertain, a journey that entails leaps and unexpected trapdoors.

I've struggled and I've floundered. I've revelled in its alien delights, its treasures, its rich elsewhere-ness. But I've also seen it as homecoming, resorted to it in times of need. And while it has sustained me, it has also, on occasion, betrayed me.

It's been a journey from awe to acquisition, apprenticeship to armed conflict, armistice to awe all over again. (Although none of it has been as linear as it sounds.) I'm not sure I'll ever make my peace with all the tripping, the falling, the plummeting it entails. But then what of those times when it stretches out in its glory—a long, breathtaking Persian carpet to the stars?

I remember early encounters with nonsense verse in Tamil, bits of doggerel in Hindi, nursery rhymes in English. I didn't have a clue what any of it meant; I loved it all the same. I remind myself of this now: the fact that the sound patterns of poetry sustained me at a time when the meaning was almost entirely incomprehensible. I loved the soaring and diving and careening of it. The fragmentary flashes of meaning were more than enough. Who wanted more?

It was my first insight into poetry as the art of verbal choreography. Unlike everyday adult speech—tedious and terrestrial—this was speech capable of being aerial and aquatic all at once. It wasn't subject to the same laws of gravity. Unlike pedestrian prose, this was language that danced.

Born in a home with Tamilian parents (both second-generation English speakers), a sister, and a grizzled cook from Kerala (who doubled up as a glorious nocturnal storyteller), life was a happy polyglottal mess of English and Tamil, with a smattering of Hindi and a rich whiff of Malayalam.

I was dimly aware of hierarchy. At the start, English seemed to be the language adults knew; I remember complaining as a three-year-old to my mother that my sister and her friends excluded me from their games by deliberately "talking English" to one another. They were, in other words, pulling rank.

But then came school and a gradual emergence into a verbal universe. English was no longer "adult" language; it was both home language and world language, though there was a mild change of flavour depending on which side of the door one was on.

Soon, the real distinction in my life wasn't about "inside language" and "outside language", or "child-speak" and "adult-speak". It was about the distinction between prose and poetry. Prose—whether English or Tamil or Hindi—was sane, staid, unsurprising, conversational, comfort food. Poetry, on the other hand, was magic language, holiday language, dance language, music language, electric language. It was a reminder that language—

whether English or Tamil or Hindi—was, at heart, mysterious, unpredictable, sly, feral. Poetry was the language of danger. Of discovery. Of heart-stopping illumination. It was heightened, intense, pressure-cooker language. When you applied that kind of heat and pressure to language, its chemical properties changed. It became quicksilver. Language came alive.

I speak of it as a distinction of genre. But that wasn't the whole truth either. The distinction was a matter of attitude. Poetry wasn't only made. It could be found. All it took was alertness and a willingness to carry one's awe and relish of language into other areas of one's life.

"Govt Split over Aluminium" was a caption in *The Times of India* one morning. As an eight-year-old, I had no idea what it meant. But I sang the phrase to myself, tasted it, gargled it, sipped it. By the end of the day, I had made it mine. Aluminium was surely one of the most delicious words in the language—supple, elastic, versatile, capable of being enunciated with different stresses and tonalities. Who gave a damn what it meant? Even mundane journalese, it seemed, could be an occasion for verbal callisthenics. If one took speech out of one context, hurled it into another, dimmed the house lights, turned on a spot, threw it up in the air, language turned magical. The sorcery began.

I was around thirteen. It was afternoon. I was in my grandparents' home in Madras on my annual vacation, browsing through my grandfather's library. Impulsively, I pulled down a book by someone called T.S. Eliot. I had no idea who this was. I started reading. Two hours later, I was still reading. All the while I knew—exuberantly, irrefutably, thrillingly—that I was in the presence of poetry.

What was it about? I had a dim idea. And yet, even as a neophyte reader, the opacity and the density of the verse wasn't a deterrent. I could recognize it even without being able to decode it; understand it without being able to paraphrase it. Mystery was poetry's domain, and I was fine with it. I'd come home.

English, Hindi, French, Marathi—these were merely names of languages you could tame. You could learn to sound at ease in them; you could "mug them up" for exams; you could watch movies, read books in them. But poetry? You approached it with delight, with care, with attention—the way you'd perhaps approach a wild animal you wanted to befriend. This was language that entailed depth, intensity, guile. And yet, for all the obvious craft involved, this was language that resisted domestication. Poetry wasn't just about ideas or emotions, about mind or gut. It was about something that came from such a deep place in one's inner magma that by the time it emerged on the tip of the tongue, it left you singed, chemically altered. It yoked together terror and truth.

~

Then followed the more formal academic engagement with language when poems turned into Poetry and reading into Education.

Not entirely dismal, however. These were years of active acquisition, but also of absorption. They gave me the license to marinate in poetry and in that other surprisingly creative domain: literary criticism. The best critics, I began to see, were shamans in their own right, who could lead you into the inner life of a poem, to that dark cavern where its heart pumps and its life energies flow.

But above all, I realised that literature was not just about a shadow world, but a daytime universe. Poetry was as much about precision as about passion, about exactitude as about excitement, about craft as about creativity. And it was the combination of night and day that made it profound, blazing, life-altering.

A curriculum that comprised a pantheon of dead white male poets wasn't really a problem once I learnt I also had the license to be critical of it. For I had to admit there was enjoyment too. Shakespeare and Herbert, Wallace Stevens and Rilke, Neruda and Whitman—these were writers to devour. There was enough parallel study to uncover the other side of the story: how many currents flowed, unacknowledged, alongside what is considered mainstream. I was aware that literary cartography was a tricky business—imprecise, arbitrary, selective. I knew this was deeply unfair. I knew that these poets were just a fraction of the world polyphony, but I loved them all the same.

And yet, there was unease about the unacknowledged presences. I knew there'd always be other voices: peripheral voices, forgotten voices, those I'd have to strain to hear. Then there were the silenced voices, hopelessly irretrievable. The silencing made me fearful. That was perhaps my biggest fear as a sixteen-year-old: of never finding a listener. I was beginning to discover this wasn't a private adolescent anguish, but a very real possibility. English, as we studied it, had its riches. But it was the language of a chosen few, a remote and starry *devaloka*.[1]

Thankfully, I could create my own eclectic parallel reading list. Through my undergrad years, I did just that, immersing myself in Basho and A.K. Ramanujan, Elizabeth Bishop and Buson, Erica Jong and Nammalvar, Arun Kolatkar and Yehuda Amichai. But I knew how precarious this equilibrium was, how easily you could be excluded.

Many years later, in the title poem of my first book, I wrote about the act of "cleaning bookshelves" as an act of sedition. Reorganising one's shelves, stumbling upon old flyleaf inscriptions, fingering the tactility of crumbling paper and glossy coffee-table covers—the poem talked of all the magic and elation of bibliophilia. But above all, it was a poem about a literary mutiny, a quiet coup d'état. It wasn't about silencing any voices, but about shuffling around existing arrangements, and setting up conversations between writers who, I wished, could meet each other, share a drink with each other, perhaps. And so, the poem

---

1 The realm of the gods.

turned into a playful rewriting of the canon, a blurring of borders
between high art and low art, mainstream and periphery:

    Begin by respecting the logic
    that governed earlier conjunctions—

    respect the hauteur
    of the book not journeyed,

    the complicit camouflage
    of the borrowed paperback,

    the frowning grandeur of the Russian classics,
    upper shelf, upper caste,
    lost in the austerities of a glacial tapas,

    the sly tight-lipped smile
    of the coffee-table volume,
    lusciously swathed,
    venerable geisha,

    and the amber geniality
    of the leatherbound coterie,
    still fragrant with the smoke
    of old cheroots
    from colonial living rooms.

    Then trace the occult insignia of silverfish
    on paper that crumbles at a touch
    into dragonfly-wingdust.
    Rediscover the flyleaf inscription
    of a lover's ex-lover,
    damply intimate,

>   and rising somewhere
>   the crushed
>   azalea scent
>   of Manderley...

Tumbling unexpectedly
out of the mists of mothball
and nostalgia, a world
of lighthouses off the Devonshire coast
and dungeons stuffed with precious ingots—
embrace the lost world of Enid Blyton,
blessed Blyton,
beloved reactionary.

Now comes the chance to intervene,
match-make, infiltrate
old-boy networks—
allow Kerouac
to nudge familiarly
at Milton,
Mira at Shankara,
watch Nietzsche sniff suspiciously
at Krishnamurti.
And listen close,
as Ghalib in the back row
murmurs drowsily
to Keats...

>   —from "On Cleaning Bookshelves"

~

When I emerged from my master's, I gleefully followed Randall Jarrell's dictum: "Read at whim, read at whim!"

I also wanted to *write* at whim. But that wasn't so easy.

Poetry was the shortest and most direct route to the self that I knew. Also the most pleasurable. Since language was *my* way of knowing the self, English became a desperate device, an invaluable tool. I had to sharpen my implements, know the rules, learn the game. And yet, I didn't want a borrowed language. I'd spent my life believing others possessed a superior wisdom and life was elsewhere. Now I wanted to inhabit myself.

Becoming me was, however, far from easy. I hadn't realised it was going to be the journey of a lifetime, the rewards undeniable, but in their entirety, endlessly deferred.

There were years of apprenticeship—conscious and unconscious—during which I tried to write like those I admired and, scarily enough, often ended up sounding like those I disliked. There were years of séance when other voices spoke through me, unbidden and unsought. There were also years of ventriloquism, during which I writhed in envy while other poets spoke in what I recognised was actually *my* voice. And of course, there were spells of laryngitis, when I had no voice at all.

But I knew what I wanted: a language that was both familiar and startling, a voice that could whisper and still be heard, a language polished like gunmetal and yet agile enough to creep into the crevices of lullabies and the folds of old saris. I wanted a language that could speak of my love of Keats and my dislike of literary Brahminism in the same breath. A language that could speak lyrically of my grandmother's self-possession ("the secret of a world / where nayikas still walk / with the liquid tread of those / who know their bodies as well / as they know their minds") and savagely about pundits with faces "about as mediaeval as nylon" and macho intellectuals with "brains bullworked into maleness". A language that could speak of personal dream worlds ("the moonwatered stone of Egyptian temples", the zephyr in Khorasan, and medieval feelings of yearning for paramours "whose eyes smoulder like lanterns in winter") and implicate at the same time, women's compartments on peak-hour

Bombay locals, and convent schoolteachers (who spawn students that must "prefer wrens and martins to daydreaming / daffodils to Venus flytraps"). It wasn't about trying to be contemporary or postcolonial or Indian in any self-conscious way, but I was aware of a surge of power in reclaiming bits of myself I had frittered away—to "books, lovers, teachers, customs officials".

The art of the murmured voice is what I once called poetry. To keep the faith that one's murmur will be heard—despite the odds—was the most difficult challenge of all. But strangely, impossibly, the murmurs did get heard. Echoes did happen. Subtle echoes. But undeniable ones.

The responses to my first book convinced me that I could write in a language that was mine enough to be personally rewarding and shared enough to be somewhat rewarding for others. When the poems were translated into Hindi and Tamil, Italian and Spanish, I realised that there were unexpected homes for this odd Bombay–Tamil–Anglophone voice; that it could leak into other lives in ways I hadn't imagined.

And then a review appeared in *Poetry Wales*. A critic patted me in avuncular fashion on the back for my command over rhythm and sound, and then proceeded to rue the absence of an "identifiably Indian" ingredient in the work. The review was mildly annoying, but more than anything else, it fed into a deeper disquiet. As an arts writer and curator, I had started to encounter the many self-appointed gatekeepers of culture and was beginning to find out that the only way to be heard was sometimes to be a gatekeeper oneself—not a prospect I relished.

I wanted to write a poetry that could be vulnerable, that could disarm, expose its own underbelly. A poetry that could be critical of a cultural history and yet deeply implicating of the self, that could embrace contradiction, the many roiling paradoxes of the lives we lead. Somewhere between verdict and sound bite, between a culture of terminal sanctimoniousness and terminal triviality, there had to be another way, a real language, *my* language.

That's what I was looking for. But to sound provisional, uncertain, contradictory—all these were signs of weakness in a world of magisterial stances. Even to confess to a love of Keats was treason in a world of postcolonial lawmakers. To be myself, I realised, would always be fraught in a world with its own formulae for authenticity and belonging. I didn't want to surrender a hard-won quest for language merely to suit the diktats of a fundamentalist ethos. I had to reclaim my right to speak the way I wanted—assertively. The alternative was to be taken over by the cultural police.

The problem, I found, wasn't progressive or orthodox opinions; the problem was calcified attitudes, dogmatic perspectives, prescriptive worldviews. The problem was that the world resorts—particularly when challenged—to readymade language.

That was the birth of a poem about my need to resist those voices that constantly legislate on belonging, a poem that's entered more than one anthology and continues to evoke strong responses:

> You believe you know me,
> wide-eyed Eng Lit type
> from a sun-scalded colony,
> reading my Keats—or is it yours?—
> while my country detonates
> on your television screen.
>
> You imagine you've cracked
> my deepest fantasy—
> oh, to be in an Edwardian vicarage,
> living out my dharma
> with every sip of dandelion tea
> and dreams of the weekend jumble sale…
>
> You may have a point.
> I know nothing about silly mid-offs,
> I stammer through my Tamil,

and I long for a nirvana
that is hermetic,
odour-free,
bottled in Switzerland,
money-back-guaranteed.

This business about language,
how much of it is mine,
how much yours,
how much from the mind,
how much from the gut,
how much is too little,
how much too much,
how much from the salon,
how much from the slum,
how I say verisimilitude,
how I say Brihadaranyaka,
how I say vaazhapazham—
it's all yours to measure,
the pathology of my breath,
the halitosis of gender,
my homogenised plosives
about as rustic
as a mouth-freshened global village.

Arbiter of identity,
remake me as you will.
Write me a new alphabet of danger,
a new patois to match
the Chola bronze of my skin.
Teach me how to come of age
in a literature you've bark-scratched
into scripture.
Smear my consonants

> with cow-dung and turmeric and godhuli.
> Pity me, sweating,
> rancid, on the other side of the counter.
> Stamp my papers,
> lease me a new anxiety,
> grant me a visa
> to the country of my birth.
> Teach me how to belong,
> the way you do,
> on every page of world history.
>
> —"To the Welsh Critic Who Doesn't Find Me Identifiably Indian"

~

And then, one day in March 1997, language deserted me. I'd been betrayed before, but never so definitively. There are various ways I describe that experience. A near-death experience. A dark night of the soul. But I think of it as my first visceral encounter with the blank spaces on a page of poetry. I hadn't quite understood their significance until I fell headlong into one of those craters.

When I started emerging, many things in my life changed. My self-definition, for one. I was now more seeker than poet. And I was filled with the terrifying discovery that there were giant silences in my inner life that could never be permeated by language. As I emerged, it felt like I had urgently to come to terms with this deafening silence of the universe, this place where language is ashes in the mouth.

Until this time, my questions about the inadequacy of English were cultural. Could I find words to speak of the cow-hoof-dust light of a north Indian dusk? The dark camphorated recesses of my grandmother's pooja room?[2] The crackle of my mother's sari when she returned after an M.D. Ramanathan concert? I knew certain experiences could only be forded by image. Metaphor could carry you over most trans-linguistic gaps. Also, over emotional and cultural abysses.

But this was an abyss of another kind. Not despair—I was familiar with that terrain. Here, words were distant, spectral. And so was everything else—love, dreams, rages, desires, traumas. Nothing counted. This was wordlessness.

Life returned seemingly to normal in a week. But something changed, irrevocably. And the poetry began to gradually reflect that disturbingly real experience. It grew quieter, less obviously dramatic, more perforated. There were more pauses, less of an anxiety to fill in the gaps.

It wasn't about losing faith in language as much as about realising that nothing—not even my hard-won personal English—was foolproof. The ropes were frayed, the magic carpet tattered.

> To swing yourself
> from moment to moment,
> to weave a clause
> that leaves room
> for reminiscence and surprise,
> that breathes,
> welcomes commas,
> dips and soars
> through air-pockets of vowel,
> lingers over the granularity of consonant,
> never racing to the full-stop,
> content sometimes
> with the question mark,
> even if it's the oldest one in the book.

---

[2] An area for prayer.

> To stand
> in the vast howling, rain-gouged
> openness of a page,
> asking the question
> that has been asked before,
> knowing the gale of a thousand libraries
> will whip it into the dark…
>
> —"Another Way"

And even as I struggled with this betrayal, I began to dimly see its gifts. When I decongested language, allowed it to grow less fevered, more expansive, more open to bewilderment, it breathed easier. My relationship with it grew less clingy. And something else began to emerge in the holes—something that wasn't me, something truer.

It felt dangerous. But curiously, life wasn't losing its ethical concerns, its politics, its questions about dharma. It's just that as I started following a deeper imperative, some of these questions seemed to fall into perspective, growing strangely more energised.

> We thought it meant going against the grain,
> and of course, it did,
> but not with clenched teeth
> and knotted sinew
>
> but by listening just beneath the skin—
> the urgent gurgle of current,
> rife with frogspawn,
> pushing rapidly
> upstream.
>
> —"Counter"

Nor did it mean an erasure of sensuality, of the "uncensored wilderness of greed" that is the body. Earlier, writing the "spiritual" had always felt mildly embarrassing, because it seemed to reinforce stereotypes of the esoteric East. As Indian women artists, we'd had enough of that, surely? We wanted to be women with bodies, hormones, hungers, not ethereal sprites, anaemic archetypes. But now, the spaces between words uncovered a lust for a deeper life, which, curiously enough, provoked a more erotic, exuberant verse.

…I could swallow you,
feel the slurry of you
against palate
          —and throat,
ravish you
with the rip, snarl
and grind of canine
and molar, taste the ancestral grape
that mothered you, your purpleness
swirling down my gullet,
and it would be a kind
of knowing,

but you still wouldn't be
me enough…

      —from "Black Oestrus"

And perhaps even truer than lust was a growing glimpse that underlying all this—whether the need for sensuality, love, knowledge or the sacred—was the same octane. My language had to grow subtler to reach it, but subtlety didn't mean a loss of voltage.

Language didn't need to be impregnable in order to be strong, or soft in order to be vulnerable. Pauses didn't mean an absence of muscle, of spine. The more the gaps, I discovered, the stronger, the more tensile it could become.

The terrors haven't subsided. But I am more at ease with gaps than I was fifteen years ago. That brings me back to where I started: those times when language was a mystery and mystery wasn't a problem.

> …Grant me the fierce tenderness
> of watching
> word slither into word,
> into the miraculous algae
> of language,
> untamed by doubt
> or gravity,
>
> words careening,
> diving,
> swarming, un-
> forming, wilder
> than snowstorms in Antarctica, wetter
> than days in Cherrapunji,
>
> alighting on paper, only
> for a moment,
> tenuous, breathing,
> amphibious,
> before
> leaping
> to some place the voice
> is still learning
>
> to reach.
>
> Not scripture,
> but a tadpole among the stars,

unafraid to plunge
deeper
if it must—

only if it must—

into transit.

—from "Leapfrog")

I still enjoy the workshop negotiation with language, the lapidarist's art. But there is more room for awe now. And a deeper trust of language—its tides, its rhythms, its attunement to the caprices of the moon.

Poetry is about composition and craft, and always will be. But I'm more comfortable with being listener and conduit today. The real poetry is inspired eavesdropping on the self.

I've always valued metaphor for its capacity to mean different things all at once. But the dark art of poetry is darker than I imagined. The blank spaces in a poem—which rescue a poem from semantic overload—*are* the point.

English today is a bit like my body—"so alien when I try to belong, / so hospitable when I decide / I'm just visiting". And perhaps that's even all right?

It's taken forever to see that poetry "means" not in spite of its silences, but *because* of them.

Poems Matter

It was snobbery perhaps
(or habit)

to want
perforation,

to choose cotton, for instance,
with its coarse asymmetries,
over polyester
or unctuous rayon.

But this, I suppose,
is what we were looking for all along—
this weave
that dares to embrace

                air,

this hush of linen, these frayed edges,
these places where thought
runs
    threadbare,
where colours bleed into
something vastly blue
like sky,

these tatters
at peace almost
with the great outrage
of not being around.

It's taken a long time
to understand
poems matter
because they have holes.

Waking Dream

Reflections on Poetry

Randhir Khare

Randhir Khare is a national and international award-winning writer, poet, teacher, and artist who has been guiding and mentoring writers, visual artists, and performance artists of all ages for decades, helping them to write and publish books, create and display visual art, and nurture their love for dramatic performance. He has published thirty-five books of poetry, fiction, non-fiction, translations, and educational handbooks, had seven solo exhibitions of his art, written for, produced, directed, or performed in numerous stage-shows, is a well-known folklorist and storyteller, and has produced and directed a film titled *The World in a Story*. Randhir Khare's wide-ranging creative workshops, guidance sessions, and custom-designed programmes have been used in schools, professional or corporate spaces, and with non-formal interactive groups in various parts of India. A.R. Rahman has set his poetry to music.

~

It was in the mid-1980s, I remember, when a young poet brought his poems to me for my opinion and endorsement. There was something distinctly fresh and avant-garde about their tone, manner of saying, mood, and the musical balance that each of them had achieved. I was impressed and recommended a slim selection of them to a publisher. Fortunately, he felt the same, accepted the manuscript, and brought out the book. A gifted young poet had arrived. The publisher and I congratulated each other ... too soon.

A few months later, when some of the lines of his poems were still ringing in my head, I picked up *My Son's Father*, the fragmented autobiography by the distinguished poet Dom Moraes. To my utter horror, lines, phrases, and images started popping up, fresh and familiar. "Oh God," I said to myself (I have a habit of talking to myself), "here's where the young genius has been snacking."

I rang up the publisher and profusely apologised to him. He laughed and said, "He had me too because of the ingenious manner in which he pieced together the bits. There are seven other poets he's stolen from." Well, the rest of the story was embarrassing.

Another poet, much older and supposedly wiser and more "responsible", borrowed a couple of volumes by selected European poets from my bookshelf and forged an entire manuscript of poems from bits and pieces of their poetry. To his misfortune, he picked up lines from a poem by the Italian poet Eugenio Montale, one of my favourites. To crown it all, he requested me to write an introduction. I agreed and wrote an essay on the various poets he had stolen from. He vanished into the blue.

There were numerous occasions when this happened ... then the big one came. A young poet, one of my postgraduate students, wrote a poem and titled his book using the title of one of my poems, without asking me for permission to do so. To rub salt into my wound, he used the line as a refrain. At the end of the public reading where he had read the poem, he asked me, "What do you think of the poem? I think it's one of my best."

So, why do poets plagiarise? Why do they need to steal other poets' lines? Is it that they can't be bothered with even *trying* to write their own lines, so just pick up other poets' lines? Do they lack confidence in their own ability, so piggyback on others? Do they think a poem is a thingy that should look smart and witty, or obscure, or wise, and so to make that happen they pick up the best of the litter and pack them together into a sardine can? Are they afraid to dig into themselves and draw out their own feelings and ideas and sense of self and forge them into poems? Are they afraid that "their feelings" are not worth a dime? Or are they just in a hurry to be heard?

In his poem "The Circus Animal's Desertion", the Irish poet W.B. Yeats reflects on the fact that throughout his literary career he borrowed themes, ideas and concerns from Irish culture, folklore, politics, and social life to enliven his poetry with. Now, at the end of his life, he realises that he must abandon using them as sources of inspiration but instead:

> lie down where all the ladders start,
> In the foul rag-and-bone shop of the heart.[1]

In other words, he realises that true poetry comes from the self because it is the authentic voice of the poet. So why are poets afraid of being themselves and creating from the "rag-and-bone shop of the heart"? Anna Akhmatova, the Russian poet, known for the darkly sombre lyricism of her poetry (which grew from the suppression of Stalinist times), wrote in a poem addressed "To Poetry":

> Fame swam like a swan
> through the golden mist

---

[1] "The Circus Animals' Desertion". In: W.B. Yeats. *Yeats's Poems.* Ed. A. Norman Jeffares. Macmillan, 1991, 471-72. See, too, the poem by Peer Khan, "Writing about Yourself", in this volume.

> and you, love, were always
> my despair.²

I am not suggesting that all poetry should be dark and intense and tragic, all I am saying is that we should dig into ourselves and our own lives and set free the wellsprings of thought and feeling, our thoughts and our feelings. W.H. Auden in his moving memorial poem on the death of W.B. Yeats, wrote:

> Follow, poet, follow right
> To the bottom of the night,
> With your unconstraining voice
> Still persuade us to rejoice;
>
> With the farming of a verse
> Make a vineyard of the curse,
> Sing of human unsuccess
> In a rapture of distress;
>
> In the deserts of the heart
> Let the healing fountain start,
> In the prison of his days
> Teach the free man how to praise.³

Allow me to give you an analogy. Once when I was trekking in the jungles of Dang in south Gujarat, in summer, I ran out of water. The rivers and streams and waterfalls were dry, so a Bhil tribesman showed me where to drink water from. He walked to the dry bed of a stream and going down on all fours dug up the

---

2 "A String of Quatrains: To Poetry". Transl. Richard McKane. In: Anna Akhmatova. *Post-War Russian Poetry*. Ed. Daniel Weissbort. Penguin, 1974, 21.
3 "In Memory of W.B. Yeats". In: W.H. Auden. *Collected Shorter Poems 1927-1957*. Faber, 1966, 141-43.

dry earth and stones until water hidden below emerged. Then he lowered his head till his mouth touched the water, and he lapped it up like an animal.

"It's pure water from the stream's womb," he said, "cleansed by the sand and stone that it has passed through. Drink your fill but do not carry away any water. This stream's water belongs here, it has a sweetness of its own, there will be other streams on the way to quench your thirst and they will have their sweetness."

You'll ask, "What do you mean by deep? How deep should we dig for a poem?"

As deep as a dream.

A poem is like a dream.

Why?

There is an inherent mood … it may be fear, expectation, surprise, sorrow, intense passion, loneliness and so on. When you awake from a dream, you awake with a mood that feels *real*, familiar, as if it has really happened, and the mood stays with you a while. Like a poem. You read it, and when it is over, it leaves you with a mood. The feeling is authentic.

A good example is the mood that the poem "somewhere i have never travelled" by e.e. cummings conveys. Google it if you are not in the habit of reading. Read it aloud and you'll find yourself drawn into a mood that is tender, warm, intimate, and appreciative. Or one of Pablo Neruda's poems from his book *Twenty Love Poems and A Song of Despair*. The mood Neruda puts you in is at once physical as well as emotional, erotic as well as desperate. Or the poems from the collection *The Mersey Sound*, which features three of my favourite British poets, Roger McGough, Adrian Henri, and Brian Patten.

Consider then, what creates the *mood* in a dream?

What your senses absorb—the sounds, the images, the tastes, the touch, the feeling that is created. Not necessarily awakening all your senses but definitely overtly sensory in the experience it offers.

Read the poems of Erica Jong, Sylvia Plath, Gwendolyn Brooks, or for that matter the poetry of Louise Glück or Nelly Sachs, a much older poet. Carl Sandburg's poems have it too. For example, his poem "Haze" never fails to create an unforgettable mood:

> Keep a red heart of memories
> under the great gray rain sheds of the sky,
> Under the open sun and the yellow gloaming embers.
> Remember all paydays of lilacs and songbirds,
> All starlights of cool memories on storm paths.[4]

The American balladeer Bob Dylan's work does the same in many of his lyrics, for example, "Mr Tambourine Man" and "A Hard Rain's a-Gonna Fall"; so does the Canadian poet-performer Leonard Cohen in poems like "Light as the Breeze", "Suzanne", and "Bird on the Wire". Or on the other hand the soft rock lyrics of "Brain Damage" by the band Pink Floyd.

Next, we come to the narrative or action in a dream.

As you perhaps are aware, the dreamer goes through a series of experiences in a dream … moving through living places and spaces in a surreal manner—which is at the same time perfectly logical. The poem too should take the reader on a journey through the unexpected, shifting from one place to another, one action to another. The poem "Song in the Blood" by the French poet Jacques Prévert best illustrates this. Listen to Joan Baez reciting Lawrence Ferlinghetti's translation of the poem on her album *Baptism: A Journey through our Time*, it's on YouTube, check it out.

You could also read the Welsh poet Dylan Thomas's poem "Fern Hill". Read it loudly to yourself. It will take you on a magical journey. There's constant motion in the poem, it carries you away, and you willingly give yourself up to the flow.

---

4 Carl Sandburg. "Haze". https://www.poemhunter.com/poem/haze-14/

What makes a dream a dream? The presence of "Otherness". It is real and deeply felt but it is not obviously real. It's something else, somewhere else.

What makes a poem a poem? The presence of "Otherness". It is real and deeply felt but it is not obviously real. The Bohemian-Austrian poet Rainer Maria Rilke's poems "You, Darkness" and "On the Edge of Night" mysteriously create this "Otherness" in the same way as James Joyce's poem "I Hear an Army" or D.H. Lawrence's poem "Under the Oak".

How does one charge one's poetry with the spirit of a dream?

You need to be in tune with any mood that you may be in, particularly an overwhelming mood, focus on it, don't shy away, *be it*. Write it down as if you are inside it, as if it is a dream with all the necessary elements that make a dream. Let the dream take you wherever it wishes. Don't worry if you don't understand what you are writing—keep writing. Soon you will discover that it is a "waking dream". Leave the reader with a mood. If you are true to the experience of engaging with the mood in dream form, there will be images you never imagined you could cull from deep within yourself, cadences that are uniquely your own. The poem will find its way out of the passage and become itself, like the sculpture of a creature that finds its way out of a piece of driftwood that an Inuit sculptor is working on. An Inuit artist will take a piece of wood, talk to it, and speak to the creature hidden inside, then will let his small sharp knife "set it free".

Therefore, when you are turning your prose passage into a poem don't use your mind, use your sixth sense, your deep feeling. Too often do we destroy the poems we create by thinking them through, making them up, being control freaks. A bird doesn't belong in a cage, it belongs to freedom, to the air, to the skies. The power and authenticity of a poem lie in it expressing its own free will.

When Samuel Taylor Coleridge started writing his poem "Kubla Khan" he was on opium, which helped him drop his guard and articulate his "waking dream". Unfortunately, someone disturbed him, and the flow stopped. He completed the poem wide awake and detached from his waking dream. From being in the flow, the poem then became thought through. Read the poem loudly to yourself and try to find the shift in treatment. (But don't depend on opium.)

So, what is my point here?

Don't think but feel. Let the lines and images flow of their own volition through associations (because that's exactly what happens in a dream!)

Having taken you through the first baby steps of finding your poetic self, let me talk to you about how certain poems came to me through dream states.

Many years ago, I lived alone in the city of Mumbai, in a high-rise apartment block. It was perhaps the loneliest phase of my life. I felt as if I was the sole survivor in a bombed-out city. After a hectic day's work, I would return to my apartment and brood till I fell asleep. On one occasion I drifted into sleep listening to Leonard Cohen's "Light as the Breeze". Prompted by his lyrics and soulful voice I was drawn into the most mysterious dream I have ever experienced. When I awoke, I sat down and wrote a series of poems. Following that experience, I felt as if my deep consciousness had been awakened. Here are some lines from one of the poems:

> I sing of drowned sailors,
> Bones polished smooth lying on the floors of silt,
> Layer upon layer,
> In the shadows of leviathans.
> Constellations of bones wait to rise up with the land
> When waters shift and continents are born;
>
> I sing of them
> Hard on dry land, smelling of shells and silence,

I sing of them waiting to form rocks and sand,
Moving ceaselessly like the wanderings of time;
I sing of them, the drowned sailors,
Bones polished smooth lying on the floors of silt.

What does the pillar of smoke say,
Drifting along the underbelly of the sky,
I want to be a cloud? A cloud heavy with rain,
Unzipping water on a restless land.

The dead cannot turn to water.
The dead remain. Fine particles of dust. Worlds.
And inside those worlds, more worlds and worlds beyond.
Beyond, within, deep down within.

I sing of drowned sailors,
I sing of the rain that fills the oceans
Moving across the city like angels.
Feet sweeping rooftops.

Hair trailing wet over the hoof-prints of the wind.
Bells stop ringing in factories and the hooters are silent,
Waiters and watchers at lonely windows turn and smile,
Remembering returns and reunions
And the meeting of bodies and the drowning of eyes.[5]

And so began a journey of rejuvenation, a celebration of poetry created by waking dreams.

I think this happened because I was willing to feel vulnerable. And when one is willing to feel vulnerable and not be afraid of feeling, the most powerful visions wrought from a pure feeling of

---

5   Randhir Khare. "I Sing". In: *Live Encounters—Poetry & Writing*. May 2021, 14. At https://issuu.com/liveencounters/docs/live_encounters_p_w_may_2021issuu

trust are awakened. I believe that T.S. Eliot's "The Waste Land" came from there. So, too, "A Night with Hamlet", a poem by the Czech poet Vladimir Holan.

There are a couple of lines from Holan's poem "Horoscope" that make a lot of sense here:

> we understand simplicity only when the heart breaks,
> And we are suddenly ourselves, alone and fateless.[6]

Another powerful example of the waking dream was when my poem sequence "Green Is the Colour of Memory" first began. I was in my first marriage, which tasted of foreverness. After several tumultuous relationships, I had finally found my ideal soulmate. However, in the fourth year of our marriage I began getting up at midnight and writing for three hours. My wife and I were both astonished by what I was writing … experiences of death and dying, of entering dream worlds, strange portents, unknown signs and symbols and words that came from the depths of despair. Every night I experienced this waking dream and the poems kept writing themselves through me.

Three days after the sequence was complete, she lost her life in an automobile accident. It took me years to really understand that the poems had been born from a waking dream, in which a deep reality finally found its way out and expressed itself. And nearly two decades after that I had the courage to publish the poem sequence in *River Day*, a volume of my poems.

Having taken you, dear reader, thus far, I'd like to say that whatever the subject and theme of your poem may be, try writing it in a waking dream state in which your mind lets go of its controls, and your feelings and senses forge a language of their own. Remember, as I mentioned earlier—you are not writing the

---

6 "Horoscope". In: Vladimir Holan. *Selected Poems*. Transl. Jarmila and Ian Milner. Penguin, 1971, 19.

poem, the poem is writing itself through you. So, prepare yourself, and don't be afraid to be vulnerable. When a master flute player was teaching a pupil, he said, "If you really want to play the flute, be in harmony with it, become the flute and the very bamboo it is made of."

Read poems that you love, old and new; read them out loud, enjoy their images, metaphors, feelings, cadences; they may not be yours, but they will open in you whole new worlds that you never imagined existed. The late Russian–American poet Joseph Brodsky was perhaps one of the most inspiring teachers of poetry. He made his students read poetry and didn't encourage them to talk about poetry. He wanted them to experience the poems they read, their sound and their feeling. Do that—it will trigger in you deep associations and widen your poetic sensibility.

Another suggestion: keep a small Dream Notebook and put down whatever you may remember from a dream. That will help you, sooner or later, to make your own creative reservoir.

Keep your senses alert and alive when you are awake. Be present in your experience. Be in the *now*, however boring, tedious, and fragile it might be. And don't be afraid to use words that sound right to you.

Find your own way in the darkness, I can't hold your hand, I'm stumbling too.

Why Poetry Needs to Mess with Your Head[1]

Francis Jarman

Who needs poetry?

Well, TV advertisers do, for a start, also all those people who buy greetings cards with rubbishy poems and pictures of puppies, kittens, or roses.

Totalitarian regimes believe that poetry lends their turgid pronouncements or wicked doings gravitas. In much the same vein, national anthems cannot do without poetry.

Even ordinary Joes like to fall back on rhyme for momentous happenings like declarations of love or best man's speeches at weddings.

To be honest, is any of that poetry? Maybe we can find better words to describe it. Verse (often collocated with "leaden")? Jingles? Doggerel?

So why should anyone take poetry seriously, if it is only TV wallpaper, or an accompaniment to events that, later, you will probably look back on in embarrassment? Can you make

---

1 Based on a lecture originally given at the University of Hildesheim.

money out of it? Not unless you're the State Poet of the People's Democratic Republic of Somewhere. Or you have a contract with a major advertising agency. When did you last hear of a professional poet?

I won't say much more about the specifics of *writing* poetry. Of all the forms of literature, poetry lends itself least well to the training approach. You can teach yourself the rudiments of the craft, by studying the great masters and examples of their work, and you will soon discover whether you have a gift for "rhyming" or not, but something else is needed too, an individual wellspring, like the electricity that makes the machine you have constructed jump into life. W.B. Yeats wrote: "We make out of the quarrel with others, rhetoric, but of the quarrel with ourselves, poetry."[2]

Writing poetry is an infuriating occupation, bringing mostly frustration but, very occasionally, deep satisfaction too. However, the "quarrel" that Yeats refers to is a personal matter—there is no creative writing workshop to make you a poet or give you your money back. Only you can do that, and when you find yourself on that journey, you will know why.

But poetry also has a purpose for the reader or listener (bearing in mind that many poems only reveal their power when they are read aloud): its purpose is to shake you up, freak you out, turn you on, discombobulate you (great American word, that), and mess with your head. Poetry is the bad boy of literature. It ought to affect you in such a way that some part of your life, however tiny, is never the same again.

In 1904, Franz Kafka wrote to his friend Oskar Pollak:

> Altogether, I think we ought to read only books that bite and sting us. If the book we are reading doesn't shake us awake like a blow to the skull, why bother reading it in the first place? [...] What we need are books that hit us

---

2 W.B. Yeats. *Per Amica Silentia Lunae*. Macmillan, 1918, 29.

> like a most painful misfortune, like the death of someone we loved more than we love ourselves, that make us feel as though we had been banished to the woods, far from any human presence, like a suicide. A book must be the axe for the frozen sea within us. That is what I believe.³

A touch hyperbolic, but he does have a point. And for "book", now substitute "poetry".

Great poetry needs to have qualities that are lastingly powerful and vigorous, outliving fashion, so that it is not merely an in-your-face reaction to the conventional. Dada, the Angry Young Men, the Beats, and the Punks were sensational phenomena of their day—but we have moved on, and the shock effect has faded.

So—print it on T-shirts and tell the world: "Poets do it better."

F.R. Leavis effectively said as much, though in rather more sober language, back in 1932.

> Poetry matters because of the kind of poet who is more alive than other people, more alive in his own age. [...] The potentialities of human experience in any age are realised only by a tiny minority, and the important poet is important because he belongs to this (and has also, of course, the power of communication). Indeed, his capacity for experiencing and his power of communicating are indistinguishable; [...] He is unusually sensitive, unusually aware, more sincere and more himself than the ordinary man can be. [...] And poetry can communicate the actual quality of experience with a subtlety and precision unapproachable by any other means.⁴

---

3   Quoted in Ernst Pawel. *The Nightmare of Reason: A Life of Franz Kafka* (1984). Farrar, Straus & Giroux, 1992, 158.
4   F.R. Leavis. *New Bearings in English Poetry: A Study of the Contemporary Situation* (1932). Penguin, 1963, 19-20.

If you don't agree that we need poetry, please stop reading now.

If you do agree, the next question would be: How do you *know* that it is poetry? (And not simply some fancy rhyming junk.) Verse doesn't have to be bad, but it is characterised principally by its *structure*, and its ideas, whereas poetry is characterised by its *imaginative power*. Poetry's effectiveness for expressing thoughts and feelings comes about because its language is carefully chosen, both for its sounds and its associations. Coleridge defined poetry as "the best words in the best order" (whereas prose was merely "words in their best order"),[5] and he asserted that

> it would be scarcely more difficult to push a stone out from the pyramids with the bare hand than to alter a word, or the position of a word, in Milton or Shakespeare (in their most important works at least), without making the author say something else, or something worse, than he does say.[6]

We also have the poet A.E. Housman's often-quoted test based on the listener's or reader's *reaction*:

> I received from America a request that I would define poetry. I replied that I could no more define poetry than a terrier can define a rat, but that I thought we both recognised the object by the symptoms which it provokes in us. [...] Experience has taught me, when I am shaving of a morning, to keep watch over my thoughts, because, if a line of poetry strays into my memory, my skin bristles so that the razor ceases to act. This particular symptom

---

5   Samuel Taylor Coleridge. *Specimens of the Table Talk of the Late Samuel Taylor Coleridge*. Vol. One. John Murray, 1835, 84.
6   Coleridge. *Biographia Literaria, Or, Biographical Sketches of My Literary Life and Opinions* (1817). Ed. George Watson. Dent/Dutton, 1965, 12.

is accompanied by a shiver down the spine; there is another which consists in a constriction of the throat and a precipitation of water to the eyes; and there is a third which I can only describe by borrowing a phrase from one of Keats's last letters, where he says, speaking of [his great love] Fanny Brawne, "everything that reminds me of her goes through me like a spear". The seat of this sensation is the pit of the stomach.[7]

Gokul Madhavan, who teaches Sanskrit at Harvard, quotes this on his blog, and points out

[...] how beautifully Housman describes the involuntary physical reactions that Sanskrit theorists have called the *sāttvika-bhāvas*: *stambha* (stupefaction), *sveda* (perspiration), *romāñca* (horripilation), *svara-bhaṅga* (voice-cracking), *vepathu* (trembling), *vaivarnya* (pallor), *aśru* (tears), and *pralaya* (loss of consciousness).[8]

Poetry can achieve such effects in different ways: by the sheer *power and beauty of the language*, for instance, as in the great lyrical moments in Shakespeare's plays (Caliban's "Be not afeard; the isle is full of noises" speech in *The Tempest*[9] is one such example, and there is the love poetry in *Romeo and Juliet* and *Antony and Cleopatra*, and the so-called "*Othello* Music"), or when Samuel Taylor Coleridge (or whoever it is who is speaking in the poem) works himself into a trance at the end of "Kubla Khan" (1797):

---

7   A.E. Housman. *The Name and Nature of Poetry*. Cambridge University Press, 1933, 46-47.
8   Gokul Madhavan. *Pearls at Random Strung*. At http://pearlsatrandomstrung.blogspot.de/2011/03/poetry-according-to-ae-housman.html
9   William Shakespeare. *The Tempest*, Act III, Scene 2, 133-41.

> I would build that dome in air,
> That sunny dome! Those caves of ice!
> And all who heard should see them there,
> And all should cry, Beware! Beware!
> His flashing eyes, his floating hair!
> Weave a circle round him thrice,
> And close your eyes with holy dread,
> For he on honey-dew hath fed,
> And drunk the milk of Paradise.[10]

That does it for me!

The poetry doesn't even need to rhyme or be packaged as a poem—though I have sympathy with Robert Frost in that he "had as soon write free verse as play tennis with the net down".[11] There is fine poetry embedded in many a text not commonly assumed to be such, like the magnificent seventeenth-century King James translation of the Bible. Here is the description of a war-horse, from *Job* 39: 19-25:

> Hast thou given the horse strength? hast thou clothed his neck with thunder?
> Canst thou make him afraid as a grasshopper? the glory of his nostrils *is* terrible.
> He paweth in the valley, and rejoiceth in *his* strength: he

---

10 "Kubla Khan: Or, A Vision in a Dream". In: Samuel Taylor Coleridge. *The Complete Poems*. Ed. William Keach. Penguin, 1997, 249-52. See also the article by Randhir Khare, "Waking Dream: Reflections on Poetry", in this volume.

11 Robert Frost. *Collected Poems, Prose, & Plays*. Ed. Richard Poirier and Mark Richardson. The Library of America, 1995, 809. Less well known is the exchange that Frost had with his contemporary Carl Sandburg, a renowned proponent of free verse, who responded that "you can play a better game with the net down", to which Frost replied, "Sure you can [...] and without the racket and balls—but it ain't tennis" (quoted in Joseph T. Thomas, Jr. *Poetry's Playground: The Culture of Contemporary American Children's Poetry*. Wayne State University Press, 2007, 4).

goeth on to meet the armed men.
He mocketh at fear, and is not affrighted; neither turneth he back from the sword.
The quiver rattleth against him, the glittering spear and the shield.
He swalloweth the ground with fierceness and rage: neither believeth he that *it is* the sound of the trumpet.
He saith among the trumpets, Ha, ha; and he smelleth the battle afar off, the thunder of the captains, and the shouting.

There is another wonderful description of a horse in the *Upanishads*, of roughly the same period as the *Book of Job*, here in Wendy Doniger's translation:

The head of the sacrificial horse is the dawn; his eye is the sun; his breath the wind; and his gaping mouth the fire common to all men [...]. When he yawns, lightning flashes; when he shakes himself, it thunders; and when he urinates, it rains. His whinny is speech itself.[12]

A more modern example of "disguised poetry" can be found at the beginning of Lawrence Durrell's novel *Justine* (1957):

In that early spring dawn
With its dense dew
Sketched upon the silence which engulfs a whole city
Before the birds awaken it
I caught the sweet voice
Of the blind muezzin[13] from the mosque

---

12 Wendy Doniger. *The Hindus: An Alternative History*. Speaking Tiger, 2009, 190.
13 The prayer leader, who calls the believers to prayer, usually from the minaret tower of the mosque.

Reciting the Ebed
A voice hanging like a hair
In the palm-cooled upper airs
Of Alexandria

"I praise the perfection of God
The Forever-Existing"
(This repeated thrice, ever more slowly,
In a high sweet register)
"The perfection of God, the Desired, the Existing
The Single, the Supreme
The perfection of God, the One, the Sole
The perfection of Him
Who taketh unto himself no male or female partner
Nor any like Him
Nor any that is disobedient
Nor any deputy, equal or offspring
His perfection be extolled"

The great prayer wound its way
Into my sleepy consciousness
Like a serpent
Coil after shining coil of words
(The voice of the muezzin sinking
From register to register of gravity)
Until
The whole morning seemed dense
With its marvellous healing powers
The intimations of a grace
Undeserved and unexpected
Impregnating
That shabby room where Melissa lay
Breathing as lightly as a gull
Rocked

> Upon the oceanic splendours
> Of a language she would never know[14]

I have written this out here in the form of a poem, but in Durrell's novel it is ostensibly a prose text.

Sometimes the *thoughts* expressed in the poem are so breathtaking that they even survive translation (as much great poetry unfortunately does not). There is a three-line Persian poem that describes how, at birth, we come, naked, from the dark, and how we return there, naked, when we die. It ends: "Come to my arms, naked in the dark."[15] The marvellous little poem packs birth, death, sex, and existential angst into a mere twenty-one words.

Even when it isn't causing all kinds of physical reactions, Housman-style, great writing can still shake you up by its unexpected *appositeness*, the "Aha! effect" (not unrelated to the famous "eureka moment", and the Joycean "epiphany"). A simple metaphor like "the milk of human kindness" (from *Macbeth*) is simultaneously surprising and brilliantly true. Shakespeare makes it look easy but, asked to come up with a metaphor for kindness, who (geniuses aside) would ever think of milk?

Here is the point—a simple phrase shifts our perception. And this is what poets do: they give us a different view of things. E.M. Forster described the great modern poet of Alexandria, C.P. Cavafy, as "a Greek gentleman in a straw hat, standing absolutely motionless *at a slight angle to the universe*" (my emphasis).[16]

Coleridge explained this gift of the poets to make, out of the banal and the familiar, something fresh and new:

---

14 Lawrence Durrell. *Justine* (1957). Faber, 1968, 27.
15 "Naked out of the Dark". Transl. Kenneth Rexroth. In: *The Faber Book of Epigrams and Epigraphs*. Ed. Geoffrey Grigson. Faber, 1977, 233.
16 E.M. Forster. "The Poetry of C.P. Cavafy". In: *Pharos and Pharillon* (1923). Michael Haag, 1983, 91.

To carry on the feelings of childhood into the powers of manhood; to combine the child's sense of wonder and novelty with the appearances which every day for perhaps forty years had rendered familiar [...].[17]

Other poets have warned that it is a gift to be used with care, since "humankind cannot bear very much reality" (T.S. Eliot).[18] Emily Dickinson even saw indirectness as a protective kindness:

> Tell all the Truth but tell it slant—
> Success in Circuit lies
> Too bright for our infirm Delight
> The Truth's superb surprise [...][19]

Where poets go, theory will follow. The Russian formalist Viktor Shklovsky (1917) introduced the term *defamiliarisation* (Russian, "*ostranenie*"), for the "making strange" that is at the root of all art.[20] In the theatre, there is Brecht's "*Verfremdungseffekt*" (which has been variously translated as the alienation, distancing or estrangement effect), by which the audience are discouraged from losing themselves in emotional identification, so as to be able to react with critical intelligence to what is being presented on the stage.[21]

Defamiliarisation may not in itself be sufficient.

The best-known example in modern English poetry is Craig Raine's puzzling "A Martian Sends a Postcard Home" (1977), which contains lines like the following:

---

17 Coleridge. *Biographia Literaria*, 49.
18 This appears in both *Murder in the Cathedral* (1935) and *Burnt Norton* (1936).
19 Poem #1263 in *The Poems of Emily Dickinson (Variorum Edition)*. Ed. R. W. Franklin. Harvard University Press, 1998.
20 See "Art as Technique". Transl. Lee T. Lemon and Marion J. Reis. In: *Literary Theory: An Anthology*. Ed. Julie Rivkin and Michael Ryan. Third edition. Wiley & Sons, 2017, 8-14.
21 "Distancing Effect". At https://en.wikipedia.org/wiki/Distancing_effect

In homes, a haunted apparatus sleeps,
that snores when you pick it up.

If the ghost cries, they carry it
to their lips and soothe it to sleep

with sounds. And yet, they wake it up
deliberately, by tickling with a finger.[22]

A telephone, of course. Amusing—yes. Clever, intriguing—certainly. But does it pass the Housman test?

As well as being entertained, we need to be shaken and stirred by our poets (with a bit of help from other writers, of course), because if they don't do it who else is going to?

Gerontologists know that people who stay intellectually active tend to live longer. We also lead better and more satisfying lives when we are challenged occasionally and shaken out of our groove.

Our heads *need* to be messed with, every so often.

---

22 In: *The Penguin Book of Contemporary British Poetry*. Ed. Blake Morrison and Andrew Motion. Penguin, 1982, 169-70.

Writing Scrumptious

Using the Bengali Meal Plan as a Guide

Ramona Sen

Ramona Sen is one of the co-founders of Allcap Communications, a content and communications company based in Kolkata. Her first novel, *Crème Brûlée*, was published by Rupa Publications and her novella, *Pot Luck*, by Juggernaut Books. She honed her appetite on the food beat as a reporter for *t2*, *The Telegraph*, India. Her musings on food have been published by *Borderless Journal*, *The Bangalore Review*, and *My Kolkata*, *The Telegraph*.

~

Have you noticed that chefs and food writers tend to have a similar montage of childhood memories? They will reminisce fondly of spending winter holidays at their aunt's, engaging in the prep for *Koraishutir Kochuri*,[1] in which the spicy green paste and fried-just-right batter have allegedly spoilt them for the dish anywhere

---

[1] Fried, puffy bread, stuffed with a paste of green peas, flavoured with asafoetida.

else for the rest of their lives. They will speak animatedly of waking up every Sunday to the aroma of onion browning in a pan, which inevitably augured a rich mutton gravy for lunch—the kind that has remained unmatched by renowned restaurants for the better part of their adulthood.

But at some point, usually at the threshold of late adolescence and early adulthood, the secret-recipe-littered path of these young gourmands diverges into microwavers and oven-roasters, whole-bread-eaters and sandwich-side-cutters, or cold-food-snackers and elaborate-meal-whipper-uppers. In the flush of impatient youth, the two are unlikely to get along. The first kind might admire a firm-but-flaky pie crust, but not at the cost of time, sweat, and hunger pangs. The second kind, while appreciative of efficient time-management, will find a two-minute-mug-cake a culinary crime. And so begin the makings of a food writer and a chef.

A decade later, they will be only too happy to be in each other's company. There's always a chef on the lookout for a food writer who can tell their aioli from their mayonnaise. Does that perhaps make a food writer an epicure who failed as a chef? When it comes to writing about food, I've found that it helps to use the Bengali meal courses as a handy template and, Anatole's your uncle, the piece is ready to be served!

First course: *Teto*. Or, the bitters

The bitter truth lies not just in the fried *neem pata*[2] but also in the knowledge that you simply don't know as much as the chef. Take notes. Ask questions. If you are allowed to, watch the chef at work as closely as you used to when your grandmother was sorting the vegetables for a traditional *shukto* (vegetable

---

2   Neem leaves, which are bitter to taste and widely regarded as a medicinal plant in Bengal.

stew) into those to be parboiled and those to be fried. When you notice seemingly inconsequential details that go into the preparation, you will know why those flavours come together in a way which will lead you to your Anton-Ego-Ratatouille moment.[3] "You learn a lot about someone when you share a meal together," said the late American celebrity chef Anthony Bourdain. And you certainly learn a lot watching someone putting their soul into cooking.

Second course: *Bhaja*. Or, the fries

Here, we balance out the astringent flavours of the first course while preparing the palate for the second. Cut to the crisp, like the *macédoine* of bhindi[4] sizzling in the pan (see how you can slip in a new term which you picked up from the chef?)—throw your audience a fun fact from the kitchen to crunch up, while they wait for you to elaborate on all the dishes you are about to embark on. Not all your readers will be visiting the restaurant to try the meal of your choice, so keep the chef talking and extract a couple of trick cards from their chef's hat. Help your more enthusiastic readers discover what makes scrambled eggs the right sort of creamy, or guide young cooks on how to brine their French fries well.

For instance, Mina Holland, deputy editor of *Guardian Feast*, leaves vital clues about the baking process while writing about a chef's new bread—"She devised a way to give spent bread a new lease of life, whizzing it up into breadcrumbs before making a stewy 'porridge' ... (the) softer texture must be down to Bado's[5] porridge invention, and makes for slices

---

3 Anton Ego is a mean, hard-to-please food critic in the 2007 Pixar movie, *Ratatouille*, where a taste of the ratatouille at Gusteau's restaurant ignites a memory of the dish his mother used to make.
4 Okra, or lady's fingers.
5 Roz Bado, head baker at Gail's, a bakery chain in London.

of bread that invite nothing more than salted butter."[6] It's far from a recipe but curious home chefs will immediately have ideas on how they can repurpose their own stale bread into something freshly edible.

Third course: *Dal, shaak* and *torkari*. Or, pulses and vegetables

Take a leaf out of your mother's fridge—don't dismiss this seemingly humdrum course. It's more than just a filler till you get to the good parts; it's the backbone of your piece. Simplicity of language stripped of jargon or technical details of the meal will give your readers the information they are looking for. Step into their shoes for a moment and ask yourself what you absolutely *must* know, before you delve into what you *want* to know.

After you have mentioned the location and described the cuisine, order five dishes across the menu. As a food writer you are beholden to make a diverse selection, instead of simply sticking by your personal palate. And when you do this often enough, you will find yourself surprised by a craving for macchiato, when all you've ever ordered is plain ol' cappuccino. Other details that are par for this course include information on prices (midweek happy hour, ladies' nights, etc.), ideal timings (if you happen to know that fresh bread arrives an hour after a boulangerie opens, it deserves a mention), variations of the menu such as weekend specials, and intel on when the kitchen is likely to send out free hors d'oeuvres as a surprise for its patrons.

You can also decide if you want to write about a single aspect of eating only, making that your focus. Food critic Robert Sietsema, for instance, has made it his business to know everything about sandwiches through the years, which allows him to be the last

---

[6] https://www.theguardian.com/food/2018/nov/21/waste-bread-gails-is-making-the-most-of-yesterdays-bake

word on sandwiches. "The beauty of the sandwich-based column is that it can naturally extol cheaper food. And it's also a vehicle for talking about cultures other than European ones. I began with an essay about the Earl of Sandwich and how it's bullshit that he actually invented the sandwich. I mean, he may have popularised a certain kind of sandwich, but the sandwich itself is something that's been invented across the globe in various forms," said Sietsema, in an interview in 2020.[7] No-nonsense and reliable, like a sturdy sandwich, Sietsema debunks myths, recognises the influence of culinary cultures other than his own, and extols the importance of a meal which cuts across social classes, all in one fell swoop of the butter knife.

Fourth course: *Maach-mangsho*. Or, fish and mutton

Now you can get to the meat of the piece. Here's where you can hope to be entirely honest about your lasting thoughts and fleeting impressions. Especially if this is one of those times you're visiting an eatery without letting the proprietors know. Since you're done with the facts, it's time to get to the fat—what do you *really* think of the noodle bowl where the egg yolk isn't runny enough, or the lemon butter sauce which is a tad too tangy? Did you perhaps discover a plain *sucre* crêpe which took you back to childhood by recreating the taste of butter and sugar in a sandwich peculiar to your mother's tiffin box? It's an Anton-Ego-Ratatouille moment!

Let your readers know if requests for off-the-menu sauce will make the chef irascible, if the lighting is too low for aspiring writers to work on their poetry, if the stoneware is classic or kitschy, if the Mozart is too Muzak, and if the corner table at the end of the room is the best seat because the position allows privacy while also allowing you to catch the waiter's eye.

---

7   https://bombmagazine.org/articles/robert-sietsema/

The detailing is what will remain with your overseas readers who might not be familiar with the cuisine or landscape that you take for granted. Take the late Jonathan Gold, for instance, who was known to not mince his words—"The slice of American cheese, if you have ordered a cheeseburger, does not melt into the patty, but stands glossily aloof from it, as if it were mocking the richness of the sandwich rather than adding to the general effect," wrote Gold in the *Los Angeles Times*, about a neighbourhood hamburger restaurant.[8]

Penultimate course: *Tok*. Or, sour

The Bengali meal needs a dash of this to aid digestion. Chancing upon food which transforms a bland-boiled-potato day into a sweet-potato-fries day is always uplifting for the soul. But do consider using this course to temper down your enthusiasm—a spoonful of the papaya chutney makes the mutton curry go down! Despite your paroxysms of pleasure at the gastronomical artistry you might have just witnessed, like all the arts, the culinary board is entirely subjective—one person's chicken is another person's tofu. Moderation, for the most part, will help your readers rely on you more. While adequately garnishing your piece with compliments, a dash of playfulness might help an unfavourable opinion land gently.

Mimi Sheraton, known for being the first woman to review restaurants for the *New York Times*, and who passed away in 2023, was particularly adept at being disparaging with a sense of humour. "If it is true, as used to be said, that oversalting means the cook is in love, at least one cook at Le Cirque must be head over heels," is one of her more famous snubs of an "haute cuisine restaurant" in the Mayfair Hotel.

---

8   https://www.latimes.com/archives/la-xpm-1993-10-07-fo-42909-story.html

Last course: *Mishti*. Or, dessert

Save the sweetest mouthful for the end. Health aficionados might be divided over sugar but as the official recommender of joy, you owe it to the world to recount in excruciating detail the density of the flourless chocolate cake, the alternating layers of an entremet dessert, or the particularly moist centre of a hardened encasing of fried milk. Rest assured, even those devoted to "clean" eating will know what's good for them and be willing to take a chance on the sweetmeat you endorse.

Dessert is never a waste, as anyone who has watched Nigella Lawson in her kitchen knows. Having proclaimed herself to be more of an "eater" than a chef, her description of custard in her book *How to Eat: The Pleasures and Principles of Good Food*[9] encapsulates just how sensual the act of eating dessert really can be: "The custard should be firm but not immobile; when you press it with your fingers, it should have a little wobble still within. Soft, warm and voluptuous—like an eighteenth-century courtesan's inner thigh."

Bhaat, or staples

And there you have your piece. The one thing common to every course of the Bengali meal is rice. The rice is your staple—the storyline of your piece. Are you the protagonist of your own story, the lonely writer who wanders into an empty bistro? Or is the chef the principal character, that mad scientist creating magic over the stove? Is it perhaps that one dish, the superstar of the menu—a seven-layered sandwich or a six-storey-tall cake—whose progression you follow from kitchen to table? Lay the table and rest assured your readers will find their places.

---

9 Chatto and Windus, 1998.

Naptime

If you really want to follow the Bengali rule of thumb, it's the *dupurer bhaat ghoom*[10] which will make things a lot better. Let the piece rest and revisit it later. Those edits you will want to make when you've digested the meal are vital. Eventually though, the proof of the pudding will be in your readers' eating, not in the writing.

---

10 Afternoon siesta, usually rice-induced.

On Translation

Jerry Pinto

Jerry Pinto is a Mumbai-based, prize-winning Indian writer of poetry, prose, and children's fiction in English.

~

Not far from where the parrot sings, there was a land called Monolingua. It was inhabited by Monolinguals who never felt as well as they could be. They weren't unhealthy; just not as bright and happy as they might be.

They consulted their shaman, a she-man, and she said, "You need salt from Altalingua."

Altalingua was on the other side of a fast-flowing river called Meaning. This was a wonderful river that fertilised their land and gave them water to drink, but it was also tricky; there was the Current of Misunderstanding and the Whirlpool of Connotation and the rapids of Literal Interpretation. However, a call went out for volunteers, and a young carrier offered her services. The older and wiser shook their heads. It was a stupid thing to do, they thought. But the carrier was young and foolish and wanted something more, something better, more vibrant, more alive, more words, more sounds, a lot more.

She set off across the river in a boat made of wood, and on the other side, she was welcomed by the Altalinguals. They were delighted to see her, and when she explained that she needed some salt, they said they were willing to let her have as much as she needed but by their laws, she would not be allowed to carry it in any container, receptacle, or bag.

"How am I supposed to carry the salt across?" she asked.

"That is your problem, not ours," said the Altalinguals.

The young woman spent the night in prayer to the Goddesses of Vox, and in the morning the answer came in the form of a cloud. In the fluffy forms sailing overhead, she saw something that looked like a boat. And she realised she would have to abandon the boat in which she had come and make a boat of salt.

And so the young carrier fashioned a boat of salt and put it into the River of Meaning, which immediately began to put out little investigative tongues of water, licking at the boat. She jumped in but even before she had picked up the oars, the salt began to dissolve. The carrier began to paddle frantically. The river was fast, and the water took large chunks from her boat.

When she got to the other side, not much of the boat was left.

The Monolinguals were not happy.

"How little of the salt you brought across!" they sighed.

The carrier shrugged.

She would try again.

And they would complain again.

I do not remember the moment when I started translating. I do not think anyone ever remembers this moment, so deeply human is it, so intrinsic to every process of language. In every act of language, some translation must occur. Somewhere in the brain, neurons fire across synapses. These electrical circuits draw on memory and imagination, what we know and what we don't, what we think and what we feel, and we must take all this sensory and conceptual material and use words to construct phrases and phrases to build sentences. Somewhere muscles are moved around in the throat. Breath must be drawn up and forced across the vocal cords. The tongue plays its part, the palate, the teeth. And words emerge. Now sounds fare forth and arrive at their destination, another tympanum, if they are lucky. They create another series of neuronal firings, more translations in reverse order and more reactions: a dog may sit down, a friend may smile, a foe may frown. More translations.

I live in a city that exists only in a state of translation. Its name is a debate of translations: is it a good bay or a goddess? Choose and your choice, whether Bombay or Mumbai, places you somewhere, for your auditors. They've translated your choices and aligned you somewhere.

To my left lives a Gujarati family. On my right, lives a Marathi family.

In between?

I was in the third standard in Victoria High School, Mahim, when I was asked what my mother tongue was. There was some kind of form that had to be filled out, and my class teacher wanted to know.

I went home and asked my mother.

"English," she said. "Your mother dreams in English, your mother screams in English."

I knew what she meant. Frederick Algernon Trotteville alias "Fatty" of Enid Blyton's Five Find-Outers was outed when he pretended to be French by a bad guy who simply hurt him so that he cried out in English.[11] The language of your pain is the language of your heart and brain.

I went back and told my teacher.

"English?" she snorted. "Are you Anglo-Indian?"

"No," I replied.

"Then you cannot say English is your mother tongue. Where are you from?"

---

11 Enid Blyton. *The Mystery of the Secret Room*. Methuen, 1945.

"Mahim?" I said.

"You're one sample! Your name is Pinto. Are you Goan or Mangalorean?"

"Goan," I said.

She wrote down Konkani.

It was my first lesson in how you could or could not claim a language.

~

Some people translate because there's money in it. Not literary translators. They don't do it for the money because there isn't enough money in it. Not in India.

Translators don't do it for the royalties. Arunava Sinha, the one-man Bengali translation industry, was on stage with some translators at the Samanvay Literary Festival,[12] India's most precious literary space in my mind, for it is where languages meet on an equal footing and talk to each other. He began moderating the session with a question: how do we get them to buy the books we translate?

No one had any answers though Gillian Wright, who translates from Hindi to English, suggested subterfuge. Don't tell them it's a translation. Keep the translator's name off the cover. Do you see the translator's name on the cover of a Gabriel García Márquez novel?

Translators therefore don't do it for the fame. How could they? Tintin, the comic book you loved? The series was not originally written in English, you do know that? Who translated Tintin? The Asterix & Obelix series were originally written in French. Who translated those magnificent puns? Come on, surely

---

12 Samanvay is "an annual celebration of writing in Indian languages. The festival has aimed at generating dialogue across Indian languages at various levels and has emerged as the only literature festival dedicated exclusively to Indian languages" (*Wikipedia*).

you know. Those guys gave you hours of pleasure, but you didn't care to remember their names. I have to say that, until I became a translator, I didn't either.

They don't do it because the writers of the original works care. I was on stage with Amir Or, an Israeli poet, at the Tata Lit Live festival in Mumbai. He read some poems in Hebrew and then he read them in English. I asked him who had translated his poems. He said, "Many people." He did not remember. Other writers don't care much either. A recent book of poems carries epigraphs from Rumi and Neruda. Both are English poets, you see. Because the poet and his publishers did not think fit to put the translator's name in.

So I should have been prepared for a complete lack of understanding.

I wasn't.

~

I had just translated *Cobalt Blue* (Penguin India, 2013) by Sachin Kundalkar. The author had read the translation, and he had said, "You have made it into a poetic thing," a compliment I held close to my heart as we went over five or six corrections. Then the book was launched, and I was on stage with my translation. I had read a section of it out at a reading, and then the floor was thrown open to questions.

The first question was: "Do you really speak Marathi well enough to translate?"

I was so startled by this that I did not know how to respond. I wanted to say, "I stuck the whole thing into Google Translate and when it came out the other side, I printed it out and put my name on it."

I stumbled through a response. I said something self-deprecating and defensive about how I wasn't sure how well I knew English, and when I got to the level of competence I wanted in that language, I should deal with another language and that language would no doubt be Marathi. The person asking the question sank back into her seat, not wholly convinced.

I have often thought of this question because it has come at me at any number of readings or panel discussions on translation.

I believe it has something to do with my name.

Were my name Jaiteerth Pant, I don't think anyone would ask this question. But a Roman Catholic man from Goa? Should he be translating Marathi?

And since the question is asked again and again, I have tried several variants of the same answer.

"Who can say they know a language? There will always be a word lurking on the next page of the dictionary, ready to slay your sense of superiority."

"The quotidian world for me is English. I make pilgrimages to other languages and return bearing blessings as pilgrims do."

I have given up trying to answer the question honestly because I do not think the question is asked honestly. I have some idea of why it is asked, but this is perhaps not the best place to air those ideas.

One day, if I am brave enough to be vulnerable, I might say: How can you ask that question of a writer? Do you not know that most writers often feel overwhelmed by the infinite variety of a single language? Do you not know that most writers often struggle with how inadequate all linguistic resources are when they are seeking to conjure up the specificity within? And how when they invent a new character, they struggle with the language that they must deploy to make her come alive? How they weigh each word she uses so as to be sure she would say such a word in such a place and time? And how much more they struggle when they are taking a character, composed only of words, and transplanting him into another? He may be as vibrant as a Falstaff,[13] she may

---

13 Falstaff: A humorous figure in several Shakespeare plays; Vasantsena: A beautiful and talented courtesan, the protagonist of Sudraka's Sanskrit play *Mrcchakatika* (date uncertain); Orlando: The sex-changing central character in Virginia Woolf's 1928 novel of that name.

be as multivalent as Vasantsena, he may be as she as Orlando, but in the act of translating it becomes clear, s/he is only words, and if they are the wrong words, no one will laugh at Falstaff, no one will be seduced by Vasantsena, no one will be disoriented into the multiple possibilities of Orlando. This is more responsibility than anyone can assume, should assume. I have assumed that responsibility, knowing what it means. You want to know whether I know enough words?

I want to say: Do you know what it takes to become a translator? It takes the wanting. You must want to. That's a good beginning. If you want to, you start and when you fail, you learn. And you always fail. But you learn to fail as well as you can, and you learn to fail with grace.

I have now translated a book from Hindi and a book from Konkani. I expect to be interrogated on the size of my vocabulary in these languages as well. Or perhaps my surname will spare me the word count when I confront an audience with a Konkani translation.

How my first translation from Hindi happened is an odd story, a story almost of predestination. *Em and the Big Hoom*, my first novel, dealt with the four Mendes-es, a family held in thrall by the central protagonist Em, who is bipolar.

When it came out in 2012, I began doing a series of readings. I found that many of these became fraught with emotion. Strangers would stand up ostensibly to ask questions but would then talk about how mental illness had ruined their families; or how they were so sorry for what they had done. I didn't know how to handle this outpouring of emotion, but a wise female friend said, "Tell them to write. It seems to have helped you."

I began to say that at readings until someone said, "What will happen if we do write? Will it be published?" I said we could do an anthology, maybe? And eventually *A Book of Light: When a Loved One has a Different Mind* (Speaking Tiger, 2016) was born.

One of the last pieces to come in was by Sukant Deepak, the son of the Hindi playwright Swadesh Deepak. I had heard of Swadesh Deepak, I had seen a production of *Court Martial* at the Prithvi Theatre in my city and had been startled by its compression and its rage. I did not know that Swadesh Deepak had suffered a nervous breakdown, that he had been "cured" by a series of electroshock treatments at the All India Institute of Medical Sciences, Chandigarh, and that he had then written about this in *Maine Mandu Nahin Dekha: Ek Khandit Collage* (*I Have Not Seen Mandu: A Fractured Collage*). The book came out and was well received; Deepak even wrote a play afterwards. Then the illness returned, and unable to bear it, Swadesh Deepak got up one morning, left his home, and never came back.

He vanished into India.

When I read Sukant's piece, I was moved and astonished, but I was wearing my editor's hat. I made a mental note to try and find the book, but any reader will tell you that there are hundreds of books about which mental notes are made and then misplaced. They get lost in the snowstorm of these notes.

But at this time I was also helping my friend Shirin Sabavala organise the archive of her husband, the painter Jehangir Sabavala. In the middle of beautiful books on the Impressionists and volumes of French poetry was a copy of *Maine Mandu Nahin Dekha*.

"May I borrow this?" I asked Shirin impulsively.

"Of course," she said. I borrow books from friends, but I return them religiously, so I am trusted. On the bus going home, I opened the book idly and began to read, and suddenly I got sucked in, I vanished into Swadesh Deepak's world.

I missed my stop for the first time in years and had to backtrack, but that gave me more time to read. When I got home, I was about halfway through, but I was completely transfixed. I had never read anything like it. I was on Facebook at this time, so I simply reached out to Sukant Deepak on Facebook and said, "You must translate this book."

His reply was simple, "I can't. Too personal."
I did not think. I simply wrote back. On Facebook messenger. "Then may I?"
He said, "Please."

~

The first book I translated came out of my horror at the state of India's rural schools. It was the tenth year of the Sarva Shikshan Abhiyan,[14] and the government sent out examiners to see how the children were doing in school. Most of those examiners must have come back with pabulum, the usual predictable stuff, but one man went out and actually checked. Heramb Kulkarni watched as teachers explained mathematics incorrectly, and he took photographs of blackboards on which teachers had worked out sums wrong. He gave a one-sentence dictation to students in Chandrapur—one of Maharashtra's poorest districts—and found that most of them could not spell simple words after eight years of Marathi-medium education. He took pictures of Adivasi[15] students being made to clean the teachers' homes. He wrote a book, *Shaala Aahe Shikshan Naahi* (*We Have Schools but No Learning*).

The book caused a storm. My assistant, Santosh Thorat, brought me a copy, and I read it with growing horror. I had long worked with MelJol, an NGO that worked in the sphere of child rights, and by denying them a good education, these children had been denied the right to development. Santosh told me that his father-in-law, Ajit Wakde, was keen on translating the book. I encouraged him to do it.

---

14 A government programme aimed at achieving universal primary education for children in India.
15 Literally "first inhabitants", a term used to describe the indigenous people of India, the so-called Scheduled Tribes.

And Mr Wakde did but when I read it, I realised that my friend Shanta Gokhale[16] was right. You cannot correct a translation, you can only translate it afresh. With his permission, I began to do that, and soon we had a draft on which we agreed.

A small press agreed to publish it and never did.

The editor at the small press thought she was preparing a fresh book for publication. She asked questions of the original author as if she were expecting him to write a new book. It was a breach of etiquette in a way, but these things happen. Some books simply die on the way to the press.

My first translation did not come out.

~

This should have been discouragement enough. But around this time, I was studying the Urdu script and learning to read and write in it. I was also reading Hindi and Marathi poetry every day, and one day, I happened on an article in *The Indian Express* in which Shanta Gokhale had been asked to name some of the Marathi-language books she had read and liked recently. She mentioned *Cobalt Blue* by Sachin Kundalkar. I went for a walk and bought the book. I began reading it, and the first lines began to play in my head. They were easy to understand, the book is spoken to us in the voices of a young man and a young woman, neither of whom is literary, but that first line was not an easy line to render into English. But some part of me was trying. I was fiddling with that sentence, teasing it, pulling it and pushing it.

Even before I had a workable solution, I knew I wanted to translate the book. A little while later, I called up Shanta Gokhale and asked, "Do you think I could translate *Cobalt Blue*?"

She said, "You!"

---

16 Shanta Gokhale: Distinguished Indian writer, translator, and critic. See her essay in this book.

There was an exclamation mark of delight at the end of her comment. Had there been a question mark of scorn, I might never have tried. It was a lesson for me as a teacher as well.

After I had finished, I read it to Neela Bhagwat,[17] who had taught me Marathi when I decided I must learn it again, and then to Shanta Gokhale. When they approved it, vetted it in their different ways, I showed it to Sachin Kundalkar. I've told you what happened after that.

~

The next translation happened because of another book. With Naresh Fernandes, now the editor of Scroll.in, I had edited an anthology on Bombay called *Bombay Meri Jaan: Writings on Mumbai* (Penguin India, 2003). We had included a passage from Daya Pawar's seminal autobiography *Baluta*, which we had taken from Arjun Dangle's magnificent anthology, *Poisoned Bread: Translations from Modern Marathi Dalit Literature* (Orient Longman, 1992).

A decade later, someone called from Penguin and asked if we would like to reconsider our anthology. So much had happened to the city since then, and we might want to add some fresh material. I was okay with that but first, I thought, we should look at what we had. I read the excerpt we had chosen, "Son, Eat Your Fill", and thought: "*Baluta* must have been translated by now. I should read it and see if there's a passage that suits us better."

Once again, I called Shanta Gokhale and asked whether *Baluta* had been translated.

"Not yet," she said.

"Then do you think I could?"

Again, she was delighted and said she would put me in touch with Pradnya Daya Pawar, who also assented, and I was off.

---

17 Neela Bhagwat: Renowned Indian Classical musician.

Baluta was a tough read. I began with a sense of confusion. It was supposed to be non-fiction, right? It was supposed to be an autobiography, right? Then why were there two Daya Pawars in the first few pages? Why were these two Daya Pawars talking to each other? What was going on?

Then the narrative evened out, and I was carried into Pawar's world, a world torn between his love of language and the way the custodians of language rejected his kind, a world torn between the familiarity of the village and the lure of the city. The result of such a life was a divided Pawar, I realised, a man split in two, a man who could contain multitudes, out of which two could certainly take the stage to speak to each other.

But there was another reason, which Pawar spells out in that first externalised internal conversation. What if you have not seen too many of your kind in the books you have loved? What if you have always been missing from the literature you have read all your life? How do you summon up the courage to write a book about yourself? How will you know that it is a book? Someone has to encourage you to do it. Someone has to get you to the sticking point. Who better than yourself? Once Pawar has got Pawar to tell Pawar's story, he has done his work. He does appear again in the end, but it is a necessary closure. For details, read the book. Speaking Tiger brought it out in 2015. The original was published in 1978.

When we launched the book at the Tata Institute of Social Sciences, Pradnya Daya Pawar said she was glad that I had translated her father's book for now her son could read his grandfather's life story.

Her son does not read Marathi.

~

For twenty-five years, I have taught at the Social Communications Media department of the Sophia Polytechnic. Each year, the students put together a magazine, which I edit and in which I allow them to write what they want to write about, because they will soon go out into the real world of the media and discover what the agendas of the media are. One of my students, Mithila Phadke, asked if she could interview Mallika Amar Sheikh. I had heard of Mallika Amar Sheikh as the author of the powerful autobiography, *Mala Uddhvastha Vhaaychay* (*I Insist on Destroying Myself*). I had also heard that she was a recluse. But Mithila Phadke was sure she could make contact and she did. The result was an interesting interview, interesting enough for me to ask Ms Phadke for her copy of *Mala Uddhvastha Vhaaychay*. This was a photocopy—originals seem few and far between—and I read it in a night. It was just one of a number of books I was reading. I did not think about translating it because I was sure Mallika Amar Sheikh must have been asked multiple times and had refused.

But over the years, I grew more and more fascinated by the figure of the revolutionary poet and singer, Amar Sheikh, Mallika's father, and when Ravi Singh asked me to be commissioning editor at Speaking Tiger I suggested that we should ask Amarendra Dhaneshwar to write a biography of Amar Sheikh. Nandu, I argued, would understand the political context; he would understand the music; he had even attended a couple of Sheikh's performances. When I put it to him, his wife, Neela Bhagwat, said we should all go and meet Mallika as she knew her well.

We went and had dinner with Mallika. The fried fish was excellent, and on our way out Mallika said: "No one is translating my book."

"I will," I said.

And I did.

~

It was at Shanta Gokhale's home—her name is a leitmotif, it would seem, in this piece—that I heard Ganesh Matkari read out his novel, *Khidkya Ardhya Ugdya*. I enjoyed its urban setting, and I thought

I could do a good English version of a book about young people working their way through the system. But before *Half-Open Windows* (Speaking Tiger, 2017) could come out, I read a column Shanta wrote in the *Mumbai Mirror* in which she mentioned a book, *Mee Meethachi Bahuli*, by one Vandana Mishra. A few days later, I bought the book and fell in love with its easy voice, its unabashed nostalgia, the Bombay it conjured up of theatrical performances and horse carriages to Borivali station. I was also delighted that it was by the mother of Ambarish Mishra, one of my colleagues from the brief time that I worked at the *Times of India*. Mrs Mishra was born Sushila Lotlikar. Her father died when she was two, and her mother had to train as a midwife to keep the family in food. Then someone threw acid on her back, and she ended up bedridden. The family went back to the poverty line, but Sushila, who was then thirteen years old, stepped up. She went to Pandit Altekar's drama school and got a job at the Bhangwadi theatre, as a Gujarati stage actor. For a while, this kept the family going, but since she was only getting second leads, Sushila moved on to the Marwadi[18] stage where she was a huge hit. Then her mother told her that time was ticking and, at the height of her career, she retired to marry Pandit Mishra. She was twenty-one.

At the time she wrote her book, she was in her eighties, and so I worked ferociously at it. She did live to see her book come out in English as *I, the Salt Doll* (Speaking Tiger again) but not long enough for me to capture some of her charm on film. She rarely got out of bed by the time I went to visit her, but she was vibrant, vital, and as much of an actor as she had ever been. To have captured that on celluloid would have been an act of translation that might have made the world a richer place. But the life of any creative person is always littered with lost opportunities.

~

---

18 Marwadi, Marwari: An ethnic group originally from Rajasthan but now found throughout India.

My encounter with Baburao Bagul began with *Poisoned Bread* too. That is what books do. They spawn other books. I read "Death Is Becoming Cheaper" there and was struck by its peculiar picaresque quality. It remained with me, and when I found myself reading *Jevha Mee Jaat Chorli*, I realised that Bagul was an extraordinary writer. His descriptions are almost beautiful, Romantic even; the action is savage and described with modernist severity. Death stalks these stories; translating them was painful, but the only way through was through. I told myself repeatedly that this was experienced reality; what must lived reality be like? The book won the Bangalore Literary Festival's Atta Galata Bookstore Prize for Fiction, which made me very happy. I could not go to Bangalore to receive it but collected my statuette the next year. On the way home, I realised it was not my statuette. It belonged to Bagul, the magnificent writer, so when I got home from Bangalore, I got a photograph taken of myself with the trophy, and then sent it off to the writer's widow.

~

The truth of the matter is that we only have a limited amount of time here. I have been lucky in that I have the ordering of my time; or at least have had for the past dozen years. I get to decide what I want to do, but I have what might be described as an approach-approach conflict. I want to write as much as I want to translate. When Dr Anjali Prabhu, then the director of the Suzy and Donald Newhouse Centre at Wellesley, asked me if I would like to come and spend a term there, I thought it might be time to focus on my own writing.

It was the winter term, which was perfect. Snow-silenced Boston. The north-easterners, taciturn at the best of times, put their heads down and hurried past the brown man in the monkey cap. The students went about their own business, acting out winter, shaking flakes from their beautiful hair and stamping elegant boots on the cobbles. I wrote and wrote and wrote and managed to get a novel in halfway shape. It felt good. I had kept my promise to my muse.

On the way back, I passed through Lillehammer, Norway, to spend some time as a guest of the Sigrid Undset foundation. And perhaps here is an object lesson in why you should read translations. I was at the Jaipur Literary festival and shared a ride with a nice young man who said he was from Norway. I said, "Ah Norway, the land of Sigrid Undset."

He goggled at me.

"You know Sigrid Undset?"

"Who doesn't?" I asked. "Didn't she win the Nobel Prize for Literature?"

"Yes," he said, pleased. "But I did not think…"

I explained that my parents had both been denied college by their circumstances (which can be translated as poverty). And so they made up for it by reading, and specially by reading the works of all those who had ever won the Nobel Prize. My father wanted to make sure his children also benefited, and so our bedtime reading was Ms Undset's wonderfully bloodthirsty sagas.

"You must come and stay with us at the Sigrid Undset Foundation," Matthias Samuelson said. He was the director of the foundation, and so I actually sat and wrote the last few chapters of my next novel in long hand in Sigrid's study while an underground stream ran beneath my feet and appeared in her garden and ran among the trees she had planted.

Ten days before I was to leave I received an email from Milind Awad, the son of Eknath Awad, the noted Dalit activist. He asked if I would translate his father's autobiography, *Jag Badal Ghaaluni Ghaav*. I looked up Milind and found that he was a professor in the English department at Jawaharlal Nehru University. I told him that I was taking a break from translation, and surely he could translate his father's book? His answer charmed me. He said he had tried translation and discovered he was no good at it. I was disarmed by this. I have found myself surrounded by a tiresome breed of men who think they can do anything, they just haven't tried. (I suspect I may be one of these.) To encounter someone with this level of self-awareness was extraordinary.

But it wasn't that. It was the book. (It is always the book.) It was the voice of Eknath Awad. It was his story. Here was a man who took several degrees and could speak English. He got a job in Mumbai but didn't want to stay in the city. He knew the fight was on in the villages, and he wanted to be in the thick of the action. And so he gave up his job and went back to struggle with those who would electrocute a Mang youth as a blood sacrifice to make sure a water body would fill up. Eknath Awad paid the price. He was stabbed in public and almost died, but he lived to tell his tale, and we are all the richer for it.

I knew I was going to translate *Jag Badal Ghaaluni Ghaav* even halfway through the book because I wanted other people to be able to read it. It's called *Strike a Blow to Change the World* (Speaking Tiger, 2018).

And this may be why we translate, because we want others to read what we have read, we want them to enjoy this too. We want them to feel what we feel.

I am an evangelist for every book I have ever translated. I want you to weep as I wept for Mallika Amar Sheikh, alone and sick. I want you to exult when Awad strikes a blow against caste. I want you to feel the same awe I did for Daya Pawar's brutal self-examination. I want you to visualise Bagul's stories as little films as they play in my head. I want you to walk with the young man on the top of the skyscraper in Matkari's novel.

And so I will go to the gym to lose some weight and end up translating women Warkari[19] poets from the thirteenth century onwards with Neela Bhagwat, a book called *The Ant Who Swallowed the Sun* (Speaking Tiger, 2019).

---

19 Warkari: Bhakti (devotional) movement in Maharashtra.

That is why I translate.

It is a moral imperative for me. We live in a nation of hundreds of languages, Dr Ganesh Devy[20] says. His best guess is 1,500 and counting. Each language is an island separated by the sea. At low tide we cross certain from where we live to where we want to go, but our crossings are driven by our agendas. I speak Hindi to the cab driver. I speak Marathi to the lady who sells me fish. Perhaps I would have spoken Konkani to my grandmother, were she alive, as so many of my students say when I ask them if they speak their home languages. If we are to understand each other, we must reach out at a higher level. We must listen to each other's hearts, not each other's wallets.

To do that we need good translations. Or else we will get those spidery lines of ECGs that are supposed to mimic the fullness, the richness, and the music of the beating of our hearts.

~

Envoi:
Over the years, I grew tired of listening to people saying: You know, so much gets lost in translation.
For them, this poem—which really has to be read aloud, shouted actually.

For all those who say translation loses so much, translation is like this, translation is like that...

A is for Akhmatova and Azmi and Andal and Allende
B is for Basho, Bahinabai and for Basavanna and Baudelaire and Beauvoir. For Bama. For Balzac. Also for a Buddha called Gautama

---

20 Ganesh N. Devy (b. 1950): Indian linguist and anthropologist, perhaps best known for the *People's Linguistic Survey of India*.

C is for Cavafy and Chughtai and Chokhamela
D is for Derrida and Dhoomil; also for Duras and Dostoyevsky
E is for Éluard and Elytis and Euripides
F is for Ferrante and Faiz
G is for Goscinny of Goscinny and Uderzo, yes Asterix and Obelix, but G is for Ghalib and Gandhiji and Goethe and Genet
H is for Hafiz and Holub, Hikmet and
I is for Ikkyu and Iqbal and Ibsen
J is for Janabai and Jesus (from Aramaic to Greek to Latin to you)
K is for Kanhopatra and Kabir and Kautilya; for Kafka, Kundera and Kis
L is for Li Po and Lal Ded and Lalić
M is for Montale and Mir and Mirabai and Manu and Manto; for Muktabai too and Musil as well
N is for Nirala and Nietzsche and Neruda and Namdeo
O is for Onoe and Osieko and Ovid
P is for Pawar (Dayaji) and Pawar (Urmilaji), for Pavese and Proust
Q is for Qabbani and Quasimodo (Salvatore)
R is for Rahim and Rumi and Rilke and Rimbaud
S is for Sappho and Sadi and Saramago and Sei Shonagon and Shelke
T is for Tukaram and Tulsidas and if those two aren't enough, Tolstoy and Tagore
U want more? U is for Ungaretti and Ugraji
V is for Veda Vyasa. I rest my case. Then Valmiki speaks. And Virgil. So I go on with Verlaine and Voltaire
W is for Wali and Wang Wei and Walser
X is for Xiu Li and Xirsi
Y is for Yevtushenko and Yavarov and Yrjana
Z is for Zauk and Zafar and Zachariah (Paul)

A Basic Recipe for Translating[1]

Bruce W. Irwin

Bruce W. Irwin graduated in mathematics before studying German literature at several universities in the United States and Germany. After a few years on the editorial staff of a research institute in Kiel, Germany, he became an instructor in a translation programme with an emphasis on technical translation at the University of Hildesheim, where he taught for over thirty-five years. He still occasionally translates professionally and, now that he has grandchildren, has started to produce illustrated bilingual children's books. His article summarises much of what he has learned, both as a professional translator and as a teacher of translation, and it addresses writers with little or no previous background in translation.

~

As translating is a special form of writing, it should not come as a surprise that many of the rules for writing other texts apply

---

[1] I wish to express my thanks to Gerald Kreissl, who provided me with numerous helpful suggestions.

to translation. However, as the source material for a translation comes from a different culture with a different language than the target text (the translation), numerous cultural and linguistic aspects must be taken into consideration by translators. One of the rules for writing, in particular for writing journalistic texts, is to apply all the question words: "why, who, where, what, when, and how".[2] That—in essence—is my basic recipe for translating. However, these questions must be asked on several levels—both for the original source text and for the target text, and questions must be asked regarding both the microtext and macrotext levels.

To elucidate the problems involved with answering these questions, examples will be provided in each case, and in keeping with the title of this essay, I will start each time with examples from the culinary field, but examples from other fields will be discussed to demonstrate a more general applicability of these principles. As writing in general and translating in particular are complex undertakings, the questions that a translator must ask usually entail a combination of several question words at the same time. *Why* a text is translated usually involves *who* it is being translated for, *where* the intended readership comes from, *what* the text is about, *when* it is to be published or read, and *how* the function of the translation can best be realised. As a result, the contents of the following six main sections overlap, just as no professional translator would try to consider each of the six sets of questions separately for any one decision that has to be made in the translation process. But without further ado, let us look at the first group of questions, the "why" questions.

---

2   See: Trina Wallace. "Employing the Five Ws (and one H)". 2020. https://www.charitycomms.org.uk/employing-the-five-ws-and-one-h; The Editors, *Columbia Journalism Review*. "Who, what, when, where, why, and how. CJR asks the question: What is journalism for?" 2019. https://archives.cjr.org/cover_story/who_what_when.php; These are of course the "six honest serving-men" of Kipling's well-known poem from the *Just So Stories*.

Why?

As most modern translation specialists consider the *function* of a translation essential to the translation process, this question word is the first ingredient in my recipe. Notable representatives of this approach to translation are Katharina Reiss, Hans J. Vermeer, Christiane Nord, and Mary Snell-Hornby. Reiss and Vermeer chose the Greek term *skopos* (aim or target) for their translation theory. Nord refers to her principles for translating as "functional translation". Snell-Hornby writes: "A translation is directly dependent on its prescribed function, which must be made clear by the commissioner (in professional practice usually a foregone conclusion)."[3]

In my opinion, the "foregone conclusion" really only applies if the other questions (who, where, what, when, how) have already been answered; if a translator knows for whom the text is to be translated and where it is to be published (in which publication, in which culture), the reason for translating may be obvious. As mentioned above, the answer to any question involving any one of the "W" and "H" words almost always requires an answer to other questions involving at least one of the others. Why a text is translated usually depends on who the text is translated for and what their needs are; who the intended readers are is determined by where they live; and so on.

If, for example, a German recipe from a cookbook for hobby chefs is to be translated into English for a cookbook for American hobby chefs, it seems obvious that the main objective of the translation is facilitating the preparation of the dish by the American readers. As the function of the original recipe was the facilitation of the preparation of the dish by the German readers of the original cookbook in Germany, the function remains the same. The translation is therefore functionally constant.

---

3 Mary Snell-Hornby. *Translation Studies: An Integrated Approach.* Benjamins, 1988, 44.

However, the function of the target, or translated, text does not have to be the same as that of the original, or source, text. If we stick with the translation of recipes as an example, the possibility of functional divergence may not seem obvious to non-translators. My friend Gerald Kreissl translated recipes from French into German for a German autobiography of Marc Haeberlin,[4] the famous chef at the restaurant Auberge de l'Ill in Alsace, France. The recipes had originally been written by Haeberlin for his own use or for other master chefs at Auberge de l'Ill. For highly trained professional chefs at a restaurant that was continuously awarded three stars by *Guide Michelin* over several decades, complete descriptions of the cooking procedures for preparing the dishes were hardly necessary. The German readers of the biography are not expected to be able to prepare them, but rather the recipes together with photographs of the dishes demonstrate the skill of Haeberlin, the complexity and scope of some of his creations, and the variety of ingredients used in preparing them.

One example[5] is a recipe for meringues filled with fresh red fruit (like strawberries), served on an almond pastry with poached rhubarb, strawberry coulis and topped with a tuile,[6] but no indication is given as to how many strawberries are necessary, how to prepare the coulis or the tuile, or even what kind of tuile would be appropriate. From the colour of the exquisitely twisted tuile in the photograph, caramel or orange tuiles are possible, but the reader can only guess.

When, in the following, I translate *excerpts* from recipes to demonstrate some of the principles of translating, rather than to provide my readers with the possibility of preparing the

---

4 Marc Haeberlin. *Die Kochlegende Marc Haeberlin*. With Stefan Pegatzky. Tre Torri, 2017.
5 Ibid. 220 ff.
6 A coulis is thin sauce made from puréed and strained fruits. A tuile is a thin, baked wafer, which is usually arced or twisted.

dishes described themselves, these are therefore also examples of functional divergence.

Who?

While discussing the "why" questions, we already mentioned some "who" questions (who are the text recipients, both for whom the original text was written and for whom the text is to be translated?). The intended text recipients dictate how any text should be written, including translations. Recipes are published for the whole spectrum of readers, from professional chefs to children, and the readership of the target text does not have to be similar to that of the source text. Detailed explanations that are left out in a recipe intended for a professional may have to be added if the translation is intended for non-professionals. The terminology used also varies from one group of readers to the next. In the culinary field, French terminology is commonly used by professionals in many non-French-speaking cultures, but not necessarily among hobby chefs, and certainly not in cookbooks for children. In some languages, such as German, children are generally addressed with the informal "you" (*du*), rather than with the formal "you" (*Sie*) that is used for adults who are not close friends. Recipes requiring complex or time-consuming procedures are usually avoided in children's cookbooks, or they are told to ask their parents for help.

For whom a text is written also determines the style used, as readers have specific expectations as to what a particular type of text should look like. This is referred to as *text conventions*, some of which may apply to an entire language, while others differ from one cultural region or group of readers (such as professional chefs versus hobby chefs) to the next. Text conventions can dictate both macrolevel text structure (like formatting) and microlevel text structure (grammar, word choice, and so on). A language-wide convention for English-language recipes at the microlevel seems to be the use of the imperative in the instructions. Theoretically, many other forms could be used in English for describing the preparation of a dish. I have seen such grammatical structures in culinary journals such as *Cook's Illustrated*; typically, authors for that journal use these forms for describing their research on perfecting recipes before providing the final recipe, which invariably uses the imperative.

Other text types in English also have very restrictive conventions. This can be seen by looking at the specifications for writing industrial standards. For instance, the British Standards Institution dictates how modal auxiliary verbs should be used:

> The auxiliary verb "shall" is used to express requirements in a specification, "should" is used to express recommendations in a code of practice or a guide, "may" is used to express permission and "can" to express physical possibility. "Must" is not used.[7]

The American National Standards Institute does essentially the same thing in its *Style Manual* and in its more recent *Style Guide-sheet*:

> The word "shall" shall be understood as denoting a mandatory requirement. "Shall" shall be used wherever the criterion for conformance with the specific recommendation requires that there be no deviation. Its use shall not be avoided on the grounds that compliance with the standard is considered voluntary. "Shall" shall not be used in any foreword, informative annex, or footnote.

---

7   British Standards Institution. *Rules for the structure and drafting of UK standards*. ("6.6.1 Verbal forms for the expression of provisions"). 2012 (6.6.1 Verbal forms for the expression of provisions) http://www.bsigroup.com/Documents/standards/guide-to-standards/BSI-Guide-to-standards-2-standard-structure-UK-EN.pdf

The word "should" shall denote a recommendation. "Should" shall be used wherever noncompliance with the specific recommendation is permissible.[8]

The correct verb form for indicating a requirement is "shall". The correct verb form for indicating a recommendation is "should". Universally accepted "standardese" does not recognize "must". Use "shall" for indicating a mandatory aspect or an aspect on which there is no option.[9]

For someone not familiar with industrial standards, these language specifications probably seem strange, as in everyday speech "must" is much more commonly used for mandatory requirements than "shall".

A wide variety of grammatical structures are used, however, in German recipes. An imperative may be used, but in German there are three imperative forms: the formal imperative (*Sieben Sie das Mehl in eine große Schüssel*), the informal imperative plural (*Siebt das Mehl in eine große Schüssel*), and the informal imperative singular (*Sieb das Mehl in eine große Schüssel*) (all ≈ "Sift the flour into a large bowl").[10] Infinitive constructions are very common in German recipes, as well as in other instructional texts, for which there is no similar sentence structure in English (*Das Mehl in eine große Schüssel sieben* ≈ "The flour into a large bowl [to] sift"). The impersonal pronoun *man* (*Man siebt das Mehl in eine große*

---

8 American National Standards Institute. *Style Manual for preparation of proposed American National Standards.* 8th ed. 1991 ("6.8 Special word usage"). At http://www2.ans.org/standards/resources/downloads/docs/ansi-stylemanual.pdf

9 American National Standards Institute. *ANSI Style Guide-sheet—2003* ("2 Correct use of 'shall', 'should' and 'must', i.e., correct form of requirements and recommendations"). At https://www.usug.org/answg/pdf/ANSI%20Style%20Guidesheet%20-%202003.pdf

10 The ≈ symbol is used to indicate approximate rather than full equivalence, which essentially never exists between a source text and a target text.

Schüssel ≈ "One sifts the flour into a large bowl") is also commonly used, as are the person pronouns *ich, sie* and *er* (*Ich siebe das Mehl in eine große Schüssel* ≈ "I sift the flour into a large bowl", *Sie / Er siebt das Mehl in eine große Schüssel* ≈ "She / He sifts the flour into a large bowl"). Examples can also be found for modal verbs (*Das Mehl sollte in eine große Schüssel gesiebt werden* ≈ "The flour is to be sifted into a large bowl"), and so on. The publisher may dictate which form is to be used or the authors may have their own preference, but German readers are not disturbed by the different styles used in recipes. Essentially the same can be said for several other languages, including French and Spanish. These differences in conventions from one language to another should make it obvious that the source text dictates neither the style nor, in particular, the grammatical structures used in the target text.

After looking at conventions for recipes on the microlevel, I now want to look at conventions on the macrolevel. The first, almost trivial, convention is the use of a title for each dish at the beginning of the recipe, and this seems to be the case in most languages and cultures. The order in which the other information is provided, however, varies greatly from one cookbook to the next, which again may be dictated by the publisher or a personal preference of the author. Foreign recipes included in a cookbook usually adhere to the layout and formatting used in the rest of the book, so the translator may be required to reorganise the information in the translation, to adhere to the layout of the book. A fairly standard layout with a long tradition in English provides a list of the ingredients separately, before giving the instructions. This layout for recipes is common in many European languages and cultures.

A completely different layout is used in the *Joy of Cooking* series of cookbooks. In the 1931 edition, Irma S. Rombauer used the convention of placing a list of the ingredients before the directions, as was common in most other cookbooks at that time. Starting, however, with the 1936 edition, she eliminated the separate list and set off the ingredients so that they stand out within the instructions. This layout has been used in all the *Joy of Cooking* cookbooks since, and copied by several other American cookbook authors. But recipe layouts are not restricted to these two formats. A recipe may be presented in steps with the list of ingredients alternating with the instructions for the steps, sometimes listed in separate columns to add more clarity.

Christiane Nord[11] emphasises the importance of loyalty, both to the original author(s) and to the intended readership. In other words, if a recipe is translated, the translator must demonstrate loyalty to the intended readership by making sufficient changes to enable the reader to prepare the dish (if that is the function of the translation), but must demonstrate loyalty to the original author by not altering the recipe so much that the dish originally created by the author is no longer recognisable. That means that besides the "for whom" questions, we also have to ask who wrote the original text or who is given as the source of the translated text. Usually, the author of the original text is given as the author of the translated text, at least when texts are translated as a whole. It is not unusual for the authors of recipe books to include recipes from other countries that they have translated, using their own style for consistency within their books and adapting the recipes for their intended readership. The following is an example of (the beginning of) such a recipe from the 1946 *Joy of Cooking*[12] in which Irma Rombauer maintains her specific formatting:

SACHERTORTE

A recipe of the famous restaurant keeper Frau Sacher, who fed the impoverished Austrian nobility long after they had

---

11 Christiane Nord. *Einführung in das funktionale Übersetzen: Am Beispiel von Titeln und Überschriften.* Francke, 1993, 8.
12 Irma S. Rombauer. *Joy of Cooking: A Compilation of Reliable Recipes with an Occasional Culinary Chat.* Bobbs-Merrill, 1946, 576.

ceased to pay. (She is the hotel proprietess [sic] in *Reunion in Vienna*.) This cake was considered worthy of her name.
Beat until soft:
½   **cup butter**
Add gradually:
½   **cup and 2 tablespoons confectioner's sugar**
Beat these ingredients until they are well blended. Put in a warm place until it is as soft as butter:
4   **ounces sweet chocolate**
Beat in one at a time:
6   **egg yolks**
[...]

From this another convention typical of the *Joy of Cooking* series becomes obvious: comments and suggestions are provided after the title, and before the instructions and ingredients are given. In other cookbooks they may be listed at the end of the recipe, or in a separate column. When translating such recipes for use in a specific cookbook, the translator may have to rearrange the order in which the text is presented to match the conventions used in the target publication.

Most German cookbooks maintain a uniform style throughout, however, some German authors prefer to vary their style and use numerous grammatical constructions. Extreme examples can be found in the culinary column of Bert Gamerschlag in the weekly magazine *Stern*. He frequently presents recipes using as many as four different grammatical constructions for instructions in the same text, while using other, often completely different, constructions in other issues. The German food magazine *essen & trinken* seems to use infinitive constructions for all its recipes, but different layouts. Lengthy recipes usually have the list of ingredients in the first column with the instructions in numbered steps in the middle and right-hand columns. Recipes of a moderate length have everything in one column. Shorter recipes are often presented with the ingredients embedded in the instructions. The magazine even mixes two formats for some recipes. As mentioned above, such variety would be theoretically possible in English recipes, but I have never seen an example in print and must assume that it would be most unusual, which means that a translator should avoid a non-uniform style in recipes in English. Many companies outside the culinary field also have their own text conventions, which are part of their corporate identity and must be taken into consideration by any translator who produces texts for them.

Where?

Some of the "where" questions are automatically answered when we answer the questions *by* whom and *for* whom the source text was written, and *for* whom the target text is to be written, but there are many more questions that deal with the source culture and the target culture for a particular translation. Regional differences exist for most languages and can play an important role for translators. Some of the regional differences in English are common knowledge and, although they may sound strange to speakers from a different region, they usually do not result in misunderstandings and may be included intentionally to provide a foreign flair. What Americans call rutabagas are usually called swedes, for example, in England. The kitchen appliance that the English frequently refer to as a cooker is usually called a stove or range in North America, whereas "cooker" in American English is generally restricted to a smaller device, such as a portable camping stove or a pressure cooker. Such differences in meaning and usage can, of course, result in misunderstandings. Unfortunately, there are many terms that are used for completely different concepts in different English dialects, so translators must be certain of the English dialect used in the source text before translating it into another language and use the appropriate terms for their target audience. Some examples of terms for food and drink that can be confusing for the British in America (or the other way around) are biscuits, chips, martinis, and muffins, as they have different meanings on opposite sides of the Atlantic. And the same goes for items of clothing:

> There is a curious but not often noted tendency for the names of articles of apparel to drift around the body. This is particularly apparent to Britons in America (and vice versa) who discover that the names for clothes have moved around at different rates and now often signify quite separate things. A Briton going into a New York department store with a shopping list consisting of vest, knickers, suspenders, jumper and pants would in each instance be given something dramatically different from what he expected.[13]

Naturally, this applies for other languages too. The terms used for rolls or buns in Germany, for example, vary greatly from one region to another: *Brötchen*, *Rundstück*, *Schusterjunge*, *Schrippe*, *Weck* and *Semmel*, to name just a few. And although the last term refers to a normal breakfast roll in Bavaria, it refers to a sweet raisin bread in northern Germany. In other words, determining where the source language text came from and where the target language text will be read can be extremely important for a translator. If the translation is to be made available to an international readership, for example on the internet, the translator is faced with the problem of making the text understandable to readers from different cultures, which may require saying the same thing in several different ways, possibly in brackets (or parentheses in American usage, where the term "bracket" is normally only used for "square brackets" = [ ] or "angle brackets" = < >).

---

13   Bill Bryson. *Mother Tongue: The English Language* (1990). Penguin, 1991, 72.

So far we have only looked at different names for the same thing in different regions, but some concepts may be completely unknown in the target culture and may require additional explanations. When dealing with cooking recipes, some ingredients may be difficult (or impossible) to find in the target culture. While *foie gras* (the enlarged liver of force-fed geese, or ducks) has a long tradition in France, for example, the practice of force-feeding and the production of foie gras are illegal in Germany and many other countries, and in some countries the sale is also prohibited, so a substitute must be suggested if a recipe calling for foie gras is to be translated for readers in a culture where it is unavailable and the translation is intended for use in preparing a dish.

Additionally, kitchen equipment may not be available in a target culture or the standardised sizes of pans may vary from country to country. A *Stollenform* (stollen pan) may be called for in a recipe for *Weihnachtsstollen*, something not readily available in countries where this German Christmas bread is not commonly baked, so an alternative method, say, shaping the dough by hand and placing it on a greased baking sheet, might be suggested. Loaf pans in the United States are generally measured in inches and increase in width as they increase in length, whereas the loaf pans available in Germany are measured in centimetres and usually have the same width for numerous lengths. A good translator cannot just convert the pan sizes to the unit of measure common in the target culture (clearly loaf pans are not sold with the measurements 27.94 x 11.43 x 6.985 cm [11 x 4½ x 2¾ in.] in Germany), a common pan size in centimetres must be used in the translation instead (for example, 30 x 11 cm).

Then there is the question of temperatures. These are usually listed in Fahrenheit in the United States, and not in Celsius. The translator of a recipe cannot, however, just convert a temperature such as 325°F into 162°C or 170°C into 338°F. The dials for setting the oven temperature usually do not have a continuous scale of temperatures, so cookbook authors tend to restrict the indicated temperatures to multiples of ten or twenty-five. In some countries, the dials on gas ovens use gas marks rather than temperatures, so a temperature may have to be converted into the corresponding gas mark, and unfortunately the gas mark scales are not the same for all countries.

Industrial standards apply to many areas of everyday life, and as they differ considerably in some countries, translations must take such differences into account. When translating instruction manuals for electrical appliances, for example, differences in the electric sockets and plugs may require changes in the target text if the reader is expected to use the manuals for installing or repairing their appliances. Electric wall sockets in the UK frequently have a small switch for turning the socket on or off, whereas sockets in many other countries usually do not. Likewise, there are fuses inside some plugs in the UK, but not in most other countries. Users' manuals often have a section of FAQs, including what to do if the electrical appliance does not work. Translating sentences such as "Check to see that the socket switch is turned on" or "Check to see if the plug fuse needs to be replaced" is counterproductive if sockets in the users' culture do not have switches and plugs do not have fuses, and could even result in a liability suit if a user tries to open a sealed plug looking for the fuse.

"Where" questions can also deal with text conventions specific to an individual culture. Which units of measure will a reader expect to find in a recipe? In the US, where the metric system is not commonly found, except in industries engaged in international business, units defined in the US Customary System are used, such as fluid ounces, cups, dry pints, teaspoons, and tablespoons. These units can cause confusion as units with the same name but a different volume are used in other English-speaking countries. Thus, one fluid ounce is equal to 29.5734 millilitres in the US, but 28.4122 millilitres in the UK or Canada, the standardised Australian tablespoon is considerably larger than the American or British versions, and the term "pint" is a standardised unit of volume ranging between 425 and 1,708 millilitres, depending on the country and the context in which it is used.

Translation problems associated with conventions for the units of measure used in different cultures are not restricted to culinary texts. The units used for indicating the fuel consumption of automobiles can also be confusing. In the US, fuel consumption is usually given in miles per gallon. Here again the US gallon is smaller than the imperial gallon in the UK. In Germany, however, fuel consumption is usually given as the number of litres of fuel consumed in driving 100 kilometres, and this is frequently shortened to just the number of litres. A car that is particularly fuel-efficient can, for example, be referred to as a *Dreiliterauto* ($\approx$ "three-litre automobile"). In English-speaking countries, a unit of volume given to describe an automobile, but without a driven distance, could easily be understood to refer to the engine displacement (normally given in cubic centimetres). As one litre is equal to 1,000 cubic centimetres, a "three-litre engine" would then have a displacement of 3,000 cm^3, which would be an extremely large engine with an unusually large displacement and thus a very high fuel consumption, exactly the opposite of what the German expression is trying to indicate. If units of measure are used in a text to be translated, the translator must be familiar with the conventions in both the source *and* the target culture regarding such units.

Another group of "where" questions deals with the place of publication or publishing house and is closely related to the "who" questions already mentioned. As indicated earlier, the publisher or commissioner may dictate the style to be used in a translation. For English, that can include spelling and punctuation. Besides the differences in spelling associated with the various dialects of English, there are orthographic variations within individual dialects. Common differences in British English include the "z"- versus "s"-spellings ("organize" or "organise") and the use of hyphenation within a word ("co-operate" or "cooperate", "nonlethal" or "nonlethal"), as well as the use of the Oxford or serial comma by some publishers. Publishers may advise that authors adhere to the first spelling listed in a specific dictionary. Thus, "organise" is the first spelling in Collins,[14] but it is "organize" in the Oxford dictionaries. Orthographic variations exist in other languages as well. A reformed system of spelling and punctuation was introduced and approved by the governments of the major German-speaking countries in 1996. Since then there have been several referendums on returning to the older orthography, and numerous authors and publishers have refused to use the new spellings, resulting in modifications of the 1996 reforms and less uniformity in spelling and punctuation than existed before 1996. Translators should be familiar with the orthographic variations in their working languages and be able to adapt their writing to suit their publisher or the commissioner of a translation.

What?

The questions related to "what" are just as multifaceted as the other questions discussed so far. On the macrolevel, the "what" questions deal with the problems of text typology, including some text conventions related to specific cultures already dealt with under "where". On the microlevel, terminology plays an important role. To understand a text, the reader or translator must recognise which concepts are represented by the words used. This can be complicated even when dealing with only one language in one culture but becomes complex when attempts are made to find equivalent terms for the same concepts in different languages and cultures. To make the problems clear, let us look at the different concepts associated with the term "bread" in different cultures.

---

14 *Collins online dictionary and reference resources*. 2020. At https://www.collinsdictionary.com/

In an advertising campaign, the international banking group HSBC Holdings plc illustrated cultural differences in some of the countries where they operate using photographs of typical breads from the Philippines, India, and Germany. Within one culture, a generic term is frequently used for a common, if not the most common, sub-concept within the generic class or group of concepts. In the Philippines people would have no problems recognising the first photograph as "bread", but a reader in India or Germany would need an explanation like "sliced Filipino loaf bread" or "Filipino sandwich bread". In similar fashion, the second photograph would need to be labelled "Indian flatbread" (*naan*), and the third photograph "German black bread" for the concepts to be identified correctly outside their original cultures. In a similar advertisement, HSBC used photographs of bread from Oman, the UK, and France, which would have to be identified more specifically as "Omani bread" (*khubz*), a loaf of white English wheat bread, and a French baguette, respectively, for them to be recognised with certainty as "bread" in another country.

In these examples, "bread" was *not* used generically, but as a substitute for a more specific concept. This use of a generic term instead of a term for a sub-concept, usually the most common sub-concept, is quite common and can lead to confusion among speakers in different cultures. In recipes the ingredients are frequently listed with generic terms like "flour", "oil", or "cheese". In order to translate the recipe for use in another culture, the translator must first recognise which type of flour, oil, or cheese would be assumed in the source culture, and which type would be assumed in the target culture if a generic term were used in the translation. If the two specific concepts are not identical, the translator must use a more specific term.

Most American recipes that call simply for "flour" expect the reader to use "all-purpose wheat flour" (called "plain wheat flour" in Britain), in other cultures the categories for wheat flour may be different and wheat flours may be less common than flours made from other grains.

Unless otherwise specified, "oil" in a recipe from the US or England can be expected to mean any mild-tasting oil, such as peanut (British: groundnut oil), corn, or sunflower seed oil, but in Mediterranean cultures "oil" is likely to refer to olive oil.

And as there are hundreds of different types of cheeses, finding an appropriate cheese for a particular recipe may be extremely difficult, particularly so if the typical cheeses for the region from which a recipe originates are not readily available in the target culture. Monterey Jack cheese is quite common in the US and is frequently used when grated cheese is called for in a recipe, but it is often difficult to find in Europe, where a mild Gouda or Edam cheese may have to be used as a substitute. More problems occur if fresh or soft cheeses are called for, such as *fromage blanc* from France or *Quark* from Germany, which are used in the recipes for cheesecakes in those countries and for which it can be difficult to find substitutes.

A generic concept may be required when a section heading has to be translated, keeping in mind that the translation has to be suitable for everything mentioned within that section. This can be problematic! Generic terms in one language rarely have an equivalent generic term in another language that includes all the same sub-concepts and no additional concepts.

For example, "bread" is defined in Collins as "a food made from a dough of flour or meal mixed with water or milk, usually raised with yeast or baking powder and then baked". Merriam-Webster defines it as "a usually baked and leavened food made of a mixture whose basic constituent is flour or meal". "Stollen" is defined by Collins as "a rich sweet bread containing nuts, raisins, etc." The definition in Merriam-Webster is "a sweet yeast bread of German origin containing fruit and nuts". So "stollen" is a sub-concept under the generic concept "bread" in American and British English. But in the German Wahrig dictionary, *Stollen* is defined as "*zu Weihnachten gebackener, langer, flacher Hefekuchen mit Rosinen, Mandeln u. Zitronat*", which might be translated as "a long, flat yeast cake with raisins, almonds and citron baked for Christmas" if the translator assumes that *Kuchen* refers to the same concept as "cake", as is indicated in most bilingual dictionaries. Whereas recipes for *Stollen* in German cookbooks are traditionally listed under *Kuchen* or possibly *Weihnachtsbäckerei* ("Christmas baked goods"), we will usually find them under the heading "Bread" or something similar in US cookbooks.

Collins defines "cake" as "a baked food, usually in loaf or layer form, typically made from a mixture of flour, sugar, and eggs", whereas Merriam-Webster defines it as "a sweet baked food made from a dough or thick batter usually containing flour and sugar and often shortening, eggs, and a raising agent (such as baking powder)". From these dictionary definitions it would be difficult to pick the appropriate category under which stollen belongs, but the definitions for stollen and the placement of the recipes in cookbooks clearly identify stollen as a bread, and not a cake. From this it should be clear that the generic terms "bread" and "cake" in English are not completely equivalent to the German terms *Brot* and *Kuchen*.

The search for a generic term can be a problem for translators in non-culinary fields too. One might think that terms such as "welding" or "soldering" would be easy to translate into another language. Many bilingual dictionaries list *Schweissen* and *Löten* as the German "equivalents". The American Welding Society (AWS), however, defines "soldering" as:

> A group of welding processes that produces coalescence of materials by heating them to the soldering temperature and by using a filler metal having a liquidus not exceeding 840°F (450°C) and below the solidus of the base metals.[15]

---

15 American National Standards Institute / American Welding Society. *AWS A3 0-85: Standard Welding Terms and Definitions: Including Terms for Brazing, Soldering, Thermal Spraying, and Thermal Cutting*, 1985.

The German standardising organisation DIN (8580: 2002-05) makes a clear distinction between the manufacturing processes *4.6 Fügen durch Schweissen* and *4.7 Fügen durch Löten* (≈ 4.6 joining by means of welding and 4.7 joining by means of soldering). DIN also divides *Löten* into two groups: *Hartlöten* ("brazing") and *Weichlöten* ("soldering"). In the AWS standard "brazing" is also defined as a "group of welding processes", but at temperatures *above* 840°F (450°C). From this it should be clear that *Schweissen* and *Löten* are not completely equivalent to welding and soldering. If, however, a generic term is clearly being used for a sub-concept in a specific text, a translator can use these terms without any problems, but the translator must be certain that this is the case. A typical example would be a German text using the term *Löten* as a joining method for electric circuitry. As the higher temperatures in brazing would ruin the circuits, the generic term *Löten* is clearly restricted to the meaning *Weichlöten* in this context, so "soldering" can be used in the translation without any problems.

A good translator must also be aware of false friends (*faux amis*). Terms that look very similar in two different languages can mislead a translator into thinking they have the same meaning, for example "praline" in American English ("a confection of nuts and sugar", Merriam-Webster) is not associated with chocolate, but *Praline* in German is a confection that contains a filling under a layer of chocolate. Even numbers and symbols can be misleading. The German words *Billion* and *Trillion* are equal to one trillion and one quintillion in English, respectively. Compared with English, decimal points and commas are reversed in German and several other European languages, so that 1.234 represents one thousand two hundred thirty-four in those languages, whereas 1,234 represents one and two hundred thirty-four thousandths, exactly the reverse of the meanings in English. In legal texts, the German term *Paragraph* is represented by the symbol § and is best translated as "section", whereas *Absatz* is the normal term for paragraph in German. The list of such false friends is enormous, and they should not be taken lightly.

When?

The importance of the "when" questions cannot be completely ignored by translators. Coupled with the "when" questions are the "where" questions concerning the type of publication in which the translation is to appear. If the text is to be published in a periodical, the time of publication (and thus the approximate time frame when the text will be read) will be known, but in books or the internet, the time frame for text reception can vary considerably from one reader to the next. Some of the "when" problems for translators are trivial, such as translating expressions like "yesterday" with an exact date if the source text and the translation do not appear on the same day in their respective periodicals. If we return to the field of culinary texts, the time when a recipe is published or read may be important if seasonal ingredients play a role. Bert Gamerschlag wrote in his 7 May 2015 food column in the weekly magazine *Stern*: "Did you know? According to an old farmers' rule of thumb rhubarb should only be harvested up to 24 June". The article with several rhubarb recipes appeared at a time when rhubarb was readily available in Germany. For publication in another country, the translator might have to take a different rhubarb season into consideration. The extreme case would be publication in the southern hemisphere, where a shift of six months is likely for many ingredients. Granted, many food items are now available year-round, but the quality of products that have been shipped from halfway around the world is frequently inferior to that of fresh local products, so professional chefs and food columnists usually stick to the appropriate seasons for food items in their regions.

In many cultures particular dishes are associated with holidays or seasons, irrespective of the seasons for harvesting the ingredients. One example of this in the US is the emphasis on cherries in February, in honour of George Washington's birthday. The connection between Washington and cherries comes from the well-known legend in which Washington as a young boy chopped down his father's favourite cherry tree and, when asked if he had done so, admitted his guilt, saying that he could not tell a lie. As a result, numerous stores have special offers on canned cherries and cherry pie filling in February, and some recipes use Washington's name to indicate that cherries are an important ingredient. As this tradition is unknown to most people from other cultures, translators must either eliminate references to Washington or add explanations for the target readership, depending on why the text is being translated and for whom.

Language is constantly changing, so when a source text was written may be extremely important for understanding it. In older texts, "oriental cooking" referred to cuisine from the Middle East, whereas in more recent texts it usually refers to the cuisine of eastern Asia. A 1927 cookbook by Mary Hahn includes a whole section entitled *Der Tee- oder Abendtisch* with recipes for cold dishes to be served for tea or supper, but a 2001 German Duden dictionary does not even include the terms *Teetisch* or *Abendtisch*, as they are no longer common usage in modern German. For even older texts, translators may have to resort to unabridged dictionaries such as the *Oxford English Dictionary* that provide information on the etymology, or history, of words.

How?

We have arrived at the last of the questions: *how* a text is to be translated. This, of course, depends on the intended function of the target text, for whom it is intended, where it is to appear, and so on. An important concept is the level of differentiation,[16] in

---

16 See Hans G. Hönig and Paul Kussmaul. *Strategie der Übersetzung: Ein Lehr- und Arbeitsbuch.* Narr, 1982.

other words, how much information is necessary for the translated text to do its job. If a recipe for "George Washington Pie" is to be translated for a German cookbook for hobby chefs, there may be no need to mention Washington at all, so a title like *Cherry Pie* might suffice. This, however, would be under-differentiated if the recipe is intended for a cookbook with recipes associated with American holidays. On the other hand, the inclusion of an essay on the cherry tree legend and its reception over the years in the US would be over-differentiation, providing far more information than necessary for the translation to function as intended. Determining what is over- and what is under-differentiation clearly depends on the intended readership, their background knowledge, and the type of publication in which the translation is to appear.

You may think that my suggested title *Cherry Pie* for a recipe in a German cookbook was a careless mistake on my part, as "cherry pie" is English and not German, but foreign foods frequently maintain their foreign names. Who would ever think of translating *pizza* or *spaghetti* into English as "cheese and tomato pie" or "long, thin, cylindrical noodles"? Some recipe titles may remain unchanged in a translation, if the dish is common in the target culture or the intended readership is adults who are interested in other cultures. But if the intended readership includes children, changes may have to be made. Food items that are uncommon in the target culture may have to be replaced with something with which a child is familiar and that fits the context. If the source text, for example, is a children's story that includes a passage in which a child buys a corn dog at a fair in America, the German translation could use a *Bratwurst* instead and maintain the function of the translation. A corn dog and a *Bratwurst* are not completely equivalent, but they are commonly consumed at fairs in the United States and Germany, respectively.

Such substitutions can be complicated if illustrations are involved (unlike a *Bratwurst*, a corn dog is on a stick, similar to a Popsicle or ice lolly). I have been preparing an illustrated children's book that includes a German translation of the song "Froggie Went A-Courting". One verse includes the text "Oh, what are you gonna have for the wedding feast? Black-eyed peas and hogshead cheese". Black-eyed peas (also called cowpeas) are not common in Germany, but in recipes for adults the English term is sometimes used. However, "black-eyed peas" did not seem appropriate in a text for German children. The translation was further complicated by the fact that rhymes were called for in the German text, which is intended to be sung to the original tune. And as an illustration shows a bowl of black-eyed peas, the German substitute concept must *look* like black-eyed peas. Despite their name, they are a type of bean and look like haricot or navy beans with black spots on them, so the translation uses *Bohnen* ("beans"). The German translation therefore employs a more generic term than the original English text, a strategy that is frequently called for in translations.

Recipes are not the only type of text in which source text terms are retained in the translation. Another group of texts where this is common is official documents translated to provide legal evidence for something in the target culture, such as documenting a marriage in another country. Many governmental institutions are unique to a specific region. To marry in the United States, the couple must first have a marriage license. The office where such licenses can be obtained varies from one state to the next. In South Dakota, for example, marriage licenses are issued by the Register of Deeds, an official who heads an office of the same name which—as the name suggests—is also responsible for issuing and recording land records, such as deeds for purchasing property. As you might imagine, the combination of a similar set of duties for one official or office would be unusual in other states and difficult to imagine in another country where the procedure for getting married does not involve a document like a marriage license. As the certificate of marriage is on the same sheet of paper as the marriage license in South Dakota, a translator may be required to translate the entire document if the translation is to be used in a court of law, since the omission of parts of an official document in a translation can result in awkward legal consequences. In other words, the translator may have no other choice but to use the term "Register of Deeds" in a translation, possibly adding a short explanation in the target language to facilitate understanding, but not so much information as to result in over-differentiation.

In discussing how a text is to be translated I am taking for granted that the translator has an exceptional command of the target language and culture, as well as a good command of the source language and culture. However, no translator can be expected to know everything that may appear in a translation text, so a good translator will need to know where pertinent information can be obtained, and which sources of that information are most reliable. Bilingual dictionaries do not provide sure-fire solutions but must be understood as a source of information that may help in making decisions, though they will frequently need to be supplemented by information from other sources. If translators are well-informed about the subject matter and can identify appropriate terminology for that field, a bilingual dictionary can be useful if the term has merely slipped their immediate memory.

Considerably more useful and more reliable information can be obtained from parallel texts, that is, texts on the same or similar subjects in the target language, and preferably written by native speakers who are experts in the subject area of the text. Parallel texts provide appropriate terms in context, so the translator can find correct collocations for specific items, and parallel texts also include other terms used in the subject area, so the translator does not have to look up each one separately, as is usually the case with bilingual dictionaries. If a translator is not fully acquainted with the subject area of the text to be translated, parallel texts can be indispensable for obtaining the necessary information. At the same time, beginning translators should be warned not to take on highly specialised texts if they do not have sufficient background knowledge in the field, or at least sufficient time for working their way into the field before having to submit their translations. On the other hand, once translators have acquired expertise in a specialised field, they generally find that they can translate faster and can frequently demand better pay for their translations, so technical texts can be a very lucrative field for translators once they have the necessary background.

As terms are not always defined sufficiently in parallel texts, other sources of information are needed. Translators should therefore be familiar with the monolingual dictionaries that are available for the source and target languages that they use, both general language dictionaries and dictionaries for specialised fields like engineering or medicine. Professional translators should avoid learners' dictionaries, as they have fewer word entries than dictionaries for native speakers. They use simplified definitions, in which ease of understanding is more important than detailed accuracy, and they frequently leave out some of the less common meanings for polysemic terms. Some excellent dictionaries are available today with free access online, including those of American Heritage and Merriam-Webster for US English, and Collins and Lexico (a collaboration between Dictionary.com and Oxford University Press) for British English. Some standardising organisations have also published glossaries with standard definitions for specialised fields.

No one is perfect, and just as with other writing processes, translators can become blind to their own mistakes, so professional translators frequently ask fellow translators to proofread their texts, or they at least allow time between completing their first draft and their final proofreading. Granted, submission deadlines may make this difficult, but such strategies will improve the quality of the final product, which may result in more translation commissions in future. For lengthy texts, teams of translators are often necessary, who should discuss questions of terminology, style, and formatting in advance to avoid time-consuming editing processes when the different sections are assembled. Before confronting such a task, members of the team should have a basic knowledge of the principles of terminology.

Translation is far too complex for me to cover all the aspects that are important for professional translators, but for those who are just starting to translate the questions dealt with here should provide useful guidelines for their future careers, and the question words "why", "who", "where", "what", "when", and "how" may help them remember some of these rules for translating. I have been living and working in Germany for almost fifty years, but most of my formal education was in the United States, so the examples I have used are primarily from the language pair German-English; however, the general principles presented here also apply to all other language pairs. Although I do on rare occasions translate into German, I prefer to translate into my native language, American English, as my command of that language and its nuances exceeds my command of German, so I can translate faster and better in that direction. In that spirit, I would advise translators embarking on the journey to avoid—whenever possible—translating professionally into a foreign language. With modern international digital communication, translators no longer need to be living in the same country as the commissioners of their translations to ensure delivery of the final product by a set time. Digital communication has also increased the percentage of translations completed by native speakers, and thus the quality of the translations.

Translation is a fascinating field, both academically and professionally. Translation studies is a relatively new discipline, so research still needs to be carried out on many aspects of the translation process. At the same time, every new text that one translates provides the translator with insights into the subject matter of the text and into the linguistic, cultural, and translational problems associated with putting it into another language. The range of topics is limitless, so the life of a translator is anything but boring. Should you be planning a translation career, I hope that you will find it just as interesting as I have.

One Small Step in Pursuit of Words
Premila Paul

Premila Paul taught English literature at the American College, Madurai, and has published on Indian literature and gender issues. Dr Paul was one of the three founding members and is currently director of the renowned Study Centre for Indian Literature in English and Translation (SCILET).

~

The Study Centre for Indian Literature in English, known better by its acronym, SCILET, was started in 1985 to encourage students and teachers to be open-minded and to appreciate quality literature wherever it originated from, including India. This involved resistance to the prevalent Eurocentric approach to the study of English Literature in Indian academia. It was important to make people aware of the existing treasure of Indian literature. To do that, the first move was to build a good library and a welcoming space for reading Indian literature and to create an academic environment for scholarly study of the subject. The idea of a resource centre—SCILET—has now emerged as an acclaimed library, the largest database on Indian literature in English in India.

Till the late 1970s, Indian literature in English, a product of Indo-English relations, was ignored by both Indian and British academia. In the '80s, global recognition came in the form of lucrative, prestigious international awards, and attractive purchase of publication, translation, and film rights. This was followed by the inclusion of Indian literary texts in the prescribed syllabi in most Indian universities.

The American College, Madurai, Tamil Nadu, India (where SCILET is located), was established in 1881 to empower the young, particularly from disadvantaged backgrounds, with education. SCILET's attempt to bring literature marginalised by academia centre-stage was in keeping with the college's mission. Madurai, the temple city, with its rich, diverse cultures, takes pride in the much-utilised SCILET library, the only one of its kind in India or elsewhere. Yet SCILET remains resolutely low-key. The self-effacing, stellar visionaries Dr Paul L. Love and Professor R. Padmanabhan Nair (the founders of SCILET) projected Indian literature and never themselves. In her tribute to Dr Paul Love, the renowned novelist Shashi Deshpande writes in *Love in Madurai* (*LIM*):[1]

> SCILET stands out as a marked contrast to most of the institutions in our country and I know that this is the impress of your personality, and of the rest of your team as well. I think SCILET also carries your personality in the way it does so much good work most unobtrusively, never drawing attention to itself. Nancy Batty (Red Deer College, Alberta, Canada), who came to you to work on my manuscripts, has now become not only a great admirer of SCILET but almost a member of your family (118).

---

1   A volume of tributes in honour of Dr Paul Linder Love.

Nancy Batty in SCILET's Visitors' Book affirms this:

> The dedication and the passion of the staff here never fails to astonish me. Working here in 2007-8 and then again in 2009 to write my book on Shashi Deshpande was one of the most rewarding and fruitful periods in my career. I hope to come back … to continue working with the collection of Shashi Deshpande's papers. This library is incredible! I leave a little bit of my heart here every time I come.

The multilingual India embracing the providential gift of English as the enabler of pan-Indian readership/communication is a natural progression of English shuffling aside its colonial trappings and transforming itself into yet another Indian language. Sahitya Akademi Awards, instituted in 1954, added a work of art written originally in English in the annual awards list in 1960 along with literary texts produced in different regional Indian languages. This emphasised the legitimacy/ownership of English as an Indian language. The Indianisation of English became part of the natural, unconscious, creative process of writers, some of them bi/trilingual; they could write in English, think in it, dream in it, and even play with it.

SCILET is now considered a nodal consultancy by colleges and universities for designing courses, basic and advanced, on Indian literature. It facilitates access to creative and critical material on the subject. SCILET can take undisputed, rightful pride in actively promoting research leading to doctoral degrees in the field of Indian literature, in India and beyond. In SCILET's Visitors' Book, the author and public intellectual Shiv Visvanathan calls SCILET a "literary ashram", and thanks and salutes it for teaching him that academic life "is still enjoyable, playful and quietly ethical". The poet Sanjukta Dasgupta calls SCILET an "academic pilgrimage site", a view shared by "all scholars of Indian Literature" (*LIM*, 101).

SCILET is proud of the proclamation of love and appreciation for it by Jerry Pinto, the recipient of many prestigious awards, including the 2016 Windham-Campbell Prize. Jerry Pinto, an enthusiastic supporter of SCILET, led a scintillating creative writing workshop for SCILET in 2015. The following are his impressions as recorded in the Visitors' Book:

> This is my first visit to SCILET and I have to say it was "Love" at first sight. I was deeply impressed by the collection and by the cross-referencing, the fact that a search for an author's works could throw up his ephemera as well as his books. It seems as if this institution is one of the few that I have visited which is in the fight against the Great Indian Project: Amnesia. We need to remember and since human memory often dies with the person and fades into the family, we need our libraries and centres such as SCILET to remind us of our collective enterprise: to be as fully human and humane as we can.
>
> I was not prepared for how hospitable and warm everyone was but it was a pleasant shock … The temple, the Mahal and Gandhi Museum were all wonders but it is SCILET that should also be listed as one of the wonders of Madurai for it catches and holds the sun in flight.
>
> I love all libraries. I see all of them as repositories of treasure, *ratna bhandars* in the Jaina tradition I believe. But SCILET has a special place in my heart, already. Truly, it is a monument to what "Love" has wrought.

SCILET is envisioned not just as a well-maintained library with a conducive reading space. Its larger goal is to build a community of readers; to bring students and creative thinkers together to discuss books and issues in an open environment. To sustain the interest of the readers, SCILET periodically organises meet-the-author programmes featuring leading writers. Students discuss their works in groups and prepare themselves to make the best use of the visit of each writer. These events help them look beyond the prescribed syllabus and absorb what the wider world has to offer. Some writers have opted to launch their newly published books at SCILET. It has been a mutually exciting experience for our students and the writers themselves, who feel gratified by the enthusiasm of the young readers.

Public intellectuals are also invited to give lectures and interact with interested students from colleges in and around Madurai. These well attended public programmes include the annual Paul Linder Love Endowment Lecture and R. Padmanabhan Nair Memorial Lecture delivered by inspiring speakers of great stature such as Gopalkrishna Gandhi, Shiv Visvanathan, Sashi Kumar, T.M. Krishna, Sudhir Kakar, Bill Ashcroft, Prakash Karat, Deborah Thiagarajan and PTR Palanivel Thiagarajan. A diverse range, from school students to octogenarians and professionals from different fields including medical doctors, attend these lectures and actively participate in the discussions that follow.

The United Nations has named 30 September as "International Translations Day" to pay tribute to the community of translation professionals. Translation has been a facilitator of cultural understanding, a vital means of connecting nations and fostering peace. Considering the wealth of valuable literature available in different regional languages and the fact that English is the only inter-state link language in India, SCILET actively promotes translation activity. SCILET periodically conducts rigorous translation workshops for this purpose, led by such renowned translators as the late Lakshmi Holmstrom, Gita Krishnankutty, Lakshmi Kannan, and Mini Krishnan, a staunch advocate of translations and former Editor: Translations at Oxford University Press.

SCILET's annual creative writing workshop is the brainchild of Dr Paul Love and Mr Robert Granner (former head, English Department, Kodaikanal International School). SCILET has been conducting this workshop in collaboration with Kodaikanal

International School (KIS) for the past thirty-three years. Each year, an acclaimed creative writer is invited to lead an intensive creative writing workshop in Kodiakanal for three days in the month of August for thirty to forty students of the American College and KIS. SCILET has been able to enthuse the young students with a welcoming call for creative writing in these days of deteriorating reading culture and an overwhelming flood of digital information. There is now an ever-increasing demand from students across disciplines for inclusion in the workshops.

The first workshop was led by the renowned poet Jayanta Mahapatra. SCILET has been lucky and blessed to get reputed writers who understand the students' insecurities and strengths. Some students are aware that they have creativity in them; some need a little nudge to recognise the spark within.

Students from the plains (Madurai) and the hills (Kodaikanal) come together to write and narrate. This creative writing workshop is a confluence of two strands of creative thinking. KIS students are younger and represent different states of India and other countries. They are heavily influenced by Western culture, and their primary language of communication is English. The American College students' imagination and writing are rooted in Tamil and bear the authenticity of their native culture. The workshop leaders make sure that their teaching does not stifle creativity or dilute authenticity. They ensure that all voices are heard, all words are read. They don't let the students sit idle during the workshop nor do they let them feel lost. For eager students, acquaintance with the books is followed by acquaintance with the authors during the meet-the-author sessions. Friendship with them becomes possible because of the workshops. Some of the students manage to forge a lasting bond with the writers, who continue to mentor them long after the workshop.

A creative writing workshop that aims not just to inspire but also to produce results requires the commitment of the workshop facilitators as well. Paul Love and Robert Granner were the best facilitators one could ever dream of. Both had a special gift for connecting with every student participant. They could instill confidence in the students, exude positivity, and spread cheer. Paul Love successfully spearheaded the workshops from 1991 to 2014. Manjula Padmanabhan, the leader of the 2006 workshop, wrote: "I would say Dr Paul Love is a gardener, though of a specialized kind: he has a green thumb for the human spirit. He is a cultivator of hearts and minds. He is a horticulturalist of words and verses" (*LIM*, 93). Though no longer with us, we still feel the abiding presence of Paul Love jubilantly applauding every leader of the workshop and the led.

However successful the writers may be, for them to be effective workshop leaders for students of different age groups and with diverse abilities is not easy. They have their moments of self-doubt as well. But they have no qualms about sharing with the students their own moments of insecurity; they also demonstrate their determination to work those moments towards authentic articulation. Kamala Das, who made a lasting impression upon the participants in the 1993 workshop, confessed:

> When I entered the sunlight [sic] quadrangle of the International School at Kodaikanal, I was not exactly bursting with confidence. I had been warned the students were hard to please … so I was a bit nervous at first … Later, I wished to confront them, shedding all guises. I told them that poetry is an act of bravery … a good poem cannot be explained or interpreted. You recognise it by the gooseflesh that erupts on your arms while reading it… (*LIM*, 79)

Edison Thomas, one of the participants, had this to say about the workshop leader's impact:

> Kamala Das was not only a tutor in the art of creative writing; she was poetic experience itself. At the workshop,

she had the ability to emote with young people's passions and pains (often more pain than passion). Adolescent vicissitudes, youthful traumas, insecure relationships, uncertain futures—were none too new to her, or her writing. Relating effortlessly with the aspirants, she embellished their creations with her expertise. Kamala Das was not there to instruct on the mechanics of writing. What was shared, indeed, in ample supply, was her genius for understanding, and an ability to live the young experience. Underlined repeatedly was the fact that all creative art had to be the product of felt experience. And the workshop saw just that—a riot of word and sound, emotion and introspection—all crystallised as very personal art. The sylvan slopes of Kodai and the verdant undulations of Swedish Hill blended into a heartbreakingly grand and fitting paean to the flair of Kamala Das, the total experience becoming an ineffable inspiration to fledgling talents (*LIM*, 82).

Decades later, Manu Joseph, who led the vibrant Silver Jubilee workshop in 2017, also insisted on honesty as a necessary ingredient of authenticity in creative expression. He exhorted the students not to hide behind their writing but to open up the self to the narrative.

The participants bond over the individual and collective struggle to overcome diffidence and express themselves freely. Creative writing is not necessarily an ego-driven act. The students willingly offer and seek support to build confidence in each other. Age, language, and culture are no barriers. There are friendly acoustics for free speech with assured safety; conducive spaces for individual dreams and collective conversation. The anxiety and fear of being judged give way to collaborative endeavour. Trained by Paul Love, a few alumni—Ganesh Babu, Joel Timothy, and David Jeyaraj, who have benefitted from years of annual workshops, Deborah

Cordonnier from Princeton University, and two teachers from KIS—take up responsible roles as facilitators each year to ensure that the workshop continues as an annual event and remains part of the institutional tradition of the American College and KIS. The facilitators also do every exercise assigned along with the students, subject their own writings to critical peer/student scrutiny, and read/perform in the final session of the workshop. The students become relaxed by the second day, and some even set the lyrics they write to music and perform. The group bonding enables the students to analyse the romanticising, dramatising, exaggerating, and underplaying aspects of each other's writings and revisit their drafts. As each word has an impact, the students are urged to work on the economy of words and to practise self-editing.

The workshop is a unique opportunity for students of both institutions to spend the whole day writing and consulting with the facilitators and with the writer in the sylvan surroundings of Kodaikanal, around the hearth and over food. Students are urged to work against a deadline to produce results. The workshop is just an inspirational beginning; the kindled interest in writing is sustained by SCILET's continued engagement with the students through monthly writing sessions throughout the academic year in SCILET.

The creative output born of these efforts is published as *Kavithalaya* each year. We are proud to have published thirty-three annual issues so far. The list of workshop leaders, from 1988 to 2023, reads like a Who's Who of Indian Literature: Jayanta Mahapatra, Shiv K. Kumar, Kamala Das, Meena Alexander, K. Ayyappa Paniker, Makarand Paranjape, Shashi Deshpande, Shama Futehally, Githa Hariharan, Gieve Patel, Arundhathi Subramaniam, Keki N. Daruwalla, Ranjit Hoskote, Manjula Padmanabhan, Lakshmi Kannan, E.V. Ramakrishnan, K.R. Usha, Sanjukta Dasgupta, K. Srilata, Murali Sivaramakrishnan, Anjum Hasan, Tishani Doshi, Jerry Pinto, Shinie Antony, Manu Joseph, Cyrus Mistry, Saikat Majumdar, Sampurna Chattarji, the

Amar Chitra Katha team (Reena I. Puri, Sanjana Kapur and Savio A. Mascarenhas), Deepak Unnikrishnan, and Samit Basu. They have all become friends and true ambassadors of SCILET around the world in reputed universities and at international literary events. The Silver Jubilee volume of *Kavithalaya* (Creativity@25) is a celebration of what the enduring collaboration between institutions can achieve. This 2018 volume is a compilation of sixty select pieces—poems, short stories, and reflective essays—by twenty-four aspiring writer-participants. The thirty years of storytelling through verse and prose has become a success story, a creative exercise that equips students with the ability, courage, and maturity for meaningful articulation. Each workshop ends with the students asking for more.

The writers themselves have recorded their appreciation for our annual creative writing workshop. The award-winning poet Tishani Doshi, who led an exhilarating workshop in 2014, wrote to Paul Love:

> …what a wonderful experience it was for me to participate in the workshop. I sensed that many of the students benefitted hugely from the time we had together, and I certainly enjoyed my time both in and out of the classroom … And let me add that what you've created—with these workshop sessions over the years—has created huge value. Creativity is too easily tossed to the wayside within our educational context, even though it is clearly the most important thing humans have to offer to the world.[2]

The workshops have derived strength from the experience of the past to sustain our present and future endeavours. Each workshop has proved to be an amazing exercise and experience in storytelling and writing to remember for a lifetime. The students

---

2 In the Foreword to *Kavithalaya*, 22nd Workshop Publication, 2014.

carry this rich experience and the valuable lessons from it into their lives and careers in journalism, advertising, writing, teaching, and so on. SCILET remains grateful to the founders, the creative writers, and all the facilitators for their immense contribution to the success of the workshops.

While talking about the creative workshop experience, Robert Granner recalls Joseph Conrad's image of an artist digging randomly, searching for a gem, and polishing the rough stone until a lasting work of art emerges:

> It sounds like pure chance, doesn't it? But you and I both know that many times, during those idyllic moments when we sat at the feet of one master poet after the other, many rough stones were polished and our *Kavithalaya* productions year after year contain not just efforts in artistry but more than a few lasting gems as well! (*LIM*, 78-79).

Robert Granner has been so passionately involved in the workshop that he has named his home in Pallangi, in the Kodai hills, "Kavithalayam"—House of Poetry, "as a personal response to those wonderful collaborative workshops and as a lasting tribute to *Kavithalaya*" (*LIM*, 80).

Many participants have given heartfelt testimony to the meaningful impact of the creative writing workshops. Thus Lila S. Jokanovic, recollecting her participation in the 1993 workshop, wrote to SCILET in 2014:

> This workshop changed my life on many different levels—it provided a safe and non-judgemental platform for young writers to explore and express our emotions. In looking back, I see this workshop as the point of confluence between teenage angst and *writing* in my own life. A small collection of words became a prose poem

about my fear of leaving India. It was not written very well, but Kamala Das, Mr Granner and Dr Love saw beyond my immaturity. They instead acknowledged—and even celebrated—my voice. From there, I was committed to writing not just as a way to tell stories, but as a tool for social growth and change.

Almost twenty-two years later, living in the United States, I continue to try and honour my earliest mentors by providing opportunities for inner city youth to experience a safe and non-judgemental space for expression. Along with other like-minded writers, we provide workshops to help teens tell their stories, strengthen their voice and point of view, and walk further into their life experience as individuals and agents of social growth. At an after-school programme in one of Chicago's most dangerous neighbourhoods—where youth are gunned down with terrifying frequency—thirty-one high-school writers sit with us four days a week with their journals open and pens scratching away. Collectively their spelling and grammar is atrocious for their age, but they are committed to learning how to end a sentence and where to simply pause because they have found adults who respect what they have to say. And what they have to say is terrible and funny and heartbreaking and heartwarming all at once. A young girl of fourteen writes about her mother on drugs while a sixteen-year-old boy writes about seeing his father shot in the head at a playground one summer evening. Another writes about her first kiss and her first fistfight.

That same girl once asked me why I cared about her or what she had to say. It was an honest question and required that I do a little soul-searching before answering. The children of Englewood are not special to me because they are downtrodden but because they are brave even though their voices have been kept silent.

A seed was planted all those years ago—there on that hilltop in India. The tree still grows, branches reaching wide and far, nourished by the words and images, thoughts ... of hundreds of voices. These young people in Englewood write their stories and reveal their vulnerabilities because of the vision and care provided by Dr Love and Mr Granner all those years ago and all those miles away (*LIM*, 108-109).

Kashvi Rekhy, another participant, wrote:

I thank Dr Love for encouraging us in the creative process at such a young age because later with Mr Granner's encouragement I went on to major in creative and screenplay writing in University of Canada. I am now writing my first book and I have the workshop to thank! The workshops made me realise my passion for writing and that it truly was a calling that I had to heed to. I have friends who are still confused about what they are impassioned about or what their calling is and that is something I don't have to struggle with because the opportunity for me to discover it was given in my teens.

Thank you, Dr Love, for giving me this opportunity to connect with my creative spirit at such a young age. I wish it would be introduced in more schools around India for it truly was a special programme. I learnt a lot and discovered a calling (which I think is an immense learning). Thank you once again (*LIM*, 107).

SCILET also publishes a professional annual journal, *Kavya Bharati* (*KB*, ISSN 0975-3559), devoted to Indian poetry written in English or translated from regional languages into English. It publishes poetry by writers of Indian origin located in different parts of India, in other countries or continents, as well as critical material on them. SCILET launched *KB* fully aware of the financial hardships involved in sustaining its publication and maintaining its circulation. Journals mushroom in India, to become extinct after only three or four issues. But *Kavya Bharati* has maintained an uninterrupted publication schedule since 1988.

Reciting poetry in regional languages has always been popular in public forums. But fiction and non-fictional prose have invaded the publication/market industry and have marginalised other genres in Indian English literature. *KB* is an aggressive response to the subordination of Indian English poetry. We are proud that *KB* remains the lone surviving and much-appreciated journal committed to the promotion of Indian poetry. Shashi Deshpande calls *KB* "a gem of a journal, a first-class one in every way, brought out almost regularly and such a joy to see and read" (*LIM*, 118). During the more than three decades of its publication, it has brought out special issues on translation, poetry of Indian women, poetry of the Indian diaspora, and four anniversary issues. In December 2018, *KB* passed yet another milestone with its thirtieth special issue, a celebration of thirty years of Indian poetry.

The plurality of India is its singularity—the sheer diversity of languages and cultures. Every issue of *KB* presents the creative voices of poets from at least fifteen Indian states, poets of the Indian diaspora from countries like Nepal, the UK, Germany, Italy, Spain, Austria, the USA, Canada, South Africa, and Kenya, and translations from at least six different Indian languages. Another striking feature of *KB* is the impressive range of the professional identity of the contributors, which include diplomats and doctors, bureaucrats and bankers, executives and ecologists, academics from at least nine different disciplines, and artists. SCILET lets the quality of the poetry decide whether it has the right to be included in *KB*, and it provides publication space for both new poets and more established ones. Some acclaimed poets like Anjum Hasan had their publication debut in *KB*. They have acknowledged their gratitude to *KB* in their interviews.

Many of the American College students are from conservative, patriarchal families, and some are from disadvantaged social backgrounds. Helping students recognise their self-worth, find their voices, and eventually realise their full potential is part of the education package they receive. SCILET's writing workshops conducted in Kodai and in Madurai and other group activities instill in them the belief that to speak one's mind is no sin; to state one's conviction is not an act of sedition but an expression of strength and a sacred duty. The young students learn to take themselves and their views seriously so that others will also take them seriously. They learn to use the potent word—whether written or spoken—not only as a means of communication or negotiation but also as a vital means of establishing their identity.

Words can turn volatile and render you vulnerable. But words can also have a huge impact, making a big difference in your life and in the lives of others. The effective use of words can help build solidarity and reaffirm core values. In the context of a democratic deficit in the domestic space or beyond, the power of words can have repercussions. But you must nevertheless dare to say, "I am speaking." Free speech must have a bright future.

The inspiring lectures and the non-competitive workshops led by acclaimed writers committed to the cause of freedom help the students assert their choices through words. The mixed group activities are confidence-building exercises for both female and male students. Choosing the humanities as a branch of academic study is sometimes seen as a less masculine option. The workshops help liberate both female and male students from patriarchal mindsets. Students realise that the liberation of women cannot be distinct from the liberation of men, and what binds them together is the desire to be free. They become peer participants, fellow organisers, and enjoy their roles as team players and as team leaders, as storytellers, performers, and facilitators.

Creative art has tremendous transformative potential and is an effective means of negotiating gender equality and spreading gender sensitivity. To introduce creativity of a different kind, SCILET organises inter-collegiate storytelling workshops led by professional storytellers and trainers. By the end of the workshops, students feel liberated to narrate their own stories, the stories of others, the emotional impact of natural disasters, social upheavals, and so on. Now there is a demand for SCILET to conduct monthly storytelling sessions and to take storytelling beyond educational institutions for therapeutic purposes.

Students find watching films—along with award-winning film directors like Sashi Kumar, Bala, Ram, Amshan Kumar, and Jill Mistry and dramatists like Mahesh Dattani and Manjula Padmanabhan, who have challenged religious, caste and gender barriers and hierarchies in their films or plays—an exciting experience. Film clips are used to urge the students to write alternative scripts that could project the cause better, lead to a better unfolding of the plot, and keep the audience both engaged and entertained. Film directors lead animated discussions on themes such as patriarchal practices that pass for time-honoured traditions, privileges and preferential treatment within families leading to feelings of entitlement, and self-denials accepted by the victims themselves as a noble way of life. Students write dialogues that could counter crude generalisation and stereotyping. In the process, they also learn to accept and respect multiple gender or sexual identities. The sessions, which usually start as combative debates, give way to conciliatory and accommodative dialogues, and suspicions and prejudices give way to sensitive understanding and healthy acceptance of transgenders as friends.

Students take the newly acquired sensitivity to the public by writing and enacting street plays to challenge domestic violence and to root out the widely prevalent harassment of women and sexual minorities and the violation of children's rights. They have also been very enthusiastic about writing scripts and performing one-act plays together with young school children. However, such public performances receive mixed responses—appreciation from a select informed group, but indifference or even disdain from some. But the student community gathers in large numbers to cheer and applaud the daring gender-sensitivity drive. It is important to engage and sensitise critics on and off academic campuses. The academics have progressed only to the extent of not condemning these events. Gender sensitivity is an ever-evolving process. There is still a long way to go for gender equality to gain ground and for every academic institution to offer gender-fair education.

SCILET-sponsored workshops and group activities in pursuit of words are far from elitist. They are tailored to meet the needs of the students. In the supportive, secure college environment, students decide that dreams should be made of sterner stuff and are meant to be realised. Sometimes they enjoy freedom in the fictional space and through the persona they create in their writings. The sacred space of the artistic world opens up possibilities of free self-expression without inhibitions. For many of our workshop participants, the progression from those moments and days of staring at the blank page to narrating their untold stories, real or imagined, on the printed page, or on stage, is a giant leap towards self-fulfilment.

A Writing Life

Anil Menon

Anil Menon's most recent work is the novel *The Coincidence Plot* (Simon & Schuster, 2023), which was preceded by a collection of his speculative short fiction, *The Inconceivable Idea of the Sun: Stories* (Hachette, 2022). His novel *Half of What I Say* (Bloomsbury, 2015) was shortlisted for the 2016 Hindu Literary Award. His debut novel *The Beast with Nine Billion Feet* was shortlisted for the 2009 Crossword Prize and the Carl Baxter Society's Parallax Award. Dr Menon's stories have been translated into more than a dozen languages, including Arabic, Hebrew, Igbo, and Romanian. He is the chief editor of *The Bombay Literary Magazine*. He currently lives in Pune, India.

~

I write novels and short stories. Which means I spend a lot of my time thinking about imaginary people and their problems. It is a strange existence, perhaps not the sort of thing you'd expect grown-ups to do. People sometimes ask me if I'd always wanted to be a writer. No, I had not. When I was eight or nine, I was very sure about what I wanted to be. I wanted to be an accountant. My friends, when asked what they wanted to be when they grew up, would reply "engineer" or "doctor". Not me. I was going to be an accountant. I couldn't wait to be an accountant. To me, accountants represented the height of cool. That's because my dad was as an accountant with Government of India's Audit Department. In the evenings, as he sipped, bare-chested, his pre-shower chai, he'd tell Amma about his day. He invariably made accountancy sound as exciting as exploring Mars or wind surfing or being a detective. His eyes would shine, his fingers would draw numbers in the air, and in the mornings, as he got ready for work, he would hum something from Vallathol or some other dead Malayalam poet. I wanted a slice of the same happiness pizza. All I had to do was to become an accountant.

Instead, I became a fiction writer. I did my graduate studies in computer science in the United States, worked as a software engineer with a number of startups for a long while, and it was all a great blast, but eventually the work began to pall. I was increasingly the oldest person in the room—in my ripe forties—and the fate of programmers put to pasture isn't a pleasant one (they are usually the last living speakers of some long-obsolete programming language). Then my startup got sold, I was "in between jobs" as they say in the USA, I had an understanding wife, a room with a view, and I was pretty sure that if I could code a distributed database query partitioner, I could churn out a bestselling novel in, say, a year or so.

In short, I decided to try my hand at fiction. I'd edited a non-fiction volume on evolutionary computation and knew something about the bizarre nature of the publication industry, but I didn't know anything about the fiction industry. Depressingly, even my mistakes were unoriginal. I sent out stories in non-standard formats, I included succinct abstracts of what the stories were about, and I had my own regime of what to italicise and underline. I wrote stuff that I now see as stylistically interesting, but hopelessly derivative.

I had never stopped reading fiction, and I was still very much a reader who wrote than a writer who read.

After some six months of getting nowhere with editors, I decided I'd given it a good try and it was time to quit and take up, say, some unsolved problem in mathematics or return to grad school and become, say, a suit. I remember the day well: 6 April 2004. I announced the decision to resign from the Writing Life to my wife in the morning, and in the afternoon got an acceptance from the Clarion West Writers' Workshop.

It was a six-week programme in Seattle, with sixteen other participants and a different instructor each week. Most importantly, a writer I admired a lot, Geoff Ryman, was going to be one of the instructors. I'd lived in Seattle for some four or five years and loved the place. I withdrew my letter of resignation and went to the workshop.

I'd never attended a workshop before and I didn't know what they were about. They're reasonably common now in all disciplines, but back then workshops were a rarity in technical fields. During my time at Clarion West, I came to realise they are a technology. The human mind isn't ergodic.[1] A toss of sixteen coins cannot be distinguished from one coin tossed sixteen times. Coin tossing is ergodic. But sixteen minds mulling over a narrative for an hour isn't the same as one mind mulling over it for sixteen hours. Workshops, at their best, teach us to look at things from outside our selves.

An example may be helpful. In his book *Never Split the Difference*, Chris Voss, the FBI's top hostage negotiator, writes about how hard it is to listen. To really listen. Hostage negotiation teams always work in groups, so as to compare notes on just what has been said after a discussion. A single ear, writes Voss, misses too much. It is also true of reading. A book is an encounter with

---

[1] "Ergodic theory is a branch of mathematics that studies statistical properties of deterministic dynamical systems" (*Wikipedia*).

a mind, and many minds are needed to help piece together just what is being said or not being said.

My relationship with text, with *stories*, changed drastically during the workshop. I had always been a voracious reader. I read everything and anything I could lay my hands on. I read with my own eyes and never allowed anyone to dictate what I should read and shouldn't. But fluent readers have a problem. They immerse in the text too easily. The machinery is invisible to them. At Clarion West, for the first time in my life, I was thinking about the machinery.

Actually, "machinery" is the wrong word. There is no right word, I think. A story is unlike anything else.

At Clarion West, I dissolved my old relationship with stories. All learning, says Shaw in one of his plays, is accompanied by a feeling of loss. The workshop got me started on writing fiction, but it also took away my old sentimental relationship with stories. I use the word "sentimental" with respect. The word is used as an insult these days, but about three hundred years ago, we had a subtler understanding of the concept. For me, sentiment and its innocent employment is the best gift a reader can offer a writer. To approach something sentimentally is to approach it with trust. I am not capable of that kind of innocent, sentimental, trusting response any more.

Perhaps it's not unlike awakening from the Matrix. If I'm moved deeply by a fiction, I can sense a part of "myself" wondering how the affect was effected. When sentiment goes, what is left is suspicion. I've become wary of all fictions.

The more I engage with fiction, the clearer it has become that we understand very little of how it does whatever it does. We don't know what a story is, we don't know why stories have such a grip on us, and we don't know what to tell new writers who want to write stories only they can write. English departments generally have little interest in the construction of fiction, and the disreputable task is outsourced to profitable but low-status writing centres. Literary academics are mostly interested in literature's effects, and these effects are usually studied in a haphazard and error-inviting manner. To use a fashionable word, the approach is performative.

Practitioners aren't of much use either. Most of the material one finds in writing workshops (and this included Clarion West) is herd wisdom. It's a collection of superstitions, traditions, lore, and minor and major misconceptions all passed off as craft. It's not without value—herd wisdom *is* wisdom—but the advice is so laden with bias, personal preferences, parochial reading habits, cultural expectations, and overgeneralisations that it is advisable for a new writer to take every advice as a hypothesis. What writers-who-teach have invented is a kind of folk theory—one deeply rooted in Western aesthetics—to teach people how to write fiction. Like most folk theories, it is useful but probably wrong.

This isn't a particularly new insight. Donald Barthelme famously remarked that "the writer is one who, embarking upon a task, does not know what to do".[2] Given these circumstances, writers seem to learn largely by imitation. Knowingly or unknowingly, they imitate the writers they admire or like to read. I've always admired the stylists and experimentalists—G.V. Desani, Raja Rao, Salman Rushdie, Anthony Burgess—but recently, I've begun to learn from Urdu writers like Naiyer Masud, Surendra Prakash, Khalida Asgar, Hasan Manzar and others.

It is easy for a writer to become a phony. Win a few awards, and a novelist is expected to pontificate on women's rights, the latest X (formerly Twitter) spat, the effect of Trump's policies on geopolitics, the role of fiction in shaping the concept of X (freedom, self,...), this or that subaltern literature, the post-COVID world, and other such incredibly complex topics.

---

2 Donald Barthelme. "Not-Knowing". In: *The Georgia Review*, Vol. 39, No. 3 (Fall 1985), 509.

As a writer from the subcontinent, I can be called upon (and quite reliably, may I add) to hold forth on all things involving India. I'm also open for business on multicultural issues—my skin colour grants me special authority. In India, I can't talk about Dalit issues without feeling self-conscious, but outside India, it's a different matter. Apart from my expertise as an Indian SF expert, I am a Hinduism expert, an Indian history expert, a caste system expert, a communal violence expert and contemporary politics expert. It's quite economical to invite me for literary festivals, because I can be deployed on so many different panels.

In other words, it is easy for a writer to become a phony. A sense of humour offers some protection. I've noticed a sense of entitlement in some authors, and I try to watch out against developing one. I've come to accept my story can't work for all readers. That's just the way it is. It is a bit like jokes. Some people may find a joke so funny, they fart or burst a seam, while others will stand around looking puzzled. These days I just try to write a story the best I can, and not worry too much about how it will be received. The interesting thing is that once you adopt this attitude, you not only start to write better stories (by one's own measure), but good things begin to happen. Your story may sell millions of copies or win prestigious awards or get translated into dozens of languages, or best of all, motivate readers to come up and say, "You know, I loved your story."

I write all kinds of fiction, but I'm generally linked with science fiction. A literary tag, assigned at the start of a career, can have the unwelcome fidelity of Herpes. As Babasaheb Ambedkar, one of the makers of the Indian Constitution pointed out, a division of labour soon becomes a division of labourers. This is especially the case with the English language where a relative clause can be easily turned into an adjective. A writer who works *in* genre X quickly become an X writer. I started out in science fiction, and no doubt my obits will bury me as one. I enjoy reading and writing SF, but as with every genre, its techniques aren't suitable for all stories.

SF in India is odd in the same sense that a foetus is odd. It is new, it is under development, and it is funny-looking. Indian SF, perhaps best defined as SF works by writers of Indian origin, seems to be emerging from its long thralldom to American SF. There are a number of interesting works to point to, but as yet, I don't see signs of a literature that's unique to the subcontinent. Of course, such models of nationalist literary development are obsolete in an age where identity is increasingly a matter of choice, not geography.

When I think back to my own "thralldom", what I remember is the absence of questions rather than the presence of any dominant framework of answers. It never occurred to me to question what words like freedom, individuality, rationality, science, technology, consciousness, etc., meant. I had no idea what South Asian civilisations had been up to for the past 3,000 or 4,000 years, and it never occurred to me that they might have evolved a completely different perspective from Europeans. I was thunderstruck to learn that it is only in the last quarter-century that Western philosophy has approached anything remotely comparable in sophistication to Buddhist models of language and consciousness. I knew more about Roman history than I did about the Chola or Chera empires, and I saw nothing peculiar about this state of affairs. Nor did I find my incompetency in Malayalam, Hindi or Sanskrit particularly problematic.

When I went about Bombay or Delhi, I only saw all the ways in which they weren't New York or London. In his autobiography, Nirad Chaudhuri talks (proudly) about how he had no need of maps when he visited London. I had a similar experience when I visited New York City. There is no visiting the United States for the first time any more than a Hindu can read the Ramayana or Mahabharata for the first time. Ironically, it was my native world that I learned to see for the first time.

When I realised that my head was full of conceptual furniture I didn't remember buying, I went through all the phases described by Fanon in his *Wretched of the Earth* regarding the "native writer's" development:

> In the first phase, the native intellectual gives proof that he has assimilated the culture of the occupying power. [...] In the second phase we find the native is disturbed; he decides to remember what he is [...]. But since the native is not a part of his people [...] he is content to recall their life only. [...] Finally in the third phase, which is called the fighting phase, the native [...] shake[s] the people, [H]e turns himself into an awakener of the people [...].[3]

Actually, there's a final phase. The writer, native or not, just gets on with their bloody writing. The person whom the world cannot do without hasn't been born yet. The world will muddle along, with or without you. The acceptance of the total inexplicability of existence, of one's irrelevance to history, and indeed, of one's astounding inessentiality in the cosmic scheme of things, provides all the quiet and inner calm a writer needs to write.

Remember I said I wanted a slice of the happiness pizza. Well, it tastes great. When I talk about writing, my eyes shine, my fingers gesture in the air, and I try to convince everybody to be a writer. But truth is, happiness can be found in doing anything well. Life's a buffet. Taste widely and eat to your heart's fill.

---

3 Frantz Fanon. *The Wretched of the Earth* (*Les damnés de la terre*, 1961). Translated by Constance Farrington. New York: Grove Press, 1963, 222-23.

Copyright / Acknowledgements

Copyright to the individual essays remains with the contributors. All contributions are original texts, created for this publication, with the following exceptions:

Francis Jarman. "Writing for the Stage."
Originally published in Robert Reginald (ed.). *Choice Words*. The Borgo Press, 2010, and revised for this publication.

Jerry Pinto. "On Translation."
A shorter version, "What Is Your Mother Tongue?", appeared online in *Seminar: The Untranslated in Translation—A Symposium on the Linguistic and Non-Linguistic Force of Translation*, February 2020.

Arundhathi Subramaniam. "Poems Matter Because They Have Holes."
A version of the essay was published as a monograph entitled *English*, part of the KEYwording series edited by Madhusree Dutta for the Living Archive project of Arsenal—Institute for Film and Video Art, Berlin. A shorter version appeared in the magazine *IQ*. The poems are from Arundhathi Subramaniam's *Where I Live* (2009), Bloodaxe Books, UK, and *When God Is a Traveller* (2014), HarperCollins, India, and Bloodaxe Books, UK, 2014.